T0319946

EU Economic Governance and Globalization

EU Economic Governance and Globalization

Edited by

Miriam L. Campanella

University of Turin, and Ministry of Economy, Rome, Italy

Sylvester C.W. Eijffinger

Tilburg University, The Netherlands and Centre for Economic Policy Research (CEPR), London, UK

Edward Elgar
Cheltenham, UK • Northampton, MA, USA

Published by
Edward Elgar Publishing Limited
Glensanda House
Montpellier Parade
Cheltenham
Glos GL50 1UA
UK

Edward Elgar Publishing, Inc.
136 West Street
Suite 202
Northampton
Massachusetts 01060
USA

A catalogue record for this book
is available from the British Library

Library of Congress Cataloging in Publication Data

EU economic governance and globalization / Miriam L. Campanella, Sylvester
  C.W. Eijffinger, editors.
     p. cm.
   Includes bibliographical references and index.
    1. European Union countries — Economic policy. 2. Foreign trade regulation
— European Union countries. 3. Industrial policy — European Union
countries. 4. European Union countries — Economic integration. 5. Monetary
policy — European Union countries. 6. Monetary unions — European Union
countries. 7. Globalization — Economic aspects — European Union countries.
8. European Union countries — Foreign economic relations — United States.
9.United States — Foreign economic relations — European Union countries.
I. Campanella, Miriam, 1944– II. Eijffinger, Sylvester C. W.

HC240.E738 2003
337.1'42–dc21   2003049214

ISBN 1 84064 920 8

Contents

Figures

Tables

Contributors

Miriam L. Campanella is a lecturer in International Political Economy at the University of Turin (from 1995) and holds a Jean Monnet Permanent Course on 'EMU Policies and Institutions' (1999). She has studied at MIT Center for International Studies (1980–86), where she has been a guest several times. In 1997, she held a Fulbright chair at the University of Pittsburgh. With a background in International Politics and International Political Economy, she has contributed to the field of European studies, and has focused on the conflicting rationales of the EMU policies and institutions. She has made the most of strategic interaction analysis in explaining EMU fiscal discipline, ECB–ECOFIN interaction and the European Commission agenda setter's prerogatives. Since December 2001, she has been appointed to the Ministry of Economy in Rome, where she has been involved in the EU budget reform. In a recent study, she went to suggest that EU budget reform should accomplish with the standards of a minimalist financial federalism. A study on 'Tackling the EU Budget Reform: subsidiarity, stabilization function and the allocation of strategic public goods in a multi-tiered financial regime' is on course for publication.

Sylvester C.W. Eijffinger gained his master's degree in Economics and Econometrics (Cum Laude) at the Free University of Amsterdam in 1983 and doctorate in Economics and Econometrics at the same university in 1986. He is currently Professor of European Financial Economics at the Center for Economic Research and the Department of Economics of Tilburg University (since 2000), Jean Monnet Professor of European Financial and Monetary Integration (chair endowed by the European Commission) and chairman of the Educational Programme, 'International Economics and Finance', at Tilburg University (both since 1998). Sylvester Eijffinger's research interests and publications are primarily in Monetary Policy. He has been Professor of Monetary Economics (part-time) at the Department of European Economic Studies of the College of Europe (since 1994) and a Research Fellow of the Centre for Economic Policy Research (CEPR) since 1998.

Chad Damro is currently a Jean Monnet Fellow in the BP Transatlantic Programme at the European University Institute in Florence, Italy. His general research interests focus on economic relations among the advanced industrialized economies, the international political economy of multilateral relations in the World Trade Organization, international regulatory cooperation and transatlantic economic and political relations. He has written on European Union competition policy, EU–US competition relations and EU–US environmental relations. His current research investigates the role and influence of firms in transatlantic cooperation in individual merger and non-merger cases.

Kjell A. Eliassen is a Professor of Public Management and director of the Centre for European and Asian Studies at the Norwegian School of Management – BI in Oslo and Professor of European Studies at the Free University in Brussels. He has published 12 books and several articles on European and Asian Affairs. His latest book is *European Telecom Liberalisation*. He has been a visiting professor at several European, American and Asian universities. During the last three years he has built up a part-time Master of Management programme in Infocom in Asia, in cooperation with leading Asian universities, representing the Norwegian School of management. He has been closely involved with Fudan University in Shangai and the Chulalongkorn University in Thailand, both in doing research and in the development of management training programmes.

Michele Fratianni is the W. George Pinnell Professor and chair of Business Economics and Public Policy at the Kelley School of Business of Indiana University in Bloomington, USA. He has taught also at the Catholic University of Louvain, the Università Cattolica of Milan, the Università Sapienza of Rome, Marquette University and the Free University of Berlin. He has also been an economics adviser to the European Commission in Brussels, and senior staff economist with the US President's Council of Economic Advisers. He is a recipient of the Medal of the President of the Italian Republic for scientific achievements, the Pio Manzú Center Gold Medal, the Scanno prize in economics and the St Vincent prize in economics. He is the managing editor of *Open Economies Review*, editor of the Ashgate series on *Global Finance* and author of 21 books and over 100 articles that have appeared in the main economics journals. His latest book is *Storia Monetaria d'Italia* (Monetary History of Italy), published in 2001, and his latest journal articles are 'The Konstanz Seminar on Monetary Theory and Policy at Thirty', *European Journal of Political Economy*, September 2001, and 'International Financial Architecture and International Financial Standards', *Annals of The American Academy of Political and Social Science*, January 2002. He is currently working on issues of international finance and financial architecture.

Edin Mujagic received his master's degree in Economics from the Faculty of Economics and Business Administration of Tilburg University, The Netherlands, in August 2002. Areas of interest include central banking, monetary economics, European monetary and fiscal policy, international finance and macroeconomics.

Catherine B. Monsen is a doctoral fellow at the Norwegian School of Management (NSM), Department of Public Governance. Her main research interests include regulation, European telecommunications policy, strategic management and organization. She holds a master's degree in International Marketing and Strategy from the NSM.

Alberta Sbragia received her PhD from the University of Wisconsin-Madison in 1974 and wrote her dissertation as a Fulbright scholar on Italian politics. Her teaching and publications have focused on the development of the European Union as well as on comparing US and European public policy, with particular attention to public finance and international environmental policy. Her current work focuses on understanding the development of the European Union as a structure of governance within the analytic framework of comparative federalism. She is the director of the European Union Center and the Center for West European Studies. She is also a UCIS Research Professor of Political Science, a member of numerous editorial boards for American, Canadian and European journals, and participates in the educational activities of The Atlantic Council of the United States. She is the editor of *Euro-Politics: Institutions and Policy-making in the 'New' European Community* (1992).

Martin Staniland is a professor in the Graduate School of Public and International Affairs, University of Pittsburgh. His research interests include the effects of liberalization on the EU airline industry and the history of state ownership and privatization in the industry. His publications include *What is Political Economy?* (1987), *Government Birds: the State and Air Transport in Western Europe* (forthcoming) and various articles and conference papers on regulation and airline strategy.

Nick Sitter is Associate Professor in the Department of Public Governance at the Norwegian School of Management BI, where he teaches EU political economy and public policy. He holds a PhD from the Department of Government at the London School of Economics and Political Science, and has lectured on EU, East and West European politics and history at the Central European University, the American University, Kingston University and Reading University. Research interests and publications cover EU public policy and regulation, European integration, comparative party systems and Euroscepticism.

Mehmet Ugur is Jean Monnet chairholder in the Political Economy of European Integration and program coordinator for MA European Public Policy at the University of Greenwich, London. His research interests include theory of regional integration, globalization–integration linkages and external economic relations of the EU.

Introduction

Miriam L. Campanella and Sylvester C.W. Eijffinger

INTRODUCTION

Regulatory policies, harmonization, targets as well as peer pressure are ingredients of what this book refers to as EU economic governance. Each has its roots in the Jean Monnet method of integration which aimed at narrowing gaps and differences, overcoming conflicts, inducing cooperation and eventually furthering a truly European polity. It should not matter how many and what institutions take part in this historical task of building a peaceful and integrated Europe. Whether they be supranational or intergovernmental, elected or bureaucratic, national or subnational, private corporations or social organized interests, the arena is perceived to be large enough to accommodate the representatives of all groupings, which favor the project.

Since its foundation, however, the European Commission was granted major visibility on the European scene as its mission was deemed, in the troubled after-war period, to forge compromise in a context of reciprocal diffidence (Magnette, 2001, p. 31). Empowered with a treaty-bound role as agenda setter for the Council of Ministers, the Commission has had a monopoly of regulatory legislation modeled along consensus-oriented decision-making lines where alternative paths are often neglected in favor of thoroughgoing compromise (Kohler-Koch, 2001; Magnette, 2001). Yet the integrationist influence of the Commission is often limited by the ability of national governments, in the IGCs or in the Council of Ministers sessions, to alter the proposals or to disregard the suggestions of the Commission when drafting treaties or directives. Prerogatives transferred to EU level do not 'involve the sort of geographically wide-ranging externalities and free-rider problems that would justify transferring the policy to a central entity' (Alesina and Wacziarg, 1999).

The Commission's governance of EU affairs is based on two major strategies. A first strategy consists of its ability to get a wide range of actors involved, and in drawing on toolkits of consociative governance such as power-sharing and consensus-oriented decision making to find 'common' solutions. The second strategy is based on its monopoly of the expert advice given to the Council of Ministers and to the European Parliament. The Commission behaves as the 'main expert, and therefore it happens to look for greater transfer of policies to the EU level' and eventually under its control (Alesina and Wacziarg, 1999). The European Commission as an information provider can strongly affect the multi-level configuration of governments, made up of supranational, national and subnational levels of authorities, in that it can generate an overexpansion of programs.

Centralization and deeper integration have not yet delivered the flexibility considered necessary to cope with globalization. Based on regulatory policies and rule-bound institutions, the EU economy appears to be too rigid and poorly equipped to turn the differences between its member economies into an asset when faced by global shocks and competition. In addition, economic literature disputes the extent to which integration has really generated flexibility. The concentric model – as defined by Michele Fratianni (see Chapter 1 of this book) – justified on the basis of a 'two-level game' in which the EU helped national governments to embrace market-oriented reforms in the face of reluctant constituencies, seems to have generated more centralization than flexibility, with too little room for subsidiarity. This seems in line with Alesina and Wacziarg (1999) who argue that centralization and the transfer of prerogatives to EU level 'have gone too far'.

The EU integration model has clearly made EU member economies more alike now than they were a quarter-century ago, when country-specific patterns of government–economy relations in industrial policy, competition or macroeconomic policy were by and large the rule in many EU countries. Indeed, it is now less feasible to speak of a German (or Rhineland) model, a Gallic model, a British model, an Italian family-based model – all of which were to some extent a long way from the free-market model epitomized by the United States. With the completion of the single market and the transfer of major policy functions such as competition policy and monetary policy to EU level, and with the intra-EU convergence through harmonization and peer pressure in areas such as privatization and fiscal policy, a European model seems to be entering the scene (Cohen and Pisani-Ferry, 2002). However, it is still doubtful whether the process will move ahead towards a fully-fledged free-market economy, or whether it will lead to a model of 'social market economy', an overpraised equilibrium of embedded capitalism pleasing to both right-centrist and left-centrist coalitions in the old Europe. Rule-bound policies enshrined in international treaties or treaty-like texts, whose revision requires unanimity or supermajority (a qualified majority), inevitably produces an 'element of inertia in Europe which is absent in the US' (ibid.) and favors vested interests at the expense of new entrants, whether they be new competitors, Eastern

European countries or simply new generations. Eastern enlargement negotiations are likely to test not only the existing political and economic equi-
libria, but also whether the EU economic institutions and policies are really
seriously about getting rid of those vested groupings which make the Union
unattractive to new economic enterprise. At stake here is not only the
adjustment of national economies but also that of the whole EU economy
so as to be able to face international competition.

Against such a background, the editors have asked some outstanding
scholars to offer, from the perspective of their respective fields, an assessment of the way EU governance has affected national patterns of behavior,
whether it has succeeded in strengthening the EU countries in the global
economy, and whether the central monetary institution of the newborn currency area is gaining ground on the US Federal Reserve's long-established
reputation. Some key sectors such as telecommunications, air transport,
currency competition, taxation, transatlantic relations and monetary policy
of the newly installed European System of Central Banks are the issues
selected. For each of these, the authors have offered original analyses and
stimulating conclusions which are bound to appeal to political scientists
and economists, policy and decision makers in public and private executive
bodies in Europe, in the USA, and in other regions of the world. The
authors have deliberately adopted issue-based analyses and have avoided
the tendency to engage in 'school of thought' debates common among
European Studies scholars. Such an approach has been adopted because an
overuse of stylized theories would have run the risk of relegating the issues
being analysed into a purely academic debate, and suppressed the positive
intent inspiring the book.

In Chapter 1, Michele Fratianni focuses attention on the model of EU
governance and finds that the 'concentric model' adopted should bear the
blame for some of the incoherence in the EU economic governance. By pursuing the twofold aim of simultaneously deepening and widening, the EU
policy makers have ended up squashing the differences among members as
well as empowering some members at the expense of others, an approach
which has ended up by delaying the introduction of the single currency, and
may now slow down the process of enlargement to admit new members.
This is because it has made it extremely expensive for some members to
comply with the Maastricht criteria and is likely making it even more
expensive for Eastern European states to take on board EU economic regulations and standards. In a flexible approach, member states would,
instead, express preferences and qualify for membership of the different
clubs. When policy coordination is adopted, a problem of governance
quality arises.

In Chapter 2, Mehmet Ugur introduces the notion of governance quality, defined as 'the extent to which the public authority supplies (. . .) public goods in an efficient and non-discriminatory manner'. The quality depends on the interaction between actors, and especially on the extent to which the 'public authority is not captured either by state bureaucracy or by non-state actors'. If we adopt the above definition as a benchmark to assess EU governance, Chapters 2 to 4 can be seen as attempts at assessing the extent to which EU governance has delivered those 'public goods' such as tax harmonization, air transport and telecommunications – all of which are essential policy areas bearing upon competition and competitiveness. Mehmet Ugur argues that, when considered as increased cross-border mobility, institutionalized European integration may lead to higher governance quality. One reason is that the regional authority's institutional capacity facilitates intra-bloc conflict resolution by devising transparent criteria for cost/benefit distribution. The other reason is that policy convergence codified at the regional level reduces the probability of policy reversals (that is, cheating) because it limits the capacity of national bureaucracies and/or non-state actors to capture the policy-making authority.

In Chapter 3, Martin Staniland points out how important the perception of globalization and liberalization processes 'closer to home' has been in prompting the EU member governments to embrace extended policy coordination and to delegate the governance of the air transport industry to the EU level. Liberalization of the air transport industry has turned out to be an unexciting affair. It has not produced 'head-to-head competition on many routes (notably domestic routes) that were traditionally the preserve of the flag-carriers (. . .) Further, the development of alliance systems (. . .) has led to the reinforcement of hub-and-spoke systems at major airports which are typically congested, thus creating serious barriers to entry for would-be new entrants'.

In Chapter 4, Kjell Eliassen, Catherine Monsen and Nick Sitter subscribe to a relatively positive assessment of EU governance of telecommunications. They find that there 'has been a shift from "government" at the national level to supranational 'governance' and this has entailed a considerable degree of liberalisation'. They recognize that the Commission has to a large extent driven developments in the EU telecoms governance regime, 'albeit within the parameters that the member state preferences allow. The power and influence of industry, governments, regulators and the Commission have evolved over time, producing a "governance" regime characterised by negotiation, compromise etc., in line with the notion of "EMU governance". However, this is not to say that a fully-fledged open market has been established'. In sum, the balance 'between sector regulation and competition remains open, and the sector is set to undergo further technologically driven change'.

In Chapter 5, Chad Damro and Alberta Sbragia focus attention on a rather hot topic in the EU's international economic relations: the transatlantic dimension. In their account, there is a clear understanding of the strategic significance of the transatlantic market place as 'it represents the largest and most important bilateral economic relationship today'. The EU and the USA are the world's largest industrialized economies, collectively accounting for roughly 56 per cent of global gross domestic product. The authors hint at the fact that both the 'indicators of trade and FDI reflect the growing size and interdependence of the transatlantic marketplace. In fact EU–US economic relations account for the world's largest bilateral economic relationship, generating around $1 billion of trade and investment per day (European Commission, 2002a)'.

A new framework of transatlantic economic governance is taking place and, although the new framework will continue to rely on the WTO system to resolve disputes in traditional trade conflicts, a system of transatlantic economic governance that 'emphasises *dispute prevention* seems better suited to manage transatlantic regulatory conflicts. Such a system of governance will require complementary bilateral and multilateral approaches to regulatory dispute prevention, such as maintaining and expanding bilateral Mutual Recognition Agreements and multilateral recommendations, codes and standards'.

In the heterogeneous institutional environment of EU governance, problems of legitimacy, accountability, and transparency appear especially critical when it comes to monetary policy. Compared to the US Federal Reserve, the European System of Central Bank(s) seemed unusually rigid and self-centered. In Chapter 6, Sylvester Eijffinger and Edin Mujagic focus attention on European Central Bank monetary policy, and offer evidence of it as moving in the direction of positive resilience in relation to the US Fed. Their analysis draws on the monetary dialogue between the ECB and the Committee on Economic and Monetary Affairs (ECON) of the European Parliament, in which they see a convincingly interinstitutional dynamic developing. According to their account, the ECB has shown a high degree of responsiveness to the criticism that the experts of the Committee have directed at the ECB officials. As they note, there is 'some degree of influence running from Brussels to Frankfurt. It is important to note that although the word "influence" has been used here, it should not be interpreted as that the ECB is or has been put under any formal pressure'. The case study is especially intriguing at a time when the international financial community and the public at large are experiencing a growing need for accountability and transparency. Eijffinger and Mujagic emphasize, 'As central banks have enormous powers but are led by technocrats and enjoy a high degree of independence, the society is calling for more accountability and transparency from them as well. The price for being independent is apparently, and quite rightfully we might add, the obligation to explain and give a full account of actions taken and their outcomes'.

Similarly, Miriam L. Campanella challenges the idea that the ECB is a self-centered monetary institution. In the final chapter, she offers a perspective where the ECB seems prepared to respond to the demands of economic governance, and to moderate its monetary stance, when it has been deemed necessary to assist the Eurozone's sluggish growth. The monetary policy, including the growth of M3 above its reference value, has shown the ECB to be at least as sensitive and responsive to economic governance as its elder sister, the US Federal Reserve. Such a policy could lead to a major problem, as it could result in the bank falling into the 'liquidity trap' if responsiveness gains the upper hand. Accommodation of monetary looseness in the absence of structural adjustments, though intended to counter deflationary movements, can end to swap price stability over real and long term economic growth.

The authors of this book have provided a realistic analysis of European governance and have avoided too much stress on the bickering between supranational and intergovernmental jurisdictions. The focus has been on actors at EU level and intergovernmental level, in their effort to adjust some failures of the model of social market capitalism they have inherited from previous decades. Although in some chapters of the book assessment of EU economic reforms is deemed still to be suboptimal, in others focusing on monetary policy, the ECB convergence towards its elder sister model, the US Federal Reserve, leads to a certain optimism about the strength of the EMU process.

REFERENCES

Alesina, Alberto and Romain Wacziarg (1999), 'Is Europe Going Too Far?', NBER Working Paper no. 6883.

Cohen, Elie and Jean Pisani-Ferry (2002), 'Economic Policy in the US and the EU: Convergence or Divergence?', paper prepared for the Harvard Conference on EU–US Relations, 11–12 April.

Kohler-Koch, Beate (2001), 'The Commission White Paper and the Improvement of European Governance', in Christian Joerges, Yves Mény and J.H.H. Weiler (eds), *Mountain or Molehill?: A Critical Appraisal of the Commission White Paper on Governance*, Jean Monnet Working Paper no. 6/01, Florence: European University Institute.

Magnette, Paul (2001), 'European Governance and Civic Participation: Can the European Union be politicised?', in Christian Joerges, Yves Mény and J.H.H. Weiler (eds), *Mountain or Molehill?: A Critical Appraisal of the Commission White Paper on Governance*, Jean Monnet Working Paper no. 6/01, Florence: European University Institute.

1. EU enlargement and flexible integration*

Michele Fratianni

THE ISSUES

Enlargement in the European Union (EU) threatens to stall the objective of integration deepening. Deepening and enlargement are conflicting goals. The main point of this chapter is that to resolve the conflict between deepening and enlargement the EU must introduce more flexible rules of integration; the chapter also explores how governance must evolve to allow a much larger and more diverse EU.

The original European Community (EC) was conceived primarily as a trade bloc. While it is true that the Treaty of Rome has articles defining external equilibrium, full employment, price stability and exchange rate stability as common objectives, these are too vague and cannot in any way be interpreted as a blueprint for monetary union, let alone political union. Economic and monetary union (EMU) was elevated to an objective of the EC by European leaders in the Hague Summit of 1969, three years before the accession of Denmark, Ireland and the United Kingdom. Over the years, the EC invested a great deal of its political capital in EMU. The Treaty on European Union (TEU) made a great leap forward with respect to the Treaty of Rome,[1] by imbedding the great aspirations of most EU members to be not only an economic union, but also a monetary union and ultimately, although in an as yet unspecified way, a political union. EMU is now a reality. Two more steps have to be taken to complete the integration deepening: fiscal union and political union.

The TEU changed decision making as well; the changes favored centralization and made another step, albeit a small one, towards a federal structure. Qualified majority voting was extended, and the introduction of the co-decision procedure and the extension of the cooperation and assent procedures have given more power to the European Parliament.

Enlargement of the EU is bound to slow down the deepening process just described. The membership of the Community doubled from 1958 to 1986, with the accession of Denmark, Ireland, the United Kingdom (1973),

Greece (1981), Portugal and Spain (1986). It then expanded again in 1995, with the new member states of Austria, Finland and Sweden. Another round of accession is in the making. Thirteen applications for membership are pending: Turkey applied in 1987, Cyprus and Malta in 1990, Hungary and Poland in 1994, Romania, Slovakia, Latvia, Estonia, Lithuania and Bulgaria in 1995, and the Czech Republic and Slovenia in 1996.

The European Council, at the Copenhagen Summit of July 1993, signaled its intention to open the EU doors to the 10 Central and Eastern European countries, specifying three basic requirements of membership: a stable democracy, respecting human rights and the protection of minorities; a functioning market economy; and the assumption of all obligations of membership. The European Council, at the Madrid Summit of December 1995, added the condition that aspirant countries had to undergo a suitable 'adjustment of administrative structures'. The European Council, at the Luxembourg Summit of December 1997, declared that candidate countries had not only to incorporate the *acquis communautaire* (simply, *acquis*) into national legislation but also to apply it. The *acquis* – the large body of rules and regulations of the EU – consists of 31 chapters, including free movement of goods, services, people, capital, competition policy, industrial policy, environment, consumers and health protection, financial control and EMU. The EU has negotiated accession treaties with each candidate country and is providing financial assistance in the transition period. Accession countries must accept the *acquis* in its entirety, although temporary exemptions to one or more of its chapters may be granted. The non-derogation clause was introduced to avoid aspirants 'cherry-picking' the *acquis*.

The European Council, at the Nice Summit of December 2000, changed the governance rules and speeded up the accession timetable. On rules, a hotly debated issue, the agreed-upon procedure raised the relative representation of small member states at the expense of large ones. The qualified majority hurdle rate was set in excess of the present 71.3 per cent of the votes and has to satisfy a simple majority of member states and at least 62 per cent of the EU population.

Table 1.1 shows data on population, GDP per capita measured in purchasing power standards (PPS), present and future governance rules, and a measure of under- or overrepresentation in the Council of Ministers for the EU-27. The table underscores the diversity of the aspirants relative to the incumbents. Two features in particular emerge from the table. The first is the wide income dispersion between EU-15 and the aspirants. The ratio of the highest to the lowest per capita income is 2:6 in EU-15 and 7:5 in EU-27. Note that the per capita income data are based on purchasing power parity to eliminate distortions due to price level differences among countries. Income disparities are much larger when measured by the traditional GDP per capita. With the exception of Cyprus, Slovenia and possibly Malta, the aspirants are much poorer than the three poorest incumbents (Greece, Portugal and Spain) and have a relatively large fraction of the labor force working in agriculture. This implies that the aspirants would be net recipients of significant transfer payments.[2]

The second feature is the shift in the balance of power from well to do to poor members and from large to small members. This shift is not new: it started with previous enlargements. But with the move from EU-15 to EU-27 it is creating an expanding gulf between actual power and voting power in the Council. For example, on the basis of a combination of population and economic power, Germany and Poland should have, respectively, 21 per cent and 3.6 per cent of EU-27 Council votes, whereas, according to the Nice agreement, they will have 8.4 and 7.8 per cent.

The push for enlargement has more to do with politics and security matters than with economics. Germany fears political instability in Central and Eastern Europe and believes that EU membership may be decisive in transforming the former socialist countries into viable market economies with stable democracies. Opposition to expansion to the east comes from two groups. The first group consists of poor regions (Greece, Ireland, Portugal and Spain) and protected sectors, such as agriculture, which are net beneficiaries of the EU redistributive policies and fear that the new entrants will take away from the pool of common resources. Secondly, opposition comes from the old EU members that would prefer deeper integration to a larger EU.

The chapter is structured as follows. It begins by describing rules and institutions, that is, governance of the integration process, and then develops a simple model of clubs to explain how the optimal size of jurisdictions varies under different policy areas. The greatest potential for enlargement applies to the Single Market, which is the core activity of the EU: that is, the activity without which the EU would lose its *raison d'être*. Club size is likely to be smaller for other policy areas and it may be optimal that two clubs exist for a given policy area, an old monetary union and a new monetary union. Next, the case is made for flexible integration to resolve the conflict between deepening and widening. The ultimate outcome of flexible integration resembles what Casella and Frey (1992) call 'functional federalism', a decentralized system of overlapping clubs. Finally, some conclusions are drawn.

Table 1.1 Basic data on enlargement

	Pop. (mn)	GDP per capita, PPS, EU = 100, 1998	Present council Votes	Present council (%)	Future council Votes	Future council (%)	Theoretical votes Pop.	Theoretical votes Pop*GDP	Under/over-representation Pop.	Under/over-representation Pop*GDP
Germany	82	106.5	10	11.49	29	8.41	17.04	20.97	-8.63	-12.56
France	59	99.1	10	11.49	29	8.41	12.26	14.04	-3.86	-5.63
Italy	57.6	103.5	10	11.49	29	8.41	11.97	14.31	-3.56	-5.91
UK	59.2	102.5	10	11.49	29	8.41	12.30	14.57	-3.90	-6.16
Belgium	10.2	110.7	5	5.75	12	3.48	2.12	2.71	1.36	0.77
Luxembourg	0.4	173.6	2	2.30	4	1.16	0.08	0.17	1.08	0.99
Netherlands	15.8	115.3	5	5.75	13	3.77	3.28	4.37	0.48	-0.61
Denmark	5.3	119.5	3	3.45	7	2.03	1.10	1.52	0.93	0.51
Austria	8.1	109.6	4	4.60	10	2.90	1.68	2.13	1.22	0.77
Finland	5.2	101.3	3	3.45	7	2.03	1.08	1.26	0.95	0.76
Sweden	8.9	101.6	4	4.60	10	2.90	1.85	2.17	1.05	0.73
Spain	39.4	79.2	8	9.20	27	7.83	8.19	7.49	-0.36	0.33
Portugal	10	72.9	5	5.75	12	3.48	2.08	1.75	1.40	1.73
Greece	10.5	66.7	5	5.75	12	3.48	2.18	1.68	1.30	1.80
Ireland	3.7	105.5	3	3.45	7	2.03	0.77	0.94	1.26	1.09
Czech Rep.	10.3	60			12	3.48	2.14	1.48	1.34	1.99
Slovakia	5.4	46			7	2.03	1.12	0.60	0.91	1.43
Hungary	10.1	49			12	3.48	2.10	1.19	1.38	2.29
Poland	38.7	39			27	7.83	8.04	3.62	-0.22	4.20
Slovenia	2	68			4	1.16	0.42	0.33	0.74	0.83
Cyprus	0.8	78			4	1.16	0.17	0.15	0.99	1.01
Malta	0.4	na			3	0.87	0.08	0.07	0.79	0.79
Bulgaria	8.2	23			10	2.90	1.70	0.45	1.19	2.45

Romania	22.5	27	8	14	4.06	4.68	1.46	−0.62	2.60
Lithuania	3.7	31	4	7	2.03	0.77	0.28	1.26	1.75
Latvia	2.4	27	3	4	1.16	0.50	0.16	0.66	1.00
Estonia	1.4	36	3	4	1.16	0.29	0.12	0.87	1.04

Note: The GDP per capita index is based on purchasing power standards. Theoretical votes were computed either on the basis of the relative share of the population of each country relative to the total or on the basis of the relative share of (population)(GDP per capita PPS).

Source: Eurostat, *EU Enlargement – Key Data on Candidate Countries* (http://europa.eu.int/comm./eurostat).

MARKETS, INSTITUTIONS, RULES AND GOVERNANCE

Economists make a distinction between markets and institutions (for example, Casella, 1992, p. 115). Markets are places where exchanges take place using prices, without an agent coordinating these activities.[3] Institutions instead preside over goods that cannot be allocated through markets. To provide such goods – for example, public goods, club goods or common-pool resources – collective or coordinated action is necessary. Institutions resolve the problem of coordination by setting rules. Rules confer rights and obligations, but also direct participants on how to act under specific circumstances (Sandholtz, 1996, p. 15). Not all rules are written; some can be informal or based on custom. Rules also feed back on institutions, making the causality between institutions and rules bidirectional. Finally, governance encompasses the establishment and maintenance of institutions and rules.

The Treaty of Rome, the TEU, the *acquis* and the decisions of the European Court of Justice are clearly part of the integration rules in the EU; but so are informal understandings, such as the old Luxembourg Compromise – invoked when national interest was involved – which had the effect of postponing voting until consensus was reached (Nugent, 1994, pp. 144–5).[4] The Exchange Rate Mechanism (ERM) codified the rules of limited exchange rate fluctuations for those member countries participating in the European Monetary System (EMS). Many of these rules were clearly spelled out, others were not. For example, EMS participants thought that 'intramarginal' interventions (that is, interventions before the exchange rate touches the intervention limits defined by the ERM), while not compulsory, were desirable for the functioning of the EMS. In 1987, an accord was reached, the Nyborg Accord, that made intramarginal interventions of up to 200 per cent of a member's quota eligible for financing by the EMS institutions and thus forcing a country with an appreciating currency essentially to create more money. The Accord tried to formalize, though in the form of a gentlemen's agreement, a previously ambiguous and informal rule, yet the formalization did not remove all ambiguities on rules of interventions. The French interpreted the Accord as giving a participating country the automatic right to use EMS resources; the Germans interpreted it as giving the central bank of the appreciating currency the discretion to decide on individual cases (Fratianni and von Hagen, 1992, pp. 25–6).

Institutions evolve as the rules of the game change. The European Parliament and the Council of Ministers are changing as the process of democratization deepens. New policies create new institutions. EMU has ushered in a new institution, the European Central Bank (ECB), whose existence has weakened old institutions, the national central banks. The TEU is more specific on what the new institution will do than on what the old institutions will not do. But as EMU grows the rules of the game governing monetary unification will become more precise and the role of new and old institutions more delineated.

The complexity of the rules of the integration game in the EU has spun a complex web of EU institutions that defy simple categorizations. EU institutions are too strong to be thought of as international organizations and yet not strong enough to supplant national institutions. EU institutions are *sui generis* because the EU integration rules are *sui generis*. The rules, in turn, are evolving because the process of deepening is inevitably leading some member countries to question the value of deeper forms of integration.

OPTIMAL CLUB SIZE

International trade, monetary and defense arrangements can be treated as clubs. Clubs are institutions through which members fund and enjoy the benefit of an excludable public good (Buchanan, 1965; Olson, 1965; Fratianni and Pattison, 1982, 2001; Casella, 1992). The ability of a club to exclude non-members from the activity of the club is never perfect, witness the positive externality provided by NATO to non-members. The incentives to 'free-ride', however, can be minimized by specific clauses: a common external tariff in the case of a trade agreement, denying access to rediscounts, borrowing and lender-of-last-resort in the case of a monetary union, and mutual aggression pacts in the case of defense arrangements.

Let me sketch the main features of clubs. First, a club produces an output, Q. For an organization like the EU, Q is actually an array of outputs: the Q of the Single Market combines access to a common market (that is, freedom of movement of goods, services and factor inputs) and a set of uniform competition rules; the Q of EMU is a single currency and a common inflation rate. Second, each member of the club derives benefits and bears costs from being part of the club. Third, the club, as a whole, generates a collective benefit, $B_T(Q)$, and bears a collective cost, $C_T(Q)$. The optimal size of the club is obtained at the point where the marginal benefits of the club are equal to the marginal cost of the club, $B_T'(Q) = C_T'(Q)$.

Let b_i and c_i denote, respectively, the member country's share of total benefits and costs. At the optimal club size, the individual country will face $(b_i/c_i) B_T'(Q) = C_T'(Q)$. There is no guarantee that $b_i = c_i$ for each member of the club. It is quite feasible that, at the optimal club size, some club members have $b > c$ and others $b < c$. Under free and costless exit, the club preserves 'optimal' membership if members with a positive net benefit compensate members with a negative net benefit. A similar reasoning applies for a club that contemplates a membership expansion. Actual or prospective club members with an expected net positive benefit must compensate actual or prospective club members with an expected net negative benefit (assuming that the optimality condition holds for the expanded club).

Large countries tend to have large 'bs' but also large 'cs'. This is because large countries tend to lead and bear a disproportionate share of the club's costs; large costs, in turn, cannot be divorced from large benefits. Leadership in the EU is exerted by a few large countries rather than by a dominant country. Germany and France, for example, were two pivotal players in the creation of EMU. The asymmetry of power in the EU is reflected in its governance structure, with large member countries having more Council votes than small members. Furthermore, there has been a progressive shift from unanimity to qualified majority.[5]

The new decision-making rules agreed in Nice, however, have lowered the net benefits of large member countries and raised, consequently, the cost of leading. The discrepancy between economic and decision-making power is particularly acute in the EMU, where each member of the Governing Council has one vote; more on this below.

Another property of clubs is that non-members can be excluded from the benefit of the club good. If we consider goods with a high degree of externality, such as a clean environment, the optimal size of the club must be very large (possibly the world) since exclusion is not technically feasible. If, instead, we take the Single Market as a club good, access can be denied or made more expensive through the application of commercial policy. Whether the creation of a Single Market justifies a larger optimal club size depends on whether the positive effects of a larger and more competitive market for goods, services and factor inputs outweigh the negative effects of a more cumbersome decision-making procedure and the larger transfers needed to compensate sectors that are negatively affected by deeper integration. Finally, if we take EMU as a club good, exclusion is feasible for any size of clubs. Whether the EMU club should be large or small depends on two different views of money (for example, Casella and Frey, 1992, p. 644). As a means of payment and accounting standard, money is a public good whose costs to each club member fall as more people use it. The larger the money club the larger the benefits. But money can also be a tax, in the form of inflation; as such, some countries prefer a low tax, others a high tax. If there is a wide dispersion in inflation preferences, the optimal money club could be small.

CLUB SIZE AND EU ENLARGEMENT

Let me elaborate further on club enlargement, with specific reference to the impact of the eastern enlargement on the Single Market and EMU clubs. If the club were to be formed on the basis of the Single Market, club membership could easily expand from 15 to a much large number. The Single Market is the core activity of the EU and combines a common market (freedom of movement of goods, services and inputs) with a set of uniform competition standards.

Single Market

The traditional argument in favor of the welfare-enhancing properties of the Single Market comes from customs theory. So long as trade exceeds trade diversion, an incumbent will have an incentive to join the EU. There is general agreement that static trade-creating flows have outweighed trade-diverting flows in the EC customs union (Swann, 1992, pp. 119–20), but the Single Market goes much beyond a customs union.[6] A second reason for expanding the Single Market club comes from the pressure of non-member countries that feel discriminated against or threatened by the club. Baldwin (1993, p. 18) calls it a 'domino effect' and explains it as follows:

> If the bloc enlarges, the cost to the nonmembers increases since they now face a cost disadvantage in an even greater number of markets. The second round effect will bring forth more pro-EC political activity in nonmembers and thus may lead to further enlargement of the bloc.

An enlarged EU implies also higher costs. Two critical factors are at work. The first is that, for a given decision rule, the larger the membership the more difficult it is to obtain agreement and to accommodate the objectives of different interest groups. As we have already noted, EU enlargement implies a loss of decision-making power of large members in favor of small ones. Blocking coalitions will be easier to form in EU-27 than in EU-15, implying that agreement will be more costly after enlargement. The second factor is that marginal costs of decision making respond to different decision rules. Unanimity is the most costly voting rule for the club because this rule protects the minority of one. The larger the number of countries the more costly is unanimity, in the sense that one small member can prevent all other members implementing a policy of their choice. Simple majority, on the other hand, is the least costly voting rule. Typically, voting rules within a nation state are either of two types: simple or qualified majority. Simple majority applies to ordinary laws, whereas qualified majority applies to higher-level laws, such as constitutional amendments.

Unanimity, instead, applies to intergovernmental agreements where each member state wants to retain sovereign rights.

The EU is an evolving mixture of intergovernmentalism and supranationalism. Unanimity remains an important part of the club's voting procedure, yet, over the years, the pendulum has swung towards supranational decision making. The three institutions that best represent supranationalism are the Commission, the European Parliament and the European Court of Justice. The Commission has agenda power on what the Council of Ministers decides and is a busy secondary legislator, regulator and enforcer of EU laws. The European Parliament, the weakest EU institution, has gained influence relative to the Council by virtue of the so-called 'cooperation, codecision and assent' procedures that have forced the Council to act more like a partner than as an autonomous body (Martin, 1993, pp. 137–40).[7] Finally, the European Court of Justice has consistently decided in favor of integration whenever governments were reluctant to implement directives and regulations to protect national markets and specialized groups. Now the Court is also able to fine member states for violations of EU legislation.

Distributional issues play a critical role in the enlargement negotiations. Aspirants can no longer protect industries and seek compensation for the adjustment costs that fall on those industries. Incumbents understand that to expand trade they need to compensate new entrants for the adjustment costs. Thus each enlargement gives additional power to the Union to effect transfers on behalf of new entrants. The European Regional Development Fund was established in 1975 in the wake of the British and Irish accession; the size of the Structural Funds doubled after the accession of Portugal and Spain and further expanded to target the scarcely populated area of Sweden and Finland (Begg, 1997). Aside from the Common Agricultural Policy, the EU's primary transfer criterion is regional inequality: a region is undeveloped and eligible for transfers if its per capita GDP is less than 75 per cent of the Community average. This spatial approach to redistribution was further consolidated by the TEU, whose Article 2 states that one of the Union's objectives is 'to promote throughout the Community a harmonious and balanced development of economic activities'. A Cohesion Fund was established with the purpose of funding transportation and environmental projects in member states whose per capita GDP is less than 90 per cent of the Community average.

In sum, geographical expansion of the Single Market is accompanied by 'side payments' from rich incumbents to poor new entrants. These side payments are an implication of clubs theory. Furthermore, they are handled at the Union level. The centralization of redistribution eliminates the incentives for individual states to compete on taxes or secede from the Union. In the absence of redistribution, some member states would be tempted to attract resources from other states by offering advantageous tax treatment or by protecting local industries. Centralized redistribution protects the Single Market. The negative aspect of centralized redistribution is that member states have diminished incentives to implement policies that raise incomes.

The enlargements from EU-15 to EU-27 pose serious challenges to the redistribution process. To begin with, many of the aspirants are poorer than the poorest incumbents (Table 1.1). Given existing rules on Common Agricultural Policy, Structural Funds and Cohesion Fund, aspirants would be entitled to significant flows of resources.[8] The increase in the EU budget would require substantially more funding by rich incumbents. While such transfers may be part of the long-run equilibrium result, in the short run these incumbents may find it in their interest either to delay access to aspirants or to accept them under increasingly restrictive conditions. Indeed, this has already happened: the Copenhagen Summit of 1993 set three basic requirements of membership, the Madrid Summit of 1995 added the condition of 'adjustment of administrative structures' and the Luxembourg Summit of 1997 raised significantly the entry bar by imposing on aspirants not only the adoption of the *acquis* into national law but also its full implementation.

The other consequence of enlargements is that the Community average GDP will fall and push many regions of poor incumbents such as Greece, Ireland, Italy, Portugal and Spain above the 75 per cent threshold. Thus, poor incumbents would tend to resist new accessions unless the redistribution rules were revised in their favor. Such a revision would exacerbate the financial burden on richer incumbents. In sum, redistribution is going to be a critical part of the accession of the new entrants. Without a resolution of these issues the Single Market will be in jeopardy. The conclusion is that Single Market and side payments are intertwined. This is also what club theory predicts: club members with positive net benefits must compensate members with negative net benefits to preserve club size.

Monetary Union

The case for a monetary union is significantly weaker than the case for economic integration. This suggests that a monetary union club will be smaller than the Single Market club. The move from flexible exchange rates to monetary union yields two benefits, one cost and one uncertain outcome (see, for example, Fratianni, 1994, pp. 220–24). The two benefits are the lower transaction costs associated with a single currency and the resource saving from not having to cover forward contracts denominated in different currencies. The inability to vary the exchange rate represents a cost, which is higher the more unevenly distributed the shocks are in the EMU area, the more rigid real wages and the less mobile is the labor force. For the eastern countries that are undergoing a deep economic transformation, the cost of fixing the exchange rate is potentially high. Finally, there is no a priori reason to believe that the quality of monetary policy in a large EMU is bound to be better than monetary policy in all of the separate regions.

There is one fundamental reason why the ECB may not duplicate the performance of the national central bank with the lowest rate of inflation performance: preferences for inflation rather than stabilization are bound to be more widely distributed in the ECB's governing council than in a national central bank's council. The degree of dispersion is bound to widen with the number of countries participating in the EMU. The members of the ECB's governing council could rise from the current 18 to a maximum of 33 members. The relative importance of the 'periphery' in relation to the 'center' would more than double – from 12/6 to 27/6. The fact that the new periphery has a tradition of a higher inflation rate than the old periphery leads to the prediction that the inflation rate tolerance of the expanded ECB would rise.

It is worth recalling that decision making of the ECB differs from that of the Council of Ministers in two important aspects. The first is that each member of the ECB's governing council has one vote. The second is that simple majority applies. Thus, if national representatives in the ECB's governing council vote according to the national interest, and national propensities to inflate differ among member countries, the ECB preferred inflation rate will be determined by the country with the median inflation rate preference.[9] To be sure, this prediction is overly pessimistic because it ignores the Europeanization process of the ECB's council members. Nonetheless, it is instructive to keep in mind that the principle of one-country-one-vote and pure national representation are bound to raise the inflation rate relative to the country with the lowest inflation record in the EU.

Not only low-inflation countries would lose, but also higher inflation countries that tend to rely on the inflation tax as a substitute for other types of taxation. This is particularly true for aspirants whose tax-collecting institutions tend to be weak and must tolerate a higher rate of tax evasion than incumbents'.

So far, we have treated EMU as a currency union, without any consideration of the banking and financial markets. EMU, in fact, means a high degree of integration of banking and financial services. Aspirants suffer from a distinct disadvantage in this area, which in turn implies smaller optimal EMU clubs. The reason for that is that the EU follows the principle of home-country regulation and mutual recognition of national regulation, subject to a core of harmonized financial rules. Insofar as country differences are allowed, the authorities of the home country have the right and obligation of regulating banks and financial intermediaries they have licensed regardless of where they operate in the EU. Since each member accepts this principle, national regulatory standards are mutually recognized. Mutual recognition, however, presupposes that national regulators trust one another. If, instead, there are significant differences in reputation, the principle of mutual recognition will not work and the system reverts to host-country regulation.

Take, for example, the lender-of-last-resort (LOLR) function, which is closely intertwined with financial regulation and supervision. According to the Maastricht Treaty, the ECB is expected to be the LOLR if the Euro payments system were to falter; otherwise, LOLR falls under the national jurisdiction. LOLR involves a risk of financial loss that most often falls on taxpayers (Goodhart, 1999). Governments are reluctant to transfer tax revenues to foreign owners of a bank unless failure to do so creates a negative spillover at home in the form of a banking crisis. In contrast, governments are unlikely to care much about the ripples that troubled domestic banks may cause in foreign markets (von Hagen and Fratianni, 1998). Aware of such incentives, governments will be reluctant to let substandard foreign banks operate in their home market for fear that they may endanger domestic banks and elicit an LOLR response. This is the reason why the principle of mutual recognition breaks down when there are significant differences in regulatory reputation.

The aspirants' banking industry is plagued with low human capital, inferior technology, undercapitalization, non-performing loans, and inadequate regulation and supervision. Incumbents would be justifiably reluctant to extend to aspirants the rights and obligations of home-country regulation. Since integration of banking and financial services cannot be separated from currency integration, the EMU club will not be as attractive as the Single Market club to the old members. Many new members, with vastly different economic structures and higher tolerance for inflation, will find that a low-inflation rate EMU is not likely to suit their best interests.

In sum, initial conditions suggest that the optimal EMU club will be smaller than the optimal Single Market club. Three possible outcomes can emerge. The first is that the membership of EMU will be exactly the same as the membership of the Single Market club. This is the solution preferred by those who argue that the Single Market cannot be complete without a monetary union and by proponents that monetary union is an intermediate step to political unification. The second is that the membership of the EMU club is smaller than the membership of the Single Market. This is the preferred solution by those who argue that a single monetary union is not a necessary condition to complete the Single Market and by critics of the thesis that monetary union facilitates political union. The third is that there could be more than one EMU, with memberships reflecting different preferences for inflation and different banking and financial structures. This is the solution preferred by proponents of flexible integration, a theme which will be developed in the next section.

THE CASE FOR FLEXIBLE INTEGRATION

The strong message of the club model is that different policy areas require different membership size. As Casella and Frey put it (1992, p. 645): 'If clubs providing different public goods are merged to exploit economies of scale, still there is little reason to expect that the theoretical result will replicate the hierarchical, nested federalism we are most used to.' The principle that EU institutions and rules had to be accepted by all member countries was a good working principle so long as countries had common objectives and the economies had similar structures. Indeed, up to the TEU, rules and institutions had general universality: all member countries accepted all the integration rules. The speed of the integration train was identical for all, with the speed determined by the slowest moving locomotive. Maastricht changed all that.

In the bargaining process over Maastricht three different positions emerged: those who wanted EMU soon and without preconditions, those who wanted EMU later and with preconditions, and those who did not want EMU at all. The UK belonged to the last camp. Among the others, a dispute developed that was reminiscent of the controversy of the 1970s between 'economists' and 'monetarists' (Swann, 1992, pp. 192–4). Germany – with Belgium, Luxembourg and the Netherlands – was the leading exponent of the 'economic' view of monetary union, namely that economic convergence must precede EMU. France was the leading exponent of the 'monetarist' view of EMU, namely that EMU facilitates economic convergence. Germany favored a long transition period and formal convergence criteria before the final stage of EMU; France, with Italy, on the other hand, wanted EMU quickly and without strong preconditions. The two groups agreed on the desirability of the end state, but disagreed on the speed with which each member would reach the end state. The German position was consistent with a multi-speed approach to European EMU (Garrett, 1993), the French position with a one-speed approach. The UK position rejected EMU outright as undesirable.

In the end the German position prevailed, and the UK and Denmark were given opt-out clauses for not participating in EMU. The UK also broke ranks with respect to social policy. With the signing of the TEU, the long tradition of the universality of the integration rules was broken. The

TEU, in fact, accepts the principle that certain types of integration rules – those outside the Single Market – have less than universal applicability. Furthermore, the Treaty also accepts the principle that countries may reach end goals at different speeds. Multi-speed integration is an implication of the entry conditions to Stage III of economic and monetary union.[10]

The breakdown of the universality of rules was also evident during the EMS currency crisis of 1993. In the heated discussion of the ministerial meeting of 2 August 1993, the French proposed that Germany leave the EMS. The Dutch, Belgian, Danish and Luxembourg delegations protested very loudly and said that, if that were the case, they too would the leave the EMS, leaving France in the system with Spain and Portugal (*Financial Times*, 3 August 1993). The compromise was that the Exchange Rate Mechanism bands would be widened to plus or minus 15 per cent, except for the Dutch, who voluntarily preferred the narrow to the wide bands. Within a few days Belgium, Luxembourg and Denmark signaled that they too wanted to return to the narrow bands very soon (*Financial Times*, 10 August 1993). This declaration was equivalent to the formation of a fixed exchange rate club which France, Ireland, Spain and Portugal elected not to join. Indeed, these four countries formed a different kind of fixed exchange rate club, one which enjoyed more flexibility than the German-led club. A third group of member countries (Greece, Italy and the UK) elected not to participate in either club.[11]

Accession treaties have ruled out aspirants being able to obtain the derogation that the UK and Denmark obtained on monetary union in Maastricht. But how credible is this restriction in light of the fact that some member states have challenged the notion of a 'common EU vision' beyond the implementation of the Single Market? As the EU expands, the pressure for flexibility will mount, either because the economies are structurally different or because national policy preferences diverge.

Two Alternative Strategies of Integration

There are two sharp alternative strategies to enlargement. The first is full integration, with aspirants joining the EU at the level of integration reached by incumbents, including EMU, social policy and incipient forms of political integration. Not only is each member country assured of full integration, but the steps to deeper integration are structured along a precise sequence. We call this strategy the 'concentric approach' to integration. The alternative strategy is flexible integration. The basic premise of flexible integration is that great economic and political disparities between incumbents and aspirants may postpone accession to full integration to a very distant date, and the waiting period could prove too long for some aspirants. We will analyse the two alternatives with respect to monetary union (von Hagen and Fratianni, 1998).

We begin by dividing the 15 incumbents countries and 12 accession countries into three possible groups: 1, 2 and 3. Group 1 consists of the current 12 members of the EMU, sharing similar low-inflation preferences and developed banking industries. Group 2 consists of countries that, having a lesser commitment to price stability and less developed banking industries, wish to join the EMU of Group 1 to gain the credibility of low-inflation policies. In this group we would include most of the 12 aspirants. Group 3 consists of countries that, despite preferences for low inflation and well-developed banking industries, are not keen on EMU for one reason or another. The UK, Denmark and Sweden fit into Group 3.

The preferred outcome for Group 1 is to restrict membership of the EMU and endow it with a highly integrated regulatory system for banks. The preferred outcome for Group 2 is to join EMU both to gain credibility and to exert influence over European monetary policy, but not to integrate regulatory systems. Group 1 would have an incentive to exclude Group 2 from EMU because of the higher preferred inflation rate and the higher risk due to a common regulatory structure. The preferred outcome of Group 3 is neither to join EMU nor to harmonize banking regulation. Harmonization of bank regulation would reduce the international competitiveness of Group 3's banking industry. On the other hand, once EMU is in place, Group 3 would have an incentive to establish an integrated regulatory structure with Group 1 to remain competitive.

In the concentric approach integration is not only full but also structured to follow a precise sequence. This approach rules out the formation of competing functional areas; instead, all member countries have to agree ex ante on a set of entry rules (for example, the Maastricht criteria for Stage III of EMU) and on a sequence of integration steps (for example, should EMU occur before or after integrated regulatory functions?). Precise and observable entry rules eliminate the potential for discrimination by insiders against outsiders; the six entry criteria established by the Maastricht Treaty fall under this category. On the other hand, imprecise and difficult-to-observe criteria trigger discretion and the potential for discrimination by insiders against outsiders; banking and financial regulation fall under this category. The lack of precision of the TEU on banking regulation and supervision reflects the importance each member state assigns to this area and deep divisions among member states in reaching a common policy (Goodhart, 2000). Discretion on banking and financial regulation allowed Group 1 to create EMU before integrating banking regulation. It also gives an option to Group 1 to establish high regulatory standards and delay entry of Group 2 in EMU. Group 3 would support Group 1's position on the ground that monetary union would be delayed. Whether this option would be exercised depends on the payoff of an enlarged EMU to Group 1.

The payoff of an EMU enlargement could be negative for Group 1 if Group 2's banking systems were deemed sufficiently fragile to raise significantly the risk of managing a common regulatory system. In this case, Group 1 would exercise the option of erecting high enough regulatory standards to delay permanently the entry of Group 2 in EMU. On the other hand, if Group 2's banking systems were deemed more fragile than Group 1's banking systems but not enough to add significantly to the risk of a common regulatory structure, the option would be exercised to harden entry requirements, with the intent of postponing Group 2's entry in EMU. This scenario describes the game played so far in the EU. The northern group of the EU – that is, the core of EMU – accepted the principle that the southern countries, typified by Italy, could not be excluded from EMU. Tough entry standards were used to align the policies of the southern members to those of the northern members. In either case, the concentric approach to integration would prevent the emergence of a monetary periphery.

Under flexible integration, Group 1 could exclude Group 2 from EMU and Group 2 would be free to create an alternative arrangement. Group 1 and Group 3, having sufficiently similar banking structures and regulatory preferences, would decide to integrate their regulations. This would rise to at least two peripheries, a monetary union limited to Group 1 and an integrated regulatory system involving both Group 1 and Group 3. The existence of two peripheries would rule out the ECB being in charge of the integrated regulatory system. Group 2, excluded from both peripheries, would be free to create a periphery of its own, for example an EMU2, with a higher average inflation rate than EMU and a different regulatory system. Nothing would prevent EMU2, in the long run, from merging with EMU as the preferences for inflation and regulation of Group 2 converge to those of Group 1.

CONCLUSIONS

The Union is pursuing two objectives, deepening and enlargement, which are increasingly in conflict with each other. Dissent in the membership has been handled by accepting multi-speed integration and exempting recalcitrant members from participating in specific policy dimensions. The governance structure resulting from this approach is ad hoc, with certain rules and institutions having universal application and others not. More flexibility appears to be needed. Given the large and heterogeneous membership, common goals imply that only some members can pursue deep integration;

others will be relegated to shallow integration. The alternative to the current strategy is for members to participate in the integration process with different intensities and for the EU to accept partially overlapping jurisdictions.

Flexible integration breaks down one high hurdle into a lower required hurdle (the Single Market) and optional hurdles (EMU and other forms of integration). Participation in the Single Market would, in turn, facilitate the process of democratization and economic transformation in the east. The flexible integration strategy would also remove the obstacle of a distant accession date.

Enlargement presents more difficulty for monetary union than for the Single Market. Under the existing approach of full integration with a structured sequence, EMU incumbents may fear that an enlarged monetary union with a common regulatory system would generate negative payoffs. Incumbents would raise entry requirements and block expansion of EMU. Thus neither incumbents nor aspirants would want enlargement. Flexible integration provides a solution to the impasse: incumbents would be free to form their own monetary union immediately, without a depressingly long delay, and create the premises for a merger of two monetary unions in the future.

NOTES

*   This chapter extends the basic thesis developed in Fratianni (1999) from which it draws liberally.
1.   The Treaty on Monetary Union was agreed upon by the Heads of State at the Maastricht European Council in December 1991, signed by the Foreign and Finance Ministers in February 1992, and came into force in November 1993.
2.   Baldwin (1994, p. 176) concludes that 'an enlargement by 2000 that included only the Visegrad-4 would require an increase of the EU budget of about 70%'.
3.   The functioning of the price system requires an agreement among parties to respect property rights and adherence to contracts. Thus even markets require the institution of a specific legal structure.
4.   The Luxembourg Compromise was never codified as a formal decision-making procedure and was made irrelevant by the Single European Act of 1986. Yet it 'may not be quite completely dead' (Nugent, 1994, p. 145).
5.   Unanimity still applies in important fields such as taxation and social regulation.
6.   The estimates of the net gains from the completion of the Single Market range from a minimum of 2.5 per cent to a maximum of 6.5 per cent of Community GDP (Commission, 1988, p. 19). The highest estimate includes the important, but more difficult to quantify, competition and restructuring effects, but excludes dynamic aspects such as the interaction between technological innovation and competition.
7.   The cooperation procedure makes life harder for the Council. Two readings are prescribed. The first reading is similar to the opinion stage in the consultation procedure. The Council adopts a common position by qualified majority. In the second reading the European Parliament has three months to take action. If the European Parliament rejects the common position, the Council can go ahead with the common position by voting unanimously. If the European Parliament amends the common position, the

latter is sent back to the Commission for revision. Within three months the Council can either accept the amendments by qualified majority or reject them unanimously.

In both the co-decision and assent procedures the European Parliament has veto power. With respect to the cooperation procedure, the co-decision procedure starts after the Council approves the common position. The European Parliament can approve, modify or reject the Council's common position. Either one of the two last instances triggers a Conciliation Committee consisting of an equal number of Council's members and European Parliament's members. If the Conciliation Committee finds an agreement, the European Parliament and the Council must adopt the compromise, otherwise the compromise becomes null. If the Conciliation Committee does not find an agreement, the Council can approve the common position with the amendments proposed by the European Parliament; alternatively, the Parliament can reject the proposal. As the name suggests, the assent procedure requires the European Parliament to approve the proposal.

8. Begg (1997) calculates that Slovenia would receive transfers equal to 7 per cent of its GDP and Lithuania 51 per cent.
9. Using a model where (i) the inflation rate is determined by equating the marginal distortions from collecting the inflation tax and income taxes and (ii) each national representative votes according to his or her national interest, Fratianni and von Hagen (1992, p. 168) conclude that Spain would be the pivotal voter in a nine-member EMU, and that the EMU inflation rate would be one-third higher than the inflation rate preferred by Germany.
10. There are six entry conditions, relating to inflation rates, long-term interest rates, government budget deficits, government debt, exchange rate realignments and independence of national central banks.
11. Italy and the United Kingdom left the Exchange Rate Mechanism, following the turbulent exchange market events of September 1992. Greece never joined the Exchange Rate Mechanism.

REFERENCES

Baldwin, Richard E. (1993), 'A Domino Theory of Regionalism', National Bureau of Economic Research, Working Paper no. 4465, September, Cambridge, MA.

Baldwin, Richard E. (1994), *Towards an Integrated Europe*, London: CEPR.

Begg, Ian (1997), 'Inter-regional Transfers in a Widened Europe', in Horst Siebert (ed.), *Quo Vadis Europe?*, Tübingen: Mohr.

Buchanan, James M. (1965), 'An Economic Theory of Clubs', *Economica*, 32 (February): 1–14.

Casella, Alessandra (1992), 'On Markets and Clubs: Economic and Political Integration of Regions with Unequal Productivity', *American Economic Review*, 82 (2) (May): 115–21.

Casella, Alessandra and Bruno Frey (1992), 'Federalism and Clubs: Towards an Economic Theory of Overlapping Political Jurisdictions', *European Economic Review*, 36: 639–46.

Commission of the European Communities (1988), 'The Economics of 1992', *European Economy*, 35 (March).

Financial Times (1993), 'ERM Bands Produce Sort of Harmony', 3 August.

Financial Times (1993), 'Commission Determined to Hold Line on EMU Strategy', 10 August.

Fratianni, Michele (1994), 'What Went Wrong with the EMS and European Monetary Union', in Berhanu Abegaz, Patricia Dillon, David H. Feldman and

Paul F. Whiteley (eds), *The Challenge of European Integration: Internal and External Problems of Trade and Money*, Boulder: Westview Press.

Fratianni, Michele (1999), 'Governance of the EU in the Twenty-first Century', in Aseem Prakash and Jeffrey A. Hart (eds), *Globalization and Governance*, London and New York: Routledge.

Fratianni, Michele and John Pattison (1982), 'The Economics of International Organizations', *Kyklos*, fasc. 2, pp. 22–35.

Fratianni, Michele and John Pattison (2001), 'International Organisations in a World of Regional Trade Agreements: Lessons from Club Theory', *The World Economy*, 24(3): 333–58.

Fratianni, Michele and Jürgen von Hagen (1992), *The European Monetary System and European Monetary Union*, Boulder: Westview Press.

Garrett, Geoffrey (1993), 'The Politics of Maastricht', *Economics and Politics*, 5 (July): 105–23.

Goodhart, Charles, A.E. (1999), 'Myths about the Lender of Last Resort', Henry Thornton Lecture, City University Business School, 17 November.

Goodhart, Charles, A.E. (ed.) (2000), *Which Lender of Last Resort for Europe?*, London: Central Banking Publications Limited.

Martin, Lisa (1993), 'International and Domestic Institutions in the EMU Process', *Economics and Politics*, 5(2): 125–44.

Nugent, Neil (1994), *The Government and Politics of the European Union*, 3rd edn, Durham, NC: Duke University Press.

Olson, Mancur (1965), *The Logic of Collective Action*, Cambridge: Harvard University Press.

Sandholtz, Wayne (1996), 'Rules, Reasons and International Institutions', paper presented at the International Studies Association, San Diego, California, 15–21 April.

Swann, Dennis (1992), *The Economics of the Common Market*, 7th edn, London: Penguin Books.

Von Hagen, Jürgen and Michele Fratianni (1998), 'Banking Regulation with Variable Geometry', in Barry Eichengreen and Jeffrey Frieden (eds), *Forging an Integrated Europe*, Ann Arbor: The University of Michigan Press.

2. EU governance under duress? Tax policy coordination under globalization

Mehmet Ugur

INTRODUCTION

One of the issues in the debate on globalization is the extent of policy arbitrage caused by cross-border mobility and the impact of this arbitrage on the quality of governance. This chapter aims to contribute to the current debate by developing and testing a political economy model of the relationship between globalization and governance quality. The proposed model assumes strategic interaction between the state and non-state actors in a world divided into jurisdictions that compete for the loyalty of the non-state actors. It predicts that globalization, understood as increased cross-border mobility of the non-state actors, does not necessarily undermine governance quality provided that the policy issues are transparent and divisible.

We define governance as the supply by a public authority of rules, procedures and codes of conduct that regulate the interaction between state and non-state actors. The quality of governance is defined as the extent to which the public authority supplies these public goods in an efficient and non-discriminatory manner. In this context, governance quality is an indicator of the extent to which the public authority is not captured either by state bureaucracy or by non-state actors. (For similarity and differences between this definition and others discussed by the EU Commission and the European Bank for Reconstruction and Development, see European Commission, 2001; Hellman and Schankerman, 2000).

One strand in the globalization and integration debate argues that increased cross-border mobility would lead to policy arbitrage between jurisdictions. Policy arbitrage entails convergence, which limits the governance options available to the public authority. This approach can be described as 'society-centric' because it focuses on the constraints that non-state actors impose on public policy. The other strand in the debate can be described as 'state-centric'. It argues that the scope (and need) for global or national governance may not be reduced by cross-border mobility. That is because cross-border mobility is either initiated by the state or the state acts as a gatekeeper between the global and national levels.

The approach proposed here differs from existing approaches on two counts. First, and in contrast to the society-centric approaches, it demonstrates that governance quality need not be undermined by the high degree of convergence dictated by cross-border mobility. On the contrary, effective and efficient governance is more likely to be undermined by the nature of the institutions through which convergence is mediated. Secondly, and in opposition to the state-centric approach, it argues that governance quality depends not on the autonomy of the state but on how this autonomy is deployed during the interaction with non-state actors. The model underpinning these arguments is developed in the next section, after a brief review of the debate on globalization and regional integration.

A subsequent section examines the issue of tax policy coordination in the EU with respect to business and capital income taxation. As is well known, this is an area where public policy choices can be constrained by high levels of capital mobility between jurisdictions. Therefore the existing literature would predict that governance in this policy area will be either ineffective (the society-centric thesis) or inefficient (the state-centric thesis). Our evidence demonstrates that these predictions are incompatible with the emerging EU response to increased tax competition. We will demonstrate that policy convergence caused by increased cross-border mobility can go hand in hand with effective and innovative governance. We conclude with certain propositions on the implications of globalization for EU governance in policy areas characterized by a high degree of cross-border mobility.

GLOBALIZATION, REGIONAL INTEGRATION AND EU GOVERNANCE: A REVIEW AND A PROPOSAL

Globalization has become the buzzword in the study of the world economy. This chapter does not intend to order and analyse the extensive debate – an exercise already undertaken by Higgot and Reich (1998) and Held *et al.* (1999, pp. 2–20). Here, we limit ourselves to an assessment of the current debate's conclusions concerning the link between globalization and regional integration, and the implications of these processes for the quality of the national or global governance structures.

An Overview of the Debate

The key issue in the globalization debate is the extent to which effective governance may be undermined by increased cross-border movements of people, goods and factors of production, a phenomenon facilitated and encouraged by technological advances. This concern reflects the perennial conflict between the state as a territorially competent actor and the non-state actors whose competence is vertical/functional. Yet one striking aspect of the debate is the absence of theorization about the way the state interacts with non-state actors. The debate tends to derive conclusions based on exogenously given incentives and constraints rather than endogenously determined outcomes that state or non-state actors may or may not prefer ex ante. Because of the exogenous approach to policy, those who focus on the societal constraints derive *society-centric* conclusions while those focusing on the constraints imposed by the state derive *state-centric* conclusions.

The society-centric approach focuses on societal constraints that globalization imposes on effective governance. Here we are faced with two versions. The 'strong constraint' version emphasizes the universalization of the market structures. It envisages no or very little scope for policy autonomy (Ohmae, 1990, 1995; Albrow, 1996; Greider, 1997). The 'weak constraint' version puts forward two arguments. First, the level of cross-border mobility may not be as high as the 'strong constraint' thesis would suggest. Therefore Hirst and Thompson (1996) envisage a significant scope for active governance because the world economy is less global now than it was in the nineteenth century. The second argument is that high levels of cross-border mobility create significant externalities that justify public intervention. (See, for example, Dunning, 1997; Arndt, 1997; Commission on Global Governance, 1995, pp. 147–57).

The state-centric approach can also be divided into two categories. In the 'strong state' version, the state initiates, shapes or capitalizes on the process of globalization (Boyer and Drache, 1996; Ramesh, 1995). The 'weak state' version agrees that globalization may render the territorial boundaries porous, but it also argues that inter-state relations reproduce these boundaries and the structures contained by them (Armstrong, 1998; Held *et al.*, 1999). For Cox (1997), the state is a transmission belt through which liberal policy prescriptions pass from the global to the national domain. Similarly, Grant (1998) argues that the state might respond to globalization pragmatically and use it as an alibi for implementing unpleasant policies that it wishes to implement anyway (see also, Armingean, 1997).

The tendency to derive state-centric conclusions is also observable in the emerging literature on the connections between globalization and regional integration. In this literature, regional integration is analysed as a state reaction to globalization. According to Sideri (1997, p. 53), regionalization may be seen as an attempt to reduce the pace of globalization and/or minimize its costs. In the case of less developed countries, regionalization may lessen the effect of marginalization implied by globalization (Sideri, 1993). A similar view is put forward by Hirst and Thompson (1995), who indicate that trade blocs may allow member countries to withstand the global pressure on specific policy issues and to pursue policy objectives that may not be feasible when member countries act independently. Others analyse regional integration as a strategic reaction of the state to its main rivals in the world economy. For example, Streeck and Schmitter (1991, p. 149) argue that the aim of the European Union's Single Market was 'to recapture collective autonomy in relation to the US and to begin to organise a competitive response to the Japanese challenge'.

This literature cannot explain why the interaction between state and non-state actors has generated different levels of integration within different regional blocs. Nor can it predict which types of integration arrangements (deep v. shallow) are less or more capable of developing effective governance structures under globalization. For example Higgot (1998) and Stubbs (1998) highlight the differences in the extent of intra-bloc convergence in the EU, the Asia-Pacific and North America. However, neither they nor Coleman and Underhill (1998a) provide any explanation as to why these differences exist and what implications they have for these blocs' ability to deliver effective governance. Although Milner (1998, p. 21) indicates that divided government is a recipe for failure in the international coordination game, neither she nor other contributors to the volume by Coleman and Underhill (1998b) examine the implications of this observation for the quality of governance within loose (that is, less coherent) regional integration arrangements.

It must be acknowledged that the literature on globalization and regionalization has been successful in drawing our attention to significant developments that have emerged in the 1990s and will continue to unfold in the future. It has also taken the debate a step further by moving beyond the compatibility of regional integration with multilateral trade liberalization. We are now discussing, not only whether regional integration is a building or stumbling block to trade liberalization, but also its implications for governance in a global context. However, we are still far from having either a unified methodology to study the two processes or a common analytical framework from which testable hypotheses can be derived. This is due largely to a *reductionist* tendency that focuses on the state or on non-state actors rather than on the *endogenous* outcomes of the strategic interaction between them. The paragraphs below will develop an analytical framework that is based on this strategic interaction and is capable of capturing the endogenous nature of the EU's governance structures.

The Political Economy of Interjurisdictional Loyalty Shifts and Policy Convergence

We start with the maxim that no theory is better that its assumptions. Therefore it is essential that we state our assumptions explicitly. First, we assume that the world will remain divided into different jurisdictions as long as the *functionally competent* non-state actors are unable to solve the extra-market coordination problem that can be tackled only by a public authority with *territorial competence*. Therefore exit from and entry into a jurisdiction is costly – although the cost may vary over time and across jurisdictions. Secondly, we assume that the territorially competent states interact with each other and with their constituents as monopolistically competitive units. Finally, we assume that both the state and non-state actors are rational in the instrumentalist sense that they respond to the constraint/benefit structures they face in a manner that will maximize their utilities.

Given these assumptions, we will demonstrate that the state's reaction to high levels of cross-border mobility (a proxy for globalization) may or may not reflect the preferences of the non-state actors whose movement between jurisdictions is the cause of the state's reaction. We will also demonstrate that governance quality under low levels of cross-border mobility is not necessarily better than the governance quality under high levels of cross-border mobility. To do this, we will draw on Hotelling (1929), who demonstrates that the ability of customers to shift loyalty from one firm to the other does not necessarily enable them to maximize welfare. In fact, loyalty shifts may induce the firms to adopt *convergent* price, location or quality strategies that would reduce the customers' choice and, consequently, welfare. This finding enables us to hypothesize that increased cross-border mobility (that is, increased globalization) does not necessarily increase the ability of the internationally mobile actors to constrain the governments' policy choices and extract rents associated with societal capture of the public policy.

Hotelling's model is based on strategic interaction at two levels: firm–firm and firm–customer. The firm–firm strategic interaction is worked out very well and has been revisited and developed by various contributors, of whom d'Aspermont *et al.* (1979) is a good example. The analysis runs as follows: in a world where customer loyalty shifts are possible but costly, the firm's best reaction is to adopt convergent strategies in terms of the attributes that influence the customer's loyalty (price, quality, location and so on). Hotelling demonstrates that convergent prices, qualities or locations would maximize firm profits at the expense of reduced customer choice. This is a specific manifestation of a Nash equilibrium that would be sustainable provided that the customer demand for the firm's product was not perfectly elastic. In other words, convergence is the optimal choice for firms as long as the customer's cost of shifting loyalty from one supplier to the other is not zero. The extent of convergence may decline as the number of suppliers increases, but the tendency towards convergence will prevail even if the number of firms in the market is large.

The second, but less successfully worked, level of interaction is between firms and their customers. In Hotelling's analysis, the customers' quest for the lowest-cost supply (that is, maximum utility) induces the firms to opt for convergent location, price or quality choices. This outcome is suboptimal for customers as the latter are now faced with reduced choice. In addition, they are faced with reduced incentive to shift loyalty from one firm to the other with the aim of maximizing utility. It was this endogenous process that led Hotelling (1929, p. 58) to observe that firms would engage in outright competition for the loyalty of the marginal customer but without necessarily discriminating in his or her favor. What this analysis overlooks is the possibility that firms may utilize other strategies of loyalty maintenance, which may take the form of product differentiation, branding or market segmentation based on outright collusion. Hotelling considers collusion as irrelevant as it is too risky, given competition laws, and unstable, given the incentive to renege on the illicit agreement. Although this is a valid argument, the neglect of product differentiation and branding remains a major weakness of Hotelling's approach.

Despite this shortcoming, Hotelling's analytical framework may still enable us to capture the implications of inter-state competition for constituent loyalty. In fact, inter-state competition provides a highly relevant context to extend Hotelling's analysis to situations where 'market' segmentation, policy differentiation and identification with a given jurisdiction are the norm. In this context, states (or governments as proxies) compete for constituent loyalty, whereas constituents seek to maximize the utility derived from loyalty to a given jurisdiction. This context is similar to Hotelling's monopolistically competitive market, but it also differs from the latter because the monopoly power of Hotelling's firms does not result from artificial barriers to loyalty shifts. In the state system, physical border controls, different legal systems, differences in law enforcement, nationalist ideology and so on all function as barriers to loyalty shifts. These barriers result from the state's territorial/lateral competence and their incidence depends on the states' past preferences and their current methods of loyalty maintenance. Therefore Hotelling's analytical framework must be qualified by allowing for *state-specific* differences in the level of artificial barriers against loyalty shifts.

Hotelling's analysis must also be qualified in order to allow for *policy-specific* differences in the level of artificial barriers. According to Hotelling, customers switch between suppliers on the basis of transparent costs and benefits associated with loyalty shifts. In addition, these costs and benefits are determined by given preferences of the customer rather than by differences in the formation of these preferences. In the state system, however, the costs/benefits associated with loyalty shifts are not necessarily transparent. This is because switching loyalty from one jurisdiction to the other entails costs/benefits associated, not only with the policy issue that triggers the decision at hand, but also with other policies that would affect the constituent's welfare after the new jurisdiction is chosen. The costs/benefits may also be affected by loyalty-increasing variables such as ideology, patriotism and cultural identity. To the extent that this is the case, each constituent will be faced with a reduced incentive to switch loyalty to a new jurisdiction.

Using Hirschman's (1970) exit–voice–loyalty framework, we can qualify Hotelling's conclusions in three ways. First, the higher is the state's ability to block 'exit' in a policy area, the lower is the scope for loyalty shifts from one jurisdiction to the other and the lower is the extent of convergence between national public policies. Secondly, the less transparent the costs/benefits of 'exit', the lower is the incentive for switching jurisdictions, and thereby, the lower is the level of policy convergence between national jurisdictions. Finally, the extent of loyalty volatility (hence policy convergence) will be lower the stronger is the impact of loyalty-increasing variables on the constituent's choice of jurisdiction.

The Political Economy of Policy Convergence, Regional Integration and Governance Quality

In the analysis above, the extent of policy convergence between jurisdictions is a result of strategic interaction not only between states but also between the latter and their constituents. This is similar to Putnam's (1988) 'two-level game', where governments agree to international agreements or codes of conduct that are compatible with the societal constraint on international policy choices. Nevertheless, it differs from Putnam's model in two significant ways. First, Putnam's analysis is static in the sense that the game is limited to a single international agreement and it is played independently of previous games. Our analysis is dynamic: that is, the state–state and state–society interaction is a repeated game. Secondly, for Putnam the state is a self-interested Leviathan who tries to maximize its objective function subject to a given societal constraint. In our approach, the societal constraint may exist but it is not externally given. On the contrary, the repeated interaction between the state and non-state actors makes the societal constraint and, thereby, the outcomes of the state–society interaction endogenous. This is due to the fact that the results of the interaction at one stage of the game may alter the cost/incentive structure that the state and/or non-state actors face in the next stage. To the extent this is the case, the outcomes of the state–constituent interaction become less determinate and may turn out to be unintended for both actors.

The second implication of the analysis above is that the extent of policy convergence can be related to two variables bearing upon the state–state and state–society interaction: *cross-border mobility* and *transparency/divisibility* of policy issues. While cross-border mobility reflects the volatility of the constituents' loyalty to a given jurisdiction, issue transparency/divisibility reflects the extent to which the implications of a policy decision are quantifiable and state/non-state actors are unable to equate a certain policy decision with an overarching national interest that the state must defend against 'outsiders'. Therefore the higher the level of transparency/divisibility is, the less able is the state bureaucracy or non-state actors to capture the public authority. Under this condition, the public policy maker is more likely to engage in package deals involving trade-offs between gains in some areas and losses in others. As a result, policy coordination may be facilitated, the extent of convergence may be increased and the convergent policy choices may be less of a reflection of societal preferences (Ugur, 1997).

The endogenous consequences of the strategic interaction between the state and non-state actors at the national level are depicted in Figure 2.1 below. Here, the dependent variable is the endogenously determined level of policy convergence that an individual government would choose to stabilize the loyalty of its constituents. The independent variables are the extent of cross-border mobility and the level of issue transparency/divisibility.

We can see that the highest level of policy convergence occurs in cell B2, where cross-border mobility and transparency/divisibility are high. High

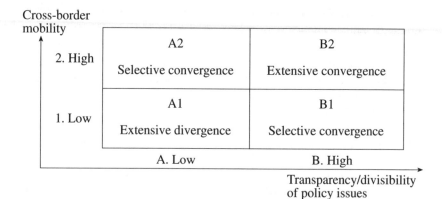

Figure 2.1   Levels of policy convergence for stabilizing constituent loyalty

cross-border mobility induces policy makers to coordinate their policies with those of other jurisdictions in order to stabilize constituent loyalty and/or minimize externalities associated with loyalty shifts. On the other hand, high levels of issue transparency/divisibility increase the feasibility of convergence. While transparency renders the impact of policy change quantifiable, divisibility implies that the costs/benefits of the policy change are distributed unequally between the relevant actors. Then the combination of high cross-border mobility and transparency/divisibility makes policy convergence preferable and less costly. It is preferable because it stabilizes constituent loyalty (that is, it reduces the ability of the non-state actors to capture the policy maker). It is less costly because transparency/divisibility facilitates the construction of winning coalitions domestically and provides a basis for negotiating the terms of the distribution between as well as within jurisdictions.

In contrast, the dominant trend would be policy divergence when the independent variables are low (cell A1). Low cross-border mobility means that there is less pressure on the policy maker to engage in policy convergence as a means of loyalty stabilization. This implies that the policy maker will be well-positioned to pick up divergent policies reflecting their preferences. On the other hand, low issue transparency/divisibility implies that either the state or non-state actors are able to equate their interests with an overarching national interest that must be defended against others. This combination causes policy makers to shy away from policy convergence and leads to a higher probability of 'societal' or 'bureaucratic' capture of the public policy.

In cell B1, the level of cross-border mobility is the same as in A1, but issue transparency/divisibility is higher. Therefore, in cell B1, we would expect relatively higher convergence compared to A1. That is because higher transparency/divisibility reduces the cost of negotiations leading to policy convergence – which is functional for reducing cross-border mobility. Finally, we expect only selective convergence in cell A2 despite the fact that cross-border mobility is as high as in B2. In contrast to the extensive convergence in B2, convergence in A2 will remain selective because issue transparency/divisibility is lower than in B2. Comparing A2 and B2, we can conclude that high cross-border mobility is not always conducive to high levels of convergence.

Having identified the endogenously determined levels of policy convergence, we can now use the same framework to analyse the governance quality that a group of countries are likely to secure with and without an institutionalized integration framework. For convenience, we will label the integration framework as EU and the group of countries as the sum of EU member states acting individually. The exercise will enable us to identify the variations in governance quality under the integration scenario (with EU) and answer the counterfactual question as to what that quality would be without integration (without EU).

Convergence quality, as indicated in the introduction, refers to the extent that the public authority is not captured either by state bureaucracy or by non-state actors. In Figure 2.2 below, we denote these captures as 'bureaucratic' and 'societal'. The extent of capture, on the other hand, is depicted by a scale ranging from 1 to 5, where 1 indicates the lowest and 5 indicates the highest level of capture. The values for bureaucratic and societal capture are added to provide an indication of the total capture level. Assuming that the optimal level of governance quality is Q, we can derive a governance quality index by discounting Q with the level of capture. Given this specification, the higher the capture level is the lower is governance quality.

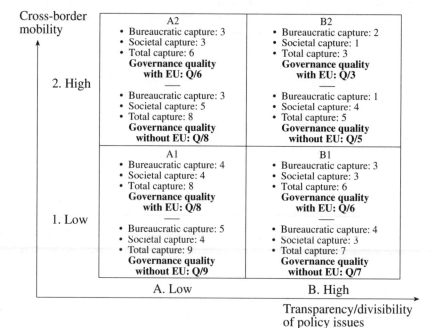

Cross-border mobility ↑	A2 • Bureaucratic capture: 3 • Societal capture: 3 • Total capture: 6 **Governance quality with EU: Q/6** —— • Bureaucratic capture: 3 • Societal capture: 5 • Total capture: 8 **Governance quality without EU: Q/8**	B2 • Bureaucratic capture: 2 • Societal capture: 1 • Total capture: 3 **Governance quality with EU: Q/3** —— • Bureaucratic capture: 1 • Societal capture: 4 • Total capture: 5 **Governance quality without EU: Q/5**
2. High		
1. Low	A1 • Bureaucratic capture: 4 • Societal capture: 4 • Total capture: 8 **Governance quality with EU: Q/8** —— • Bureaucratic capture: 5 • Societal capture: 4 • Total capture: 9 **Governance quality without EU: Q/9**	B1 • Bureaucratic capture: 3 • Societal capture: 3 • Total capture: 6 **Governance quality with EU: Q/6** —— • Bureaucratic capture: 4 • Societal capture: 3 • Total capture: 7 **Governance quality without EU: Q/7**
	A. Low	B. High →

Transparency/divisibility of policy issues

Figure 2.2   Effectiveness and efficiency of governance quality under two scenarios

The first observation that Figure 2.2 allows is that governance quality is not uniform across policy issues and levels of cross-border mobility. Focusing only on the scenario with integration (with EU), we can see that endogenous governance quality ranges from the highest level of Q/3 in cell

B2, through Q/6 in cells A2 and B1, to the lowest level of Q/8 in cell A1. Focusing on the scenario without integration, we can see that governance quality can be ranked as follows: Q/5 in cell B2; Q/7 in cell B1; Q/8 in A2; and Q/9 in cell A1. The second observation is that governance quality within each cell is higher when the scenario envisages integration (that is, with EU). The third observation is that governance quality (with and without EU) tends to improve as the level of cross-border mobility and issue transparency/divisibility increases. Hence the lowest governance quality results in cell A1, where both cross-border mobility and issue transparency/divisibility are low.

In the remainder of this section, we will first demonstrate that the specifications in Figure 2.2 are not arbitrary constructs. We will do this by explaining how these specifications follow from the analytical framework developed above and depicted in Figure 2.1. Then we will provide explanation and some evidence as to why these endogenous outcomes are relevant to EU governance in the 'real world'.

Comparing Figures 2.1 and 2.2, we can see that the capture level specified in Figure 2.2 is negatively correlated to the extent of convergence derived in Figure 2.1. That is because policy convergence emerges as a solution to two problems. On the one hand, it enables the policy maker to stabilize the loyalty of the constituents without discriminating in their favor. In other words, it enables the public authority to resist capture by non-state actors. On the other hand, it ties the hands of the policy maker by reducing the scope for discretionary policy. Therefore the ability of the state bureaucracy to shape policy in line with their interests is also reduced. Consequently, when high cross-border mobility and transparency/divisibility combine to generate policy convergence (cell B2 in Figure 2.1), the total capture of the public authority is at its lowest level – irrespective of whether the EU exists or not.

We can now open up cell B2 in Figure 2.2 and explain why total capture is lower with EU compared to the counterfactual scenario of 'without EU'. As is well known, the EU system is characterized by two properties: extensive prior bargaining on the stance of the common (that is, convergent) policy to be adopted; and legally binding rules that increases the cost of defection once the common policy has been adopted. These properties make the EU a credible commitment device that (a) ensures cost/benefit distribution between and within member states, and (b) reduces the probability of deviations from agreed convergence.

Under these conditions, the ability of the non-state actors to demand and secure special treatment is reduced. This can be described as the 'federation effect' of regional integration, whereby EU-level rules can be relied upon to deflect societal demands for special treatment (see Krugman, 1993, for a similar comment). Therefore, in cell B2, the level of societal capture is lower with EU compared to the scenario without EU. Integration also reduces the ability of national policy makers to shape the common policy in line with their preferences. As Hotelling's analysis suggests, monopolistically competing firms have to satisfice with maximizing profits over the segment of the market under their control rather than increase the magnitude of the profits by driving their rivals out. Similarly, the endogenous equilibrium in the EU requires that an EU member state must accept convergent policies that stabilize constituent loyalty across national jurisdictions. As a result of this dynamic, national bureaucracies will be less able to capture the public authority at the EU-level, even though the EU-level bureaucracy may still remain a possible source of capture risk. That is why total capture under EU (3) is lower than the total capture without EU (5), which means that governance quality under integration is higher than the case of no integration.

Now let us examine the distribution of bureaucratic and societal captures with and without integration. Focusing on cell B2 again, we can see that bureaucratic capture with EU (2) is higher than the bureaucratic capture without EU (1). This is due to the fact that, without EU, the member states act individually and engage in competitive bidding for constituent loyalty. As they do this, the member states become less able to shape the public policy in line with their preferences. Under EU, the member states also lose that capacity because of the competence delegated to EU institutions, but the bureaucracy of the latter emerges as a new capture risk – hence the higher level of bureaucratic capture with EU. The mirror image of this distribution can be seen in the case of societal capture. Without integration, societal capture is high (4), but it is very low under integration (1). Under integration, the risk of societal capture is minimized by the 'federation effect' mentioned above. Without integration, however, the risk of societal capture is high because the highly mobile non-state actors are in a position to exploit the competitive bidding policies of the individual governments who try to attract loyalty to their jurisdictions.

Space limitation does not allow us to examine each cell individually. Nevertheless, it may be sufficient to indicate that the levels of captures (hence the quality of governance structures) in all other cells are specified on the basis of the analysis above, which underpins Figure 2.1 and takes account of different levels of cross-border mobility and transparency/divisibility. Therefore we can proceed to convert the observations made above into testable hypotheses and provide some evidence regarding their relevance for EU governance.

The first observation in Figure 2.2 was that EU governance quality is not uniform across policy issues and levels of cross-border mobility. The first hypothesis (H1) that can be derived from this observation is the following: *EU governance quality will tend to improve as cross-border mobility and policy issue transparency/divisibility increase.* This hypothesis will be tested in the next section, with respect to the EU's response to increased capital mobility. Nevertheless, we can cite some evidence concerning its relevance to other areas of governance.

For example, the deepening of integration after the single market (an arrangement that reduced the barriers to cross-border mobility) has been followed by reduced societal capture on the EU's trade policy vis-à-vis the rest of world. Pelkmans (1993) provides evidence of this effect with respect to trade in textiles and clothing. Similarly, Messerlin and Reed (1995) demonstrate that the EU's anti-dumping policy has become less protectionist and converged towards that of the USA after the mid-1980s. Also, while Ugur (1998) demonstrates that the deepening of integration has been associated with a less protectionist EU trade policy in a sensitive sector such as textiles and clothing, Ugur (2000) demonstrates that EU trade policy is more likely to be compatible with multilateral liberalization compared to a trade policy of shallow integration arrangements. In addition, we know from the European Monetary System (EMS) experience that the liberalization of capital movements between EU member states was accompanied by successful management of the exchange rates, leading to a smooth transition to the single currency.

The second observation was that governance quality within each cell is higher when the scenario assumes integration, but the quality of governance without integration improves as the level of convergence increases. The second hypothesis (H2) to be derived from this observation can be stated as follows: *policy convergence may reduce the options available for the policy maker, but it will improve governance quality.* The third hypothesis (H3) that can be derived is that *governance quality (with or without EU) tends to improve as the level of convergence increases.* Owing to space limitation, these hypotheses will not be tested in this chapter. However, we would like to provide some evidence suggesting that they are relevant. The cross-country data presented by the World Bank (1996, pp. 23–8), indicate that there is a positive correlation between (a) economic performance and policy convergence caused by integration into the world economy, and (b) policy efficiency and convergent policy choices. For example, the country groups that introduced policy reform in the 1980s to increase the speed of their integration into the world economy tended to achieve higher growth rates compared to those that opted otherwise. Also the convergent policies adopted by fast integrators tended to produce better macroeconomic performance in terms of inflation rates, budget deficits and exchange rate volatility. Finally, the data indicate that the higher the extent of policy convergence was, the lower was the risk premium that the countries had to pay in the international financial market. Although this partial evidence should not be taken as confirmation of the two hypotheses, it demonstrates that they may be relevant and deserve further investigation.

TAX POLICY COORDINATION IN THE EU OR THE STORY OF IMPROVED GOVERNANCE QUALITY UNDER GLOBALIZATION

The stylized facts about European taxation policy are fairly straightforward. Increased capital mobility has induced the European governments to engage in tax competition with a view to attracting the loyalty of the mobile tax base. For example, the statutory overall (national and local) corporate tax rates in the EU member states declined from 46 per cent in 1980 to 40.5 per cent in 1992. This is very similar to the trend in the OECD area, where rates have declined from 46.3 per cent to 40.3 per cent over the same period. Also the top tax rate on interest income has fallen from 48 per cent to 36.4 per cent in the EU and from 49.6 per cent to 37 per cent in the OECD (Owens, 1993, pp. 32, 37). As a result of this tendency, the implicit average European tax rate on the relatively mobile factors of production (capital, energy, natural resources and so on) has fallen from 45 per cent in 1980 to 35 per cent in 1996. In contrast, the implicit tax rate on the less mobile factors (mainly employed labor) has increased from 35 per cent to 42 per cent over the same period (de Silguy, 1998). This trend, if unchecked, can be expected to intensify after the establishment of the monetary union as the elimination of currency risk would encourage further capital mobility between jurisdictions.

These trends lend support to the main argument of the existing literature on globalization, namely that increased capital mobility would shift the tax burden away from the mobile tax base and that the taxing capacity of the member states would diminish. In fact, this is confirmed by the OECD (1998) report, which concludes that harmful tax competition has reshaped the desired mix of taxes and public expenditures and undermined the fairness of the national tax structures.

Although such diagnosis and predictions are correct, they tend to overlook the factors that may instigate a counter-tendency towards tax policy coordination. Given that this counter-tendency is now observable in the EU, we need a more robust yet flexible approach that would enable us to predict the incidence of both competitive bidding (low-quality governance) as well as policy coordination to tackle harmful tax competition (high-quality governance). In what follows, we will demonstrate that the analytical framework developed above can enable us to account for both tendencies in the EU's capital income and corporate taxation policy.

That framework predicts that, under high levels of capital mobility and an integration scenario, the scope for good governance will be low when transparency/divisibility is low (Q/6 in cell A2). However, the governance quality will improve if transparency/divisibility increases (Q/3 in cell B2). Before the mid-1990s, two trends combined to generate low-quality European governance in the area of taxation. First, EU governments (including other OECD members) reduced the barriers to capital mobility by liberalizing capital movements (OECD, 1998). This led to increased cross-border mobility and arbitrage, which, in the EU's case, was encouraged further by the establishment of the Single Market. Secondly, EU governments tended to consider the taxation policy (with the exception of indirect taxation) as an issue of national sovereignty. This tendency led to the equalization of tax policy issues with an overarching national interest and produced an array of non-transparent rules designed to attract the mobile tax base (ibid.). As a result of both tendencies, taxation policy issues tended to correspond to cell A2 of Figure 2.2, where cross mobility is high and transparency/divisibility is low.

After the mid-1990s, capital mobility remained high and the prospect for even higher mobility became evident as the transition to monetary union set in. Unlike the previous period, however, the transparency/divisibility of the taxation policy increased, for two reasons. On the one hand, the debate on taxation – even though it was still colored by a sovereignty discourse – has acquired a technical dimension following the coordination of VAT rates after the Single Market and the fiscal convergence criteria of the monetary union. On the other hand, researchers as well as policy makers began to realize that reducing high unemployment may remain an elusive quest under the tendency of continued increase in the tax burden on labor. In addition, high unemployment was eroding the immobile tax base. Under these conditions, tax policy coordination has become less of a taboo for the member states and taxation policy issues began to correspond to cell B2 of Figure 2.2.

In line with the prediction of our analytical framework, the combination of high capital mobility and increased transparency/divisibility induced the member states and the Commission to recognize the possibility of coordinating taxation policies with a view to reducing the incentives for interjurisdictional movements without erecting artificial barriers. In the words of the Commission representative at the time, such convergence would leave fewer reasons for markets to distinguish between national jurisdictions (de Silguy, 1998). It was recognized that coordinated policy convergence could approximate the returns on loyalty to a given jurisdiction and, thereby, reduce the incentive for one-way loyalty shifts. Also EU institutions could be called upon to facilitate bargaining on the distribution of the costs and benefits that would result from policy coordination. Under these conditions, tax policy coordination became not only more desirable but also more feasible.

It must be stated at the outset that the transition from harmful tax competition to tax policy coordination has been a messy process and the speed of change leaves much to be desired. One major reason for this inefficiency has been the tendency of the member states to protect their prerogatives in the area of taxation. Another reason has been the possibility that non-EU countries may gain a competitive edge unless they are forced to undertake similar actions against harmful tax competition. Despite its drawbacks, however, the EU's achievement has been much more comprehensive than that of any other international organization, including the OECD.

The negotiations and technical work in the EU covered three major areas. First, a code of conduct for corporate taxation was drafted to combat harmful tax competition aiming to influence the company's location decisions. From the beginning, the code of conduct was envisaged to be a political declaration and not a binding directive. Secondly, a directive was drafted to reduce the scope for the flight of deposits or bond-based investments from high-tax to low-tax jurisdictions. Finally, a directive was drafted to avoid double taxation of the interest and royalty payments between associated companies. These initiatives compared very favorably with the second most advanced attempt, which was taken by the OECD and was limited only to tax policy coordination in the area of financial transactions.[1] In addition, the work carried out increased the transparency and divisibility of the taxation issues to such a level that the 'national interest' argument became less tenable than it was in the mid-1990s. This 'injected' transparency/divisibility should reduce the veto power of the member states as the suboptimality and unfairness of the past practices become more evident. As a result, both member states and the mobile tax base were forced to argue their case in public and against others in the EU, leading to a fall in the possibility of both bureaucratic and societal capture in the area of taxation.

Until the Verona meeting of the Economics and Finance Ministers (ECOFIN) in April 1996, progress was impossible in the area of direct taxation policy coordination. Therefore, by 1997, there were 18 blocked and 30 withdrawn Commission proposals owing to lack of sufficient support in the Council (*Agence Europe*, 23.8.1997, p. 2). As European integration deepened, however, there was an attitude change among the member states. In the Commission's view, this change was due to various factors. First, the deepening of European integration made tax differentials a significant factor that would influence the companies' location decisions. Secondly, the European tax system had become increasingly biased against labor, especially the less qualified segments of the labor market. Finally, the incidence of fraud and tax avoidance increased. (European Commission, 1997a). In sum, the EU's attempt at tax policy coordination was clearly inspired by the level of capital mobility and the extent of externalities generated by that mobility.

Following the ECOFIN's Verona meeting, the Commission was instructed to prepare a report on harmful tax competition between the member states. This report was published in November 1996 and formed the basis of the Dublin Summit decision to establish the Taxation Policy Group (*Agence Europe Documents*, 14.11.1997, p. 2). Other EU institutions also had an input into this debate. The Monetary Committee of the European Monetary Institute drew attention to harmful tax competition, tax evasion and further erosion in the tax base under the single currency regime to be adopted (European Commission, 1997a). Also, in early January 1997, tax policy coordination was a central theme in the debate of the European Parliament, which provided some insights into the positions of different member states (*Agence Europe*, 27/28.1.1997, pp. 6–7).

By March 1997, the Taxation Policy Group was established and held its first meeting on 11 March. It agreed to define harmful tax competition as all practices (legal or administrative) that would have a detrimental effect on other member states. It also decided that the representatives of each member state should submit a list of such measures to the Commission, which would analyse and discuss these lists with a view to securing agreement (*Agence Europe*, 10/11.3.1997, p. 8; 12.3.1997, p. 10). Until June 1997, the Taxation Policy Group held three meetings and the basis for a draft code of conduct was laid down. In the mean time, the Commission linked the work on harmful tax competition with the issues of interest income taxation, company taxation and indirect taxation and submitted its proposal to the ECOFIN in September 1997.

The Commission's proposal was based on a 'package approach', linking four elements to be negotiated simultaneously: code of conduct for business taxation, withholding tax on interest income, indirect taxation, and taxation of interest and royalty payments between associated companies. This approach had the drawback of blocking progress in a particular area should progress in other areas be lacking. However, it also had the advantage of securing agreement on the basis of package deals. The ECOFIN was not prepared to include indirect taxation in the package. Therefore the Commission's proposal had to be revised twice, leading to the exclusion of indirect taxation but a clearer definition of what the code of conduct should include and how capital income should be taxed. The code of conduct would include all business tax measures 'which affects or may affect the location of business activity in a significant way'. Business activity refers to *all* activities carried out within a group of companies and not only financial transactions. The aim was to identify and eventually roll back all measures designed to poach the tax base of other member states (European Commission, 1997b, Annex).

Aware of the sensitivity of the taxation issues, the Commissioner for the Internal Market declared just before the submission of the second proposal that the Commission was trying not to appropriate the sovereignty of the member states but to help them by pooling certain elements of the taxation policy. In other words, he was signaling that the Commission's aim was to act as an impartial broker who could facilitate package deals, which might eventually lead to binding rules. For that purpose, he also suggested that a Code of Conduct Group, consisting of member state representatives and functioning under similar principles to those of the Taxation Policy Group, should be established (*Agence Europe*, 23.8.1997, p. 2).

The package approach of the Commission was accepted in the ECOFIN meeting of 13 September 1997 in Mondorf-les-Bains, leading *Agence Europe* to comment that the Mondorf meeting 'set out premises that had hitherto been largely taboo' (*Agence Europe*, 15/16.9.1997, p. 10). The ECOFIN accepted the Code of Conduct in general but asked the commission to resolve the issue of what system should be applied for capital taxation: a withholding tax or information exchange? The third proposal of the Commission (submitted in November 1997), adopted the principle of coexistence. In this system, countries with banking secrecy laws should apply a minimum withholding tax on the capital income of non-residents; others where banking secrecy is not the norm should provide the beneficiary's country of residence with information. In either method, the incentive for granting tax-exempt treatment to non-resident investors would be reduced, if not totally eliminated.

The ECOFIN discussed the final proposal on 1 December 1997 and accepted the final version, which included a code of conduct for business taxation and the basic elements of the taxation of capital income (see *Official Journal*, C2, 6.1.1998, pp. 1–7). Nevertheless, the ECOFIN meeting also signaled the difficulties in moving forward to identify the measures that constitute harmful tax competition and determine the details of the capital income taxation directive. For example, the UK raised the issue of distinguishing between ordinary bank deposits and Eurobonds, with the aim of excluding the latter from the future directive. France indicated that the rate of withholding tax on capital income should be at least 25 per cent, which was unacceptable for Luxembourg. Belgium, Italy and Portugal stated that they would not agree to the directive on royalty and interest payments between companies unless the directive on taxation of capital income was adopted.

Under these circumstances, Monti's description of the ECOFIN decision as a historic breakthrough (*Agence Europe*, 3.12.1997, pp. 4–5) could be considered an exaggeration. However, it was not totally irrelevant. The decision signaled that the scope for a breakthrough was limited, but it also demonstrated that the EU was prepared to lay the basis for policy coordination and binding rules on an issue that had (a) generated aggressive competitive bidding in the past and (b) been treated as the ultimate indicator of sovereignty. Further developments in 1998 and the first half of 1999 demonstrated the relevance of this assessment.

During 1998, four developments were important. The first concerned the presidency of the Code of Conduct Group. On 9 March 1998, the ECOFIN agreed by majority that the president should be elected by the members of the group for two years and, if necessary, by majority (*Agence Europe*, 9/10.3.1998, p. 7). Interestingly, this decision was taken during the presidency of the UK – a champion of unanimity in tax policy matters. Although the UK was rewarded with the first presidency of the group, this was not a bad trade-off for other member states who were keener on tax policy coordination – especially given the new president's (Dawn Primarolo's) undertaking to 'put her heart into the work' of the group (*Agence Europe*, 8.5.1998).

Under Primarolo's leadership, the Code of Conduct Group performed remarkably well. It secured agreement from the ECOFIN to establish subgroups specializing in different areas. The subgroups' remit would be determined by the group itself and not by the ECOFIN. Until December 1998, extensive information was collected from the member states on all fiscal schemes that could have a significant effect on companies' location decisions. Even though phrased in general terms, the group's first report was completed before deadline. Also the information collated by the group led to the identification of five categories of harmful tax competition involving 85 harmful tax measures (*Agence Europe*, 16.7.1998, p. 6).

The group also began to examine each category with a view to ascertaining the following: (i) are tax advantages granted only to non-residents (that is, is there an attempt to poach the tax base of other member states)? (ii) Are the advantages to non-residents ring-fenced (that is, is the poaching country limiting its loss of tax revenue at the expense of others)? (iii) Are the advantages granted in the absence of real economic activity (that is, are they conducive to tax evasion by encouraging the establishment of 'brass plate' companies abroad?) (iv) Are the rules for determining company profits substantially different from internationally agreed ones? (v) Do fiscal measures lack transparency (that is, do they involve arbitrary discretion)?

The significance of these methods lies in the extent to which they were functional in cracking the black box of the national taxation policies and increasing the transparency/divisibility of the taxation policy issues. Therefore it helped to delineate the possible trade-offs in the policy coordination game. It also reduced the ability of the state or non-state actors to maintain their capture of the policy-making process at both the EU and national level.

The second development concerned the specification of the minimum withholding tax to be applied to capital income of non-residents. Despite strong objections from Luxembourg, who argued for a withholding tax rate of 10 per cent, the Commission, in its proposal of May 1998, settled on 20 per cent, which was closer to the maximum rate of 25 per cent requested by France. In addition, the Commission included a paragraph requiring the member states to ensure the implementation of the directive in the dependent territories which specialized as tax havens. Also, it included Eurobonds in the directive despite persistent objections form the UK (European Commission, 1998b; see also *Agence Europe*, 21.5.1998, p. 6).

The third development concerned negotiations with neighbouring countries and international organizations on harmful tax competition. The ECOFIN met the director of the IMF in the early days of the UK presidency to discuss a code of conduct for banking surveillance. Later on, the ECOFIN authorized the Commission to begin dialogue with neighboring countries such as Switzerland, Monaco, Liechtenstein, Andorra and San Marino with the aim of securing their agreement to a code of conduct similar to the one under negotiation within the EU. The most significant aspect of these negotiations is that the ECOFIN did not make progress within the EU conditional on the attitudes of the interlocutors. This was an indication that competitive bidding by the neighboring countries would be a factor to be taken into account, but not necessarily a stumbling block for intra-EU policy coordination.

The fourth development concerned the method of taxing interests and royalty payments between parent companies and their subsidiaries operating in different member states. The withholding tax on such payments had always carried the risk of double taxation. Countries of origin and residence both had an incentive to tax the gross amount of the payments resulting from technology transfers or inter-company financial transactions. Therefore the Commission was in favor of putting an end to double taxation with a view to facilitating technology transfer between companies as well as member states (European Commission, 1998a). However, a proposal submitted in 1990 had to be withdrawn in 1994 as agreement between member states proved impossible (*Agence Europe*, 6.3.1998, p. 8).

The tax package enabled the Commission to resubmit a new proposal with a wider coverage. The new proposal provided for the elimination of withholding tax, not only on transactions between parent companies and subsidiaries, but between all associated companies. The importance of this proposal was twofold. First, it demonstrated the extent to which the Commission could resist pressure from member states by forcing them to argue their case on the basis of transparent criteria. Of the net capital and/or technology-importing countries (that is, those in favor of maintaining the withholding tax), the Commission was in favor of granting exemption only for Greece and Portugal. It rejected similar demands by Italy and Belgium on the grounds that exemption was based on a development criterion. Secondly, the proposal demonstrated how deep integration could enable the EU and its member states to coordinate tax policy without necessarily erecting barriers against capital mobility. In fact, the aim of the proposal was to encourage capital mobility in the form of joint ventures, mergers, partnerships and technology transfer.

These developments indicated that there was indeed some scope for policy coordination. Developments in 1999, however, highlighted the difficulties involved in securing agreement and devising binding rules. The Code of Conduct Group examined the 85 measures mentioned above and decided that all should be examined in more detail to ascertain whether they constituted harmful tax competition. It also identified the member states where any particular measure was implemented. This prompted the German representative in the ECOFIN meeting of 25 May 1999 to state that there was now 'total transparency on what is done in each member-state . . . This transparency allows us to move forward to the second phase of work – i.e. identification of the illegal practices that actually enter the Code's field' (*Agence Europe*, 25/26.5.1999, p. 10). Although the ECOFIN had until the end of 1999 to decide on these measures, conflicting approaches to other elements of the taxation package could well lead to a deadlock.

Despite the difficulties, however, tax policy coordination did become part of the EU's agenda. The commitment to make progress was reflected in the declarations of the Cologne European Council, which confirmed the need to combat harmful tax competition and make the European tax system more employment friendly. The European Council also declared a desire to conclude the directive on interest income taxation and to reach an agreement on the coverage of the Code of Conduct before the end of the Finnish Presidency in December 1999 (*Agence Europe*, 6.6.1999, p. 11). However, neither the Helsinki Summit nor the da Feira Summit of June 2000 was able to resolve the outstanding issues.

One of the issues concerned the choice between information exchange and withholding tax in the area of interest income taxation. The majority of the member states where banking secrecy was not the norm preferred the information exchange principle. The withholding tax principle was preferred by a small number of member states (Luxembourg, Austria) where banking secrecy was used to attract deposits and bond-based investment from other member states. The other issue was related to the withholding tax rate to be imposed on interest income during the transition from withholding tax to information exchange. France was in favor of a rate of no less than 25 per cent, but this was considered too high by banking secrecy countries as well as others such as the UK. Finally, there was the Spanish demand for inclusion in the exemption scheme granted to Greece and Portugal in the area of royalty and interest payments between companies.

Bargaining on these issues continued until the Santa Maria da Feira Summit in June 2000. Even then these issues were not resolved. However, the da Feira Summit agreed that the deadline for wrapping up the taxation package should be 31 December 2002. This deadline was excessively generous, but it reflected a serious commitment because the conclusion of the taxation package would not be conditional on the adoption of similar measures by tax havens (Switzerland, Liechtenstein, Monaco, Andorra and San Marino). Also the member states committed themselves to promote the adoption of the same measures in their dependent territories (the Channel Islands, Isle of Man and the territories in the Caribbean) (European Council, 2000).

In the mean time, the Code of Conduct Group submitted its final report to the ECOFIN on 29 November 1999. The report was made public following the ECOFIN meeting of 28 February 2000. Although the report is incomprehensible for the layman, it provides significant insights into the way in which transparency could improve governance quality in an area shrouded in secrecy. It is evident from the report that the Code of Conduct Group was able to go beyond the lowest common denominator mainly because of the information it had at its disposal and the transparent criteria for assessment. On the basis of this information, it was able to force a revision of the initial list of potentially harmful measures submitted by the member states. It was also able to adopt a wide interpretation of the criteria set out in the Code of Conduct. The objection of the small member states to this wider interpretation was declared unacceptable. Also declared as unacceptable were the member states' arguments against the classification of certain measures as harmful tax competition (Code of Conduct Group, 1999, pp. 3–5).

As a result, 66 of the 85 potentially harmful measures were classified as harmful tax competition. Of these, 40 measures were being implemented in the member states, three in European territories for whose external relations a member state is responsible, and 23 in dependent and associated territories (*The Key*, no. 13, March 2000, p. 23). Under the Code of Conduct adopted in 1997, the member states committed themselves not to introduce new harmful tax competition measures (the standstill principle). In addition, they undertook to inform each other of existing and future measures that might fall within the scope of the Code (*Official Journal*, no. C2/4, 6.1.1998, p. 6). The Commission does not have the competence to submit proposals in this area, but it acts as coordination locus gathering information from and disseminating it between member states. The Code also provided for a rollback principle, whereby member states undertook to revise their fiscal legislation and administrative measures with a view to eliminating any harmful measures. According to the ECOFIN decision of 26–7 November 2000, the rollback must be complete by the end of 2002 and the benefits granted before that date must cease by the end of 2005 (*The Key*, no. 15, March 2001, p. 5).

As far as interest income taxation was concerned, the ECOFIN meeting of 26–7 November 2000 decided that information exchange should be the basis for preventing tax avoidance in this area. Countries with banking secrecy (Austria, Belgium and Luxembourg) will be given a period of seven years to comply with this principle. These member states must legislate for a 15 per cent withholding tax during the first three years and 20 per cent during the remaining four years. During the transition, the country applying the withholding tax will keep 25 per cent of the tax revenue and 75 per cent will be transferred to the investor's country of residence (*The Key*, no. 15, March 2001, p. 4). With respect to the taxation of interest and royalty payments, the ECOFIN agreed on the principle of taxing the beneficiary in the country of origin only. Greece, Portugal and Spain were granted a transitional period during which they can continue to tax such payments even if they are paid to companies resident in other member states. However, the draft directive also included an anti-abuse clause, which provided that interest and royalty payments subject to a low tax rate in the country of residence would not benefit from the directive (*The Key*, no. 15, March 2001, p. 4).

Given these outcomes, it can be seen that increased capital mobility, combined with increased transparency/divisibility, was conducive to policy coordination and convergence – as predicted by cell B2 of Figure 2.1. This combination was also compatible with improved governance quality (that is, reduced scope for special treatment of the mobile tax base) – as predicted by cell B2 of Figure 2.2. It is true that the process has been protracted and the withholding tax rate for the first three years turned out to be lower than the original Commission recommendation of 20 per cent. Nevertheless, their significance should not be underestimated, for three reasons. First, they have been obtained after a long period of harmful tax competition between relatively small economies which, according to the literature on tax policy competition, had no option but to continue lowering their tax rates on capital (see, for example, Razin and Sadka, 1991). Secondly, they have extended the EU's competence (in terms of legislation as well as surveil-lance) into an area that the member states had been adamant to preserve as a national prerogative. Finally, these outcomes reflect the endogenous nature of the public policy decisions, which can be predicted and explained only with the help of an analytical framework such as the one developed in this chapter.

CONCLUSIONS

The analysis above began with the observation that the current debate on globalization and regional integration has tended to focus either on the state or on non-state actors at the expense of the strategic interaction between them. Because of the 'single focus', the current debate has generated either state-centric or society-centric conclusions, which are highly reductionist and static. Focusing on state–society interaction, this chapter tried to dem-onstrate that public policy decisions (hence governance quality) at a given point in time are endogenous outcomes, which are affected not only by exog-enously given constraints and incentives but also by the outcomes of the state–society interaction in the preceding period. The chapter also demon-strated that policy convergence does not necessarily imply reduced govern-ance quality, provided that the high levels of cross-border mobility leading to convergence are combined with issue transparency/divisibility.

This is even more the case when policy convergence is mediated by and codified through the institutions of regional integration. In other words, regional integration may lead to higher governance quality compared to globalization, understood as increased cross-border mobility. One reason is that the regional authority's institutional capacity facilitates intra-bloc conflict resolution by devising transparent criteria for cost/benefit distribu-tion. The other reason is that the policy convergence codified at the regional level reduces the probability of policy reversals (that is, cheating) by limit-ing the capacity of national bureaucracies and/or non-state actors to capture the policy-making authority.

The evidence on the EU's tax policy coordination lends support to the main findings indicated above. The evidence demonstrates that the relation-ship between increased capital mobility and tax competition is more complex than what could be predicted by state-centric or society-centric approaches to globalization and integration. It is true that EU member states had been engaged in tax competition up to the mid-1990s, which led to falling statutory rates on the mobile tax base (capital) and increasing rates on the relatively immobile base (labor). The analytical framework developed in the first section of this chapter explains this trend on the basis of increased capital mobility combined with low issue transparency/divisibility, which resulted from the member states' tendency to obfuscate the fiscal regime as much as possible.

The evidence also suggests that EU member states, from 1996 onwards, began to address the problem of competitive bidding and the 'drive to the bottom' that this would entail in the area of capital income taxation. This policy reversal cannot be explained by either society-centric or state-centric approaches. The society-centric approach cannot predict or explain the policy shift because capital mobility as a constraint on public policy choices continued to be high and increasing. The state-centric approach cannot predict or explain the shift because it cannot explain why the policy objectives of the national governments changed and why this change induced cooperative rather than non-cooperative attitudes. The endogenous approach proposed above can predict and explain the policy change because it enables us to predict and explain why interaction between states and non-state actors generates a range of endogenous (that is, sometimes unintended) outcomes rather than linear and static results.

In the context of this study, one such endogenous outcome is the improvement in national and EU fiscal governance despite high levels of capital mobility. The improved governance quality is evident not only from the steps taken to eliminate harmful tax competition, but also from the fact that these steps are being taken without erecting barriers to capital mobility. In other words, possible welfare gains from policy coordination are obtained without intervening in the efficient allocation of capital within the EU. The analysis above suggests that this result is due to the change in the constraints and incentives faced by the state and non-state actors, rather than the conversion of the EU or national governments into 'enlightened' social planners, who are concerned with the maximization of European or national welfare.

The major policy implication of the analysis above is that EU governance quality under globalization (that is, increased cross-border mobility) depends on two conditions. First, the transparency/divisibility of the policy issues must be high. High transparency/divisibility ensures that the state and/or non-state actors are less able to capture the policy process and shape the policy outcomes in line with their preferences. Secondly, the EU must be able to act as a credible commitment device that facilitates the distribution of costs and benefits and reduces the probability of policy reversals (that is, free-riding).

NOTE

1. In fact, the OECD acknowledges the limited nature of its work and indicates that the EU
    package is more likely to address the issues raised by changing patterns of investment and
    trade and the interface between them. See OECD (1998, pp. 11–13).

REFERENCES

Agence Europe (1997–9), *Agence Internationale d'Information pour la Presse*,
    English edn, Luxembourg/Brussels.
Albrow, M. (1996), *The Global Age*, Cambridge: Polity Press.
Armingean, K. (1997), 'Globalisation as opportunity: two roads to welfare state
    reform', CEPR Conference Workshop 12, Berne.
Armstrong. D. (1998), 'Globalisation and the social state', *Review of International
    Studies*, 24(4): 461–78.
Arndt, S.W. (1997), 'Globalisation and trade: a symposium', *The World Economy*,
    20(5): 695–707.
Boyer, R. and D. Drache (eds) (1996), *States against Markets: The Limits of
    Globalisation*, London: Routledge.
Code of Conduct Group (1999), *Code of Conduct (Business Taxation) Report*
    (*http://ue.eu.int/newsroom*).
Coleman, W.D. and R.D. Underhill (1998a), 'Domestic politics, regional economic
    co-operation and global economic integration', in W.D. Coleman and R.D.
    Underhill (eds) (1998b), pp. 1–16.
Coleman, W.D. and R.D. Underhill (eds) (1998b), *Regionalism and Global
    Economic Integration: Europe, Asia and the Americas*, London: Routledge.
Commission on Global Governance (1995), *Our Global Neighbourhood: The Report
    of the Commission on Global Governance*, Oxford: Oxford University Press.
Cox, R. (1997), 'Economic Globalisation and the limits to liberal democracy', in
    A.G. McGrew (ed.), *The Transformation of Democracy? Globalisation and
    Territorial Democracy*, Cambridge: Polity Press.
D'Aspermont, C., J. Jaskold-Gabszewicz and J.-F. Thisse (1979), 'Hotelling's stabil-
    ity in competition', *Econometrica*, 47: 1145–50.
De Silguy, Y.-T. (1998), 'The Euro and the global financial markets', speech deliv-
    ered at SBC Wartburg Dillon Read, New York, 16 April (SPEECH/98/73,
    http://europa.eu.int/rapid/start).
Dunning, J.H. (1997), 'Introduction', in J.H. Dunning (ed.), *Governments, Globalis-
    ation and International Business*, Oxford: Oxford University Press, pp. 1–27.
ECOFIN (1998), 'Conclusions of the Ecofin Council meeting on 1 December 1997
    concerning taxation policy', *Official Journal*, no. C2, 6 January: 1–7.
European Commission (1997a), 'Towards a taxation strategy for the European
    Union', *Europe Documents*, no. 2051, 13–14 September.
European Commission (1997b), 'Towards tax co-ordination in the European
    Union', *Europe Documents*, no. 2054, 9 October.
European Commission (1998a), 'Proposal for a Council Directive on a common
    system of taxation applicable to interest and royalty payments made between
    associated companies of different member states [Com(98)67/fin.]', *Official
    Journal*, no. C123, 22 April: 9–13.

European Commission (1998b), 'Proposal for a Council Directive to ensure a minimum of effective taxation of savings income in the form of interest payments within the Community [Com(98)295/fin.]', *Official Journal*, no. C212, 8 July: 13–18.

European Commission (2001), *European Governance: A White Paper*, COM(2001)428 /final (Brussels).

European Council (2000), 'Presidency conclusions', *Press Release*, no. 200/1/00 (19.6.2000), Brussels.

Grant, W. (1998), 'Globalisation, comparative political economy and the economic policies of the Blair Government', Working Paper no. 08/98, Centre for the Study of Globalisation and Regionalisation, University of Warwick.

Greider, W. (1997), *One World, Ready or Not: The Manic Logic of Global Capitalism*, New York, Simon & Schuster.

Held, D., A. McGrew, D. Goldblatt and J. Perraton (1999), *Global Transformations: Politics, Economics and Culture,* Cambridge: Polity Press.

Hellman, J. and M. Schankerman (2000), 'Intervention, corruption and capture: the nexus between enterprises and the state', *EBRD Working Papers*, no. 58 (October).

Higgot, R. (1998), 'The international political economy of regionalism: the Asia-Pacific and Europe compared', in W.D. Coleman and R.D. Underhill (eds) (1998b), pp. 42–67.

Higgot, R. and S. Reich (1998), 'Globalisation and sites of conflict: towards definition and taxonomy', Working Paper no. 01/98, Centre for the Study of Globalisation and Regionalisation, University of Warwick.

Hirschman, A.O. (1970), *Exit, Voice, Loyalty: Responses to Decline in Firms, Organisations and States*, Cambridge, MA: Harvard University Press.

Hirst, P. and G. Thompson (1995), 'Globalisation and the future of the nation state', *Economy and Society*, 24(3): 408–42.

Hirst, P. and G. Thompson (1996), *Globalisation in Question: The International Economy and Possibilities of Governance*, Cambridge: Polity Press.

Hotelling, H. (1929), 'Stability in competition', reprinted in A.C. Darnell (ed.) (1990), *The Collected Economics Articles of Harold Hotelling*, New York: Springer-Verlag.

Krugman, P. (1993), 'Regionalism vs. multilateralism: analytical notes', in J. de Melo and A. Panagariya (eds), *New Dimensions in Regional Integration*, Cambridge: Cambridge University Press.

Messerlin, P.A. and G. Reed (1995), 'Anti-dumping policies in the United States and the European Community', *Economic Journal*, 105: 1565–75.

Milner, H. (1998), 'Regional economic co-operation, global markets and domestic politics: a comparison of NAFTA and the Maastricht Treaty', in W.D. Coleman and R.D. Underhill (eds) (1998b), pp. 19–41.

Monti, M. (1998), 'EMU, Taxation and competitiveness', speech delivered at the Kangaroo Group Conference, London, 27 November (SPEECH/98/272, (*http://europa.eu.int/rapid/start*).

OECD (1998), *Harmful Tax Competition: An Emerging Global Issue*, Paris: OECD.

Ohmae, K. (1990), *The Borderless World*, London: Collins.

Ohmae, K. (1995), *The End of the Nation State*, New York: Free Press.

Owens, J. (1993), 'Globalisation: the Implications for tax policies', *Fiscal Studies*, 14(1): 21–44.

Pelkmans, J. (1993), *Opening up the Euro-Market for Textiles*, Brussels: Centre for European Policy Studies.

Putnam, R.D. (1988), 'Diplomacy and domestic politics', *International Organisation*, 42(3): 427–60.

Ramesh, M. (1995), 'Economic globalisation and policy choices', *Governance*, 8(2): 243–60.

Razin, A. and E. Sadka (1991), 'International tax competition and gains from tax harmonisation', *Economic Letters*, 37: 69–76.

Sideri, S. (1993), 'Restructuring the post-Cold War world economy', *Development and Change*, 24(1): 7–27.

Sideri, S. (1997), 'Globalisation and regional integration', *The European Journal of Development Research*, 9(1): 38–82.

Streeck, W. and P.C. Schmitter (1991), 'From national corporatism to transnational pluralism: organised interests in the Single European Market', *Politics and Society*, 19(2): 133–64.

Stubbs, R. (1998), 'Asia–Pacific regionalism versus globalisation: competing forms of capitalism', in W.D. Coleman and R.D. Underhill (eds) (1998b), pp. 68–80.

The Key: Taxation and Customs Union (2000–2001), published twice yearly by the Taxation and Customs Union Directorate-General of the Commission, Brussels.

Ugur, M. (1997), 'State–society interaction and European integration: a political economy approach to the dynamics and policy-making of the European Union', *Review of International Studies*, 23: 469–500.

Ugur, M. (1998), 'Explaining protectionism and liberalisation in European Union trade policy: the case of textiles and clothing', *Journal of European Public Policy*, 5(4): 652–700.

Ugur, M. (2000), 'Second-order reciprocity in the age of regionalism: the EU's market access strategy and EU–APEC relations', *Current Politics and Economics of Europe*, 10(1): 73–92.

World Bank (1996), *Global Economic Prospects and the Developing Countries*, Washington, DC: IBRD.

3. Competition versus competitiveness in the European single aviation market

Martin Staniland

INTRODUCTION

In September 2001, a remarkable event occurred in the world of European air transport. The market value of British Airways (BA), the largest airline in the EU, fell to the point that it was lower than that of the Irish low-fare airline Ryanair (Cowell, 2001).[1] While this event mainly reflected the dramatic collapse of airline share prices following the terrorist attacks of 11 September 2001, it also symbolized the challenge that new entrants are offering to the established European 'flag carriers' such as BA, Air France and Lufthansa. Less obviously, it reflected the importance of intercontinental routes for the flag carriers, shown particularly in their sensitivity to any reduction in traffic across the North Atlantic.

This chapter discusses the effects of the establishment of the single market on the European airline industry. In particular, it examines the dilemmas that have faced both managers and regulators as a result of the simultaneous advent of globalization and of liberalization closer to home. These dilemmas are complicated by the need for European airlines to respond to a radically new regulatory environment within Europe while complying with a wider, international regulatory regime still governing routes that are crucial for their revenue and for such profits as they earn.

Understanding these dilemmas and the strategies adopted to cope with them provides a salutary lesson in the folly of trying to analyse commercial responses to the single market without taking account of the stakes that many European firms have in markets overseas. The size of these stakes (the chapter argues) creates a tension between two goals, both significant in the single market program: the creation of greater competition within the market and the achievement of greater competitiveness for EU airlines flying on intercontinental routes.[2]

THE EUROPEAN AIRLINE INDUSTRY

European airlines have always had a larger stake in intercontinental services than their American counterparts. From the 1920s on, the commercial strategies of the two industries diverged and they were subject to different political imperatives. The European airlines emphasized long-haul routes partly out of necessity: because of the strength of the railway networks and the relatively short inter-city routes in Europe, they had little prospect of developing major domestic and even intra-European networks.[3] But the major European governments also expected airlines to provide air services to their colonies in return for the subsidies that early airlines needed so desperately. The airlines in effect became the logistical servants of imperialism and the more-or-less willing instruments of geopolitical ambition.[4]

American airlines, meanwhile, flourished on the basis of a continent-wide domestic market and the incentives a large market provided for technical innovation. With the exception of Pan American and TWA, American carriers had little interest in international routes: scheduled transatlantic services did not begin until 1945 and were, in fact, initiated by KLM and other European carriers, eager to earn dollars for their exchange-short governments.[5] In the 1950s, however, a long-term change began to affect both European and American airlines. Decolonization first of the Dutch and successively of the British, French and Belgian empires required European airlines to switch their resources elsewhere, especially to North Atlantic routes on which traffic was increasing. The result was increasing competition on North Atlantic routes.

But such competition was contained (on all international routes) by a regulatory regime (based on the Chicago Convention of 1944) that gave governments detailed and complete control over the allocation of routes and the management of traffic and fares. Such control was exercised through an array of bilateral agreements which specified routes, the number of airlines allowed to operate on these routes, and sometimes the number of seats to be offered. Such bilaterals invariably contained strict requirements regarding the nationality of airlines, stipulating that carriers must be 'substantially owned and effectively controlled' by nationals of the country allocating traffic rights. Since most European airlines were owned by the state, opportunities for foreign investment were in fact very limited until the mid-1980s, but all states protected the nationality (and traffic rights) of their carriers by imposing legal ceilings on share holding by non-nationals.

The outcome of the Chicago regime and the system of bilaterals was typically to create a duopoly of two national carriers on particular routes. States invariably used the right of designation they had under bilaterals to designate their national airlines: since the rights typically provided for only one airline per country, the result was pervasive duopoly. Within Europe, most airlines actually created 'pools' that involved sharing traffic and revenue. Meanwhile, the airlines' trade association, the International Air Transport Association (IATA), regulated fares and conditions of service (including, on one occasion, the definition of a sandwich), subject to government approval.

By the mid-1970s, the European airline industry had been transformed into a vehicle that catered for leisure travelers as much as for businessmen and officials. Its growth was partly due to discounted fares on scheduled airlines, but mainly stemmed from a dramatic increase in charter flights. By 1972, some 31 per cent of all international air travel was being carried on non-scheduled carriers, and by 1988 some 45 per cent of airline passengers in western Europe were traveling on charter flights (Doganis,1991, p. 14).[6]

Though traffic and productivity grew, the finances of airlines remained fragile and volatile. Airlines were forced to make huge investments in new aircraft in order to stay competitive, only to find their revenues suddenly undermined by a recession, a war or a sharp increase in fuel prices. Fare wars broke out whenever the carriers found themselves with excess capacity. One result of such wars was even lower revenue; another was that many airlines (while publicly supporting the IATA fare structures) quietly disposed of large numbers of tickets to 'consolidators' (or 'bucket shops') which sold them to travelers at a substantial discount.

THE SINGLE EUROPEAN MARKET

It was, in fact, the sale of discounted tickets – challenged by the French government – that led to a key legal case before the European Court of Justice (ECJ), the *Nouvelles Frontières* case of 1986. The ECJ's judgment in this case established that the general competition rules embodied in Article 85 of the Treaty of Rome did apply to the air transport industry and it emboldened the European Commission (at a time when the design for a single market was under consideration) to challenge the protectionism endemic in this sector.

Considering the previous resistance of many member states to any liberalization of air transport, the Commission was remarkably successful in getting support for a set of three regulatory packages that by April 1997 had brought about a complete liberalization of the internal market in air transport.[7] Airlines became free to fly wherever they wished within the airspace of European Union member states, even on domestic routes: they could offer as many seats as they wished and charge fares determined solely by commercial considerations. Further, they could, subject to rules about competition and mergers, purchase equity in airlines based in member states other than their own. At the same time, a single EU regulatory regime replaced the tangle of bilateral agreements controlling traffic between member states, and airlines based in the EU were transformed into 'Community carriers'.

What was liberalization expected to achieve? According to a Commission memorandum, liberalization would 'increase airline efficiency, allow the efficient and innovative airline to benefit, encourage expansion and thus employment, and better meet consumer needs'.[8] This emphasis on efficiency was related to the broader goals of the single market in that high transport costs would clearly be an obstacle to greater economic integration.[9] Though consumer advocates invoked the value of competition, the latter (or even the threat of competition) was seen as essentially a means toward greater efficiency. Economists assumed that firms could both enter and leave markets fairly easily in this industry, so allowing routes to become 'contestable' would lead to greater competition, and with it greater choice and lower fares for passengers. To survive, airlines would have to realize greater efficiencies in their own operations.

Another major argument for the single market – that it would create strong firms able to stand up to American and Japanese competitors – was less discussed, at least in relation to air transport. Greater efficiency in the airline industry would certainly contribute to strengthening firms in other industries, by reducing the costs of transporting people and goods within Europe. But, in principle, airlines themselves would benefit from access to a market comparable in size to the American market and could, through mergers and acquisitions, engage in both horizontal and vertical integration. Larger airlines might buy up smaller airlines, creating more comprehensive networks and establishing strong 'hubs'.

The strategies of several major airlines between 1986 and the early 1990s were, indeed, predicated on the belief that only a few carriers would survive the consolidation brought on by the single market. But, however sick some European 'flag carriers' have been, they have shown a great capacity for survival. Some notorious invalids (such as British Airways, Air France and Lufthansa) have emerged reinvigorated and in this sense they reaped the bonus of efficiency forecast by supporters of the single market. The dramatic collapses of Sabena and Swissair in the autumn of 2001 quickly led to the launching of new national carriers.

Moreover, the surviving flag carriers are not 'European' in the sense of having a comprehensive presence in all markets. To understand why the predicted consolidation has not occurred, we have to consider how the particular characteristics of the European air transport industry have affected implementation of the single market.

THE EXTERNAL DIMENSION

A key characteristic of the industry is its continuing dependence on long-haul routes. In 1995, routes outside the EU accounted for roughly 30 per cent of the non-domestic passengers carried by airlines belonging to the Association of European Airlines (AEA): these routes generated roughly 60 per cent of their non-domestic revenue (AEA, 1996, p. 4).[10] Put in terms of mileage, in April 1997 some 74.4 per cent of the mileage (revenue passenger-kilometers) flown by AEA members in scheduled international air transport was on routes beyond Europe.[11] By contrast, in August 1996 only 34.7 per cent of all mileage flown by US carriers was on international routes.[12]

Such dependence has several implications. First, it explains, in an indirect fashion, the lack of consolidation in the airline industry since 1997: the restrictive nationality rules governing bilaterals mean that airlines risk losing traffic rights if their 'citizenship' is in question. Secondly, dependence on long-haul routes means that European airline managers are at least as much concerned with obtaining access to major foreign markets (notably that in the United States) as with conquering intra-EU markets. Thirdly, it explains why such managers have put forming alliances with US carriers above pursuing mergers with other European airlines.

The lack of consolidation thus arises partly from a wish to protect traffic rights. With the creation of the single market, the major EU airlines found themselves operating under a divided regulatory regime, with one set of rules governing flights within (what is now called) the European Aviation Area and another governing flights between EU cities and cities abroad. Though all bilaterals between EU member states were abolished with the creation of the single market, the Chicago regulatory regime still applies to services between member states and countries outside the EU. For the latter, airline 'citizenship' is critical. Thus, for example, TAP Air Portugal can only have traffic rights to countries outside the EU as long as it is clearly a 'Portuguese' airline. Consolidation – for example, by the merging of TAP with an EU carrier of a different nationality – would erase Portuguese citizenship and would therefore endanger traffic rights inherited by the consolidated airline from TAP.

Such exclusive nationality provisions are clearly inconsistent with the basic principles of the single market since they discourage cross-border investment and entail different trading arrangements for individual member states. The European Commission has therefore opposed fresh negotiation of bilaterals by member states and has taken action against those who have concluded so-called 'open skies' agreements with the USA. A preliminary recommendation on this issue was made early in 2002 and a formal decision is expected later in the year. But, while the Commission wants to assume authority for all future negotiation with 'third parties' such as the USA, it has not insisted on renunciation of existing bilaterals.

The Single Market legislation and the Chicago regime conflict with respect to flights outside Europe. The legislation provides – logically – that any 'Community carrier' should be able to fly from any city within the EU to cities outside it, as well as to fly within and between member states. But as long as external routes are governed by bilaterals, member state governments will be reluctant to let airlines other than those 'substantially owned and effectively controlled' by their own nationals fly on such routes, for fear that the non-EU states with which they have signed will withdraw traffic rights from their own airlines.

By extension, the bilateral system is a disincentive to cross-border consolidation. Apart from an array of legal provisions limiting the holding of equity by other nationals (including nationals of other member states), the nationality rules constitute a 'poison pill' against a foreign acquisition simply by making it commercially unattractive: the buyer would find itself facing the prospect of owning an airline shorn of its traffic rights on routes outside the EU.[13]

The persistence of a dual regulatory regime also helps to explain some of the frustration encountered by recent negotiators of airline mergers. Airline 'citizenship' was an issue in the efforts of Swissair to establish itself as a proxy EU airline through heavy investment in Sabena, and it was also a major problem in the recent failed negotiations between BA and KLM (in this case, the US government reportedly warned the Dutch government that 'KLM could lose its bilateral rights if BA took control') (Baker, 2000).

The dependence of European airlines on intercontinental traffic was also a major factor in the ramifying transatlantic alliances of the 1990s. At this time, European airline managements, already preoccupied with gaining access to the US market, found themselves facing a new problem created by deregulation in the USA. In the American market, foreign airlines had always been prevented from offering domestic flights – a restriction on so-called 'cabotage' in fact practised by all governments and sustained by the Chicago regulatory regime. But until the mid-1980s, such restrictions were not commercially threatening since only two scheduled US airlines (Pan American and TWA) were flying on North Atlantic routes and only TWA had a domestic network.

However, deregulation of the US air transport industry in 1978 had the unintended consequence of encouraging a consolidation of the American industry. From this process, three airlines (American, Delta and United) emerged controlling roughly 58 per cent of domestic traffic. Much of this traffic passed through hubs that the airlines had created in order to achieve economies of scope by the more efficient use of aircraft and other equipment. Once established, such hubs became 'fortresses' against other carriers.

In the late 1980s, these hubs (many of which were not at traditional east and west coast ports of entry) were used for expansion of international services. At the same time, the US government was pursuing a long-standing policy of liberalizing international aviation and increasing (through such liberalization) the share of traffic carried by American carriers. Exploiting loopholes in bilaterals regarding capacity, the main American airlines began to offer large numbers of seats on transatlantic routes, as well as more frequent services and fares lower than those offered by their predecessors. They also built up services from such new hinterland hubs as Atlanta, Dallas–Fort Worth and Cincinnati. The result was that by the early 1990s American carriers controlled some 71 per cent of traffic on services between the USA and France and 61 per cent of traffic on services between the USA and Germany. Only in the UK–US market, tightly regulated by the British government, did European airlines (mainly BA) enjoy rough parity.

Thus, just as the European airlines were trying to cope with liberalization within the single market, they were also facing what executives commonly described as an 'American invasion'. The responses of airlines and governments to this invasion differed sharply. In countries with large markets (such as France, Germany and the UK), the reaction was mainly defensive, involving renunciation of bilaterals and opposition to American proposals for liberal 'open skies' agreements.[14] In smaller countries (such as the Netherlands), the priority of governments and airlines was to obtain greater access to the US market: the price for doing so – offering complete access for American carriers to their own markets – was small relative to the expected gains.

Given the prohibition on cabotage and the great concentration of traffic in domestic hubs, the best available strategy for airlines such as KLM was to ally themselves with an American carrier, offering the latter access to feeder traffic from a European market in return for coordinated marketing in the American market through the US partner's main hubs. Hence KLM's alliance with Northwest, which led to an entirely new degree of commercial and operational integration between a European and an American carrier, involving notably the use of 'codesharing' and the combination of frequent flyer programs.[15] Despite some tensions at boardroom level, the KLM–Northwest alliance proved to be highly profitable to both partners.

Once established, the new alliances were valuable enough to trump projects for intra-European cooperation, best exemplified by the so-called 'Alcazar' project hatched in 1993 by KLM, SAS, Swissair and Austrian Airlines. 'Alcazar' (as the name suggests) was to be a four-sided defensive arrangement to protect smaller European airlines against the efforts of BA and other major carriers to dominate the emerging Single Market by acquiring affiliates in member states.[16] In this sense, both the threat and the response were predicated on the conventional wisdom of the time that the Single Market would lead to radical consolidation. After months of complicated negotiation, the project collapsed over the choice of a US airline as transatlantic partner for the new alliance, the Dutch preferring their existing partner, Northwest, while Swissair and probably Austrian preferred Delta. As an unidentified observer noted while the Alcazar talks were still under way: 'KLM's focus was primarily on the intercontinental market and its international partnership while the other three were interested in building a strong home market together first as a prelude to an increased market presence' (Shifrin and Sparaco, 1993).

After the collapse of the Alcazar talks, the participants naturally concentrated on pursuing transatlantic alliances, to the effective exclusion of intra-European alliances and mergers. By 1999, all the major European airlines had become members of alliances that were rapidly moving from being transatlantic to being global in scope.

With the shift in commercial strategy went a change in the debate about the problem of competition. Regulators began to worry about the antitrust problems posed by the new global alliances, instead of (or as well as) worrying about the potential threat to competition from the emergence of two or three European mega-carriers. Consolidation in Europe had been obstructed by the Chicago regulations, but it had also evaporated as a threat. European airline managements were now more concerned with building up and protecting their own home bases as hubs for global alliances and with maneuvering themselves into such alliances than with eating up other EU carriers. The mega-carriers (in the form of alliances) in effect took a transatlantic form, and in this form they began to be seen as potentially anti-competitive. Despite some recent negotiations, the general effect of the global alliances has been to reinforce the barriers between European carriers, each one of which acts as the European member of a larger team. Consolidation has simply not happened.

What both the supporters and the critics of liberalization missed when applying American experience of deregulation to Europe was, first, the difference between the American and the European regulatory environments regarding consolidation and, secondly, the significance of the European airlines' stake in long-haul international markets. Consolidation in the USA was not obstructed by issues of airline nationality or public ownership: no American airline risked loss of any traffic rights if it took over another American airline. Moreover, public ownership did not stand in the way of takeovers as it did in Europe. Finally, the US Department of Justice in the late 1980s was (perhaps regrettably) less exercised by potential threats to competition arising from mergers and acquisitions than the European Commission, watched by jealous member states, has always been.

GLOBAL ALLIANCES AND COMPETITION IN THE SINGLE MARKET

While European consumers have been spared the problems associated with consolidation into two or three huge 'Euro-carriers', the survival of national carriers and their incorporation into global alliances has not helped the cause of greater competition in the Single Market itself. At crucial moments, the flag carriers have been able to present their claims for special treatment by more or less explicitly depicting themselves as champions of European (or national) competitiveness in the face of American and Asian rivals. Such appeals have usually occurred when they have been looking for approval of 'one-time, last-time' subsidies from their government or have been trying to protect their dominant position in a European market.

The tension between 'competition' and 'competitiveness' has been especially clear in Britain where, since 1969, government policy has generally encouraged the emergence of a second long-haul carrier alongside BA. Whether the 'second force' carrier was British Caledonian, Laker Airways or (more recently) Virgin Atlantic, BA has tried to hold it at bay by depicting itself – even after privatization – as the true flag carrier. The most telling cases of conflict between the claims of competition and those of international competitiveness came in the early 1980s when BA was undergoing privatization. In 1982, the-then 'second force' airline, British Caledonian (BCAL), and other independents became concerned that, given BA's control of 83 per cent of international air services offered by British carriers, BA's privatization with all its current assets would enable it to become a private monopoly instead of a state-owned virtual monopoly (Thomson, 1990, p. 444). BCAL and the other independent airlines therefore lobbied the Thatcher government for a substantial redistribution of some of BA's assets (notably of domestic and international routes) before privatization.

Though the main conflict here was one between increasing competition and getting the highest price for BA (which, it was argued, required leaving its assets, including routes, intact), the battle quickly took on a nationalistic tone. BA stressed that 'every day [it competed] with hundreds of foreign airlines from all over the world' and it distributed stickers bearing the words, 'British Airways is winning for Britain – let's keep it that way'. In October 1984, to the disappointment of the independents, the government announced a very minor redistribution of routes, leaving BA in a virtually impregnable position and BCAL with a barely viable network. When

BCAL was subsequently forced to sell up, a further outbreak of national-ism occurred in response to an offer from SAS (with one newspaper refer-ring to 'the Viking invasion' of British aviation). In December 1987, BA absorbed BCAL, its representatives having argued to the Monopolies and Merger Commission (as Lyth notes) that such a takeover 'was necessary to build the strength necessary to stand up to the newly-emerging American 'megacarriers' (Lyth, 1998, p. 79).[17] The resilience of nationalism in this industry has been further demonstrated by the vigor put into recent efforts to replace (and, arguably, revive) Sabena and Swissair.

Privatization did not therefore reduce the nationalism sustaining the flag carrier: nor did it necessarily lead to greater competition. Thus privatiza-tion (in a liberalized market) gave BA the freedom to add routes and buy up competitors without consulting the British government and without accepting any obligations it might impose (though at least one takeover was referred to the European Commission).[18]

The threat from 'foreign competitors' was also invoked by Air France in 1990 when it bought its independent rival UTA and with it got control of the domestic carrier, Air Inter. Bernard Attali, then president of Air France, justified this takeover by reference to the flag carrier's need for a stronger domestic feeder network to improve Air France's competitive position on long-haul routes (Attali also agitated his political masters by alluding to the danger that UTA and Air Inter might 'fall into foreign hands': Attali, 1994, p. 50).[19]

Strategically, such acquisition of domestic rivals was part of a larger plan (adopted by several flag carriers) to seize market share before the single market legislation took full effect. It represented a pre-emptive strike against would-be domestic challengers and European rivals (again, on the premise that only two or three such carriers would survive).[20] Thus both Air France and Lufthansa invested heavily in new aircraft and hired new staff so as to expand their routes and capacity in the European market. At the same time, they began to buy shares in regional airlines in neighboring countries so as to draw traffic away from their rivals.[21]

However, this strategy of expansion collapsed in the face of the recession induced by the Gulf War. All the major airlines (except BA) faced huge losses that in turn led to serious reorganization. During this process, several carriers sought large subsidies from their governments (the largest being Air France's request in 1994 for FF20 billion ($3.7 billion)). Such subsidies were presented as essential for the 'survival' of the companies concerned, and the Commission's repeated agreement to granting subsidies supported the claims of its critics that it was consistently susceptible to pressures from the 'shareholders' of state-owned carriers.

Since the mid-1990s, the flag carriers (also called 'euromajors' and 'network' airlines) have concentrated heavily on two objectives. One is to reduce costs and increase productivity so as to be competitive within Europe against peers and against low-cost independent airlines (such as EasyJet and Ryanair). In this process, the organizational cultures of the 'euromajors' have been reshaped to emphasize profit and service to the customer (in place of the technically-oriented 'production'culture that was pervasive earlier). This change has been helped by varying degrees of privatization, which has been conducted in order to obtain capital and to ease relations with US alliance partners (some of whom have been uncomfortable about dealing with state-owned airlines).

The other objective is to complete and deepen global alliances (see Table 3.1): with the alliance of Alitalia and Air France with Delta, all network carriers (except Olympic and TAP Air Portugal) are now involved in global systems.[22] While this preoccupation with external alliances is a natural consequence of the continued dependence of the euromajors on long-haul traffic, it has involved a fundamental change in strategic thinking. Before, airline strategists, following the logic of the bilateral system, tended to envisage markets as discrete 'city-pairs', country–country markets, or separate 'domestic', 'European' and 'intercontinental' markets. Now, following the logic of liberalization and the alliance systems, they tend to

Table 3.1   Major airline alliances

Alliance	European members	North American members	Latin American members	Asian–Pacific members
KLM/ Northwest	KLM	Northwest Airlines	—	Malaysia Airlines
oneworld	British Airways; Aer Lingus; Finnair; Iberia	American Airlines	LanChile	Cathay Pacific; Qantas
Star Alliance	Lufthansa; SAS; bmi British Midland; Austrian Airlines	United Airlines; Air Canada	Varig; Mexicana	Singapore Airlines; All Nippon Airways; Thai Airways; Air New Zealand
SkyTeam	Air France; Alitalia; CSA Czech Airlines	Delta Airlines	AeroMexico	Korean Airlines

Source: Based on alliance listings in Baker (2001).

emphasize 'connectivity': the configuration of routes and schedules and even the deployment of aircraft so as to encourage and maximize transfer traffic through hubs. BA was a pioneer in explicitly converting to 'network maximization', mainly through its Heathrow hub. But this approach was (necessarily) applied for several decades by KLM to supplement the small Dutch domestic market by drawing on traffic from neighboring countries and it has recently been adopted by the other euromajors (most spectacularly by Air France).

While this marketing strategy is consistent with the corporate strategy of airlines in creating global alliances, it has serious implications for competition within the Single Market. Compared to its American counterpart, European air transport was always (with the exception of Germany) focused on hubs located in capital cities because of the dominance of national carriers. But the creation of competing alliance systems has increased competition between such hubs as Paris, London and Amsterdam: airlines want to achieve economies of scope by routing passengers through hubs and want to offer an extensive range of destinations within Europe, to match those offered through corresponding hubs in the USA and elsewhere. The result is (as in the USA) the dominance of hubs by network carriers which, given the congestion at all major European airports, also constitutes a serious barrier to entry both for other network carriers and for independent and start-up airlines.[23]

The networking strategy also explains three other phenomena that are sometimes identified as examples of the failure of the Single Market to realize expected levels of competition. One is the tendency for regional airlines and some low-fare carriers to become feeders to the network airlines.[24] Another is the almost complete absence of competition between national carriers on each other's domestic routes and on many intra-European routes (except for those connecting to a hub). Ironically, the innovation in the single market program that was considered most radical and threatening – cabotage – has also turned out to be the biggest flop: after a few early experiments, European airlines have forsworn the opportunity to challenge their rivals directly on domestic routes. Thus KLM's British affiliate concentrates on linking British cities to Amsterdam, while the role of BA's affiliate, Deutsche BA, in operating domestic services within Germany, was explicitly to provide 'feed' to BA's intra-European or long-haul services.[25] Domestic competition does occur, but it is provided either by alliance surrogates (such as British Midland on behalf of United and Lufthansa in the Star Alliance) or by domestic low-fare start-ups.

The corollary is limited competition on the many domestic and intra-European routes that do not serve an alliance hub as origin or destination. Air France does not fly between London and Edinburgh any more than

KLM flies between Paris and Nice, and many services that seem to represent expanded competition turn out to be (sometimes bizarre) instances of code sharing.

The third 'competitive failure' – and that which is currently most exercising the European Commission – is on long-haul services, especially across the North Atlantic. Even if the Single Market were 'completed' by allowing Community carriers of any nationality to fly from any European city to the USA (as is envisaged in the Commission's current proposal for a Transatlantic Common Aviation Area), the commercial logic of global alliances suggests that the results might be as anticlimactic as the opening of domestic routes has been. The markets concerned have already been partitioned by the alliances and it would not make commercial sense under current alliance arrangements for (say) Air France or KLM to start long-range services from Frankfurt. Apart from the special case of the UK and Heathrow, it is also unlikely that American or other non-European carriers would add significantly to their European destinations as a result of further liberalization. Open skies agreements already provide easy access to the more profitable destinations and the oligopoly conditions provided by global alliances offer profits as secure as any that airlines can earn under current circumstances.

When the European Commission has expressed concern about the anticompetitive implications of alliances both within and outside the Single Market and has proposed antitrust remedies and other ways of stimulating competition, the network airlines have responded either by denying that their strategies are anticompetitive or by complaining that the Commission's zeal for competition ignores the issue of global competitiveness. Thus, in 1998, Jürgen Weber, the chairman of Lufthansa, complained on behalf of his fellow AEA members about the Commission's zeal in promoting competition within the Single Market:

> We cannot be expected to be weak in our home markets and at the same time act as world class players in global competition. We should be able to use the tools provided by liberalization – market entry and pricing freedom – to consolidate our position in Europe, compete more strongly with each other, and hence with our rivals throughout the world.

In the same spirit, the secretary-general of the AEA declared that intervention by the Commission would 'disadvantage further the European carriers, coming from a region that has some of the highest costs in the world, against their world competitors from the US and Far East who have regional cost advantages' (Donne 1998, p. 31).

The Commission had, indeed, recognized earlier that there was a tension between the claims of 'competition' and those of 'competitiveness'. In a

1997 document, it admitted that it was 'necessary to achieve a balance between the strict control of mergers and alliances in order to make Community markets work better, and allowing EU airlines to achieve the necessary economics of scale and scope to be able to compete globally' (Commission of the European Communities, 1997, p. 4). The practical problem was therefore to ensure 'that the entry barriers created by the more successful of Europe's carriers are not so great as to stifle innovative effort' (ibid., p. 48). Its efforts to solve this problem led it to regulate on such matters as the allocation of runway slots, the use of computer reservations systems (CRSs) and frequent flyer programs, all of which were apt to favor the larger carriers, and such regulation in turn led to conflicts with the euromajors.[26] After extended debate, the Commission has recently advocated strengthening the powers of bodies responsible for allocation of slots, which is now recognized as the major barrier to entry by new carriers (Dombey and Jennen, 2001).

THE INTERNAL MARKET

Despite the commercial and political power of the network airlines, it is clear that the Single Market has succeeded in attracting new traffic to air services, stimulating services on new routes and increasing the range of 'products' available to passengers on existing routes. It has, however, been less successful in creating direct price competition for passengers seeking the same 'product' (notably business class travel).

The initial impact of the liberalization packages on traffic was particularly striking since the EU was experiencing a recession. Between 1992 and 1996, traffic on all routes in the Community grew by an average of 7.2 per cent per annum, when annual growth in GDP was only about 2 per cent. In effect, the number of passengers was 14.6 million higher than would have been predicted at the current growth in GDP (Vivier, 1999). Between 1992 and 1999, the number of cross-border routes had increased by 35 per cent.[27] But the degree of competition did not expand so dramatically. Many of the new routes were between provincial cities, and traffic on them was too thin to support more than one carrier. Moreover, the number of routes with two carriers remained static (at 37 per cent) for the first six years, while the number of international routes with three or more carriers grew from 22 to 37 (or from 3 per cent to 7 per cent). While the number of densely used inter-city routes subject to competition from three or more airlines doubled, the euromajors generally proved very successful in holding onto their shares on both these routes and the major domestic routes.[28]

On fares, the picture is also mixed. While the number of passengers benefiting from deeply discounted fares rose from 60.5 per cent to 70.9 per cent between 1985 and 1995, the cost of fully flexible business and economy tickets actually rose slightly.[29] Using revenue management techniques developed in the USA, European network airlines became adept at price discrimination, cross-subsidizing their budget fares (offered to fight off lower-cost competitors) by continuing to charge high fares to business travelers who needed to fly at short notice, on particular days and at particular times. Such travelers, willing to pay for convenience and flexibility, continue to be the main source of revenue for the network airlines, who are careful to avoid fare wars over business traffic.

Nevertheless, competition from within and from outside the Single Market had the desired effect on the efficiency of the industry. Between 1992 and 1996, the number of staff employed by the 14 euromajors fell by 23000 (9 per cent) and output increased by 35 per cent.[30] Costs also fell, in aggregate from \$1.38 per available ton kilometer (ATK) in 1990 to \$1.01 per ATK in 1994.[31] Some 94 per cent of airline managers surveyed on behalf of the Commission agreed that 'competition from EU airlines [had] affected airlines' efficiency'(Commission of the European Communities, 1997, p. 70).

INDEPENDENT AND 'NO FRILLS' AIRLINES

Pressure from established independent airlines (such as British Midland) and from new, low-cost airlines, such as EasyJet and Ryanair, has forced economies on the network carriers. These carriers (which include several, such as Deutsche BA, Buzz and Go, set up by the network airlines) have succeeded in making operational savings of as much as 50 per cent compared to the euromajors by following the model developed by Southwest Airlines in the USA.[32] This model involves at least 10 elements:

1. The use of secondary airports (such as Stansted and Luton near London, Beauvais near Paris, Charleroi near Brussels and now Hahn near Frankfurt) which impose lower user charges and are less congested than alliance hubs such as Heathrow and Charles de Gaulle.[33]
2. Operation on relatively short routes, typically under 1500 km.
3. Fleet standardization (typically around the Boeing 737) which reduces maintenance and training costs and increases crew flexibility.
4. High-density seating, excluding business class (Boeing 737–300s flown by EasyJet, BA and KLM seat 148, 126 and 109 passengers respectively).
5. High aircraft utilization (entailing up to 11 flying hours or as many as

10 flights daily per aircraft, compared to around seven hours for BA and other euromajors).

6. Heavy use of online or phone reservations systems to avoid payment of commissions to travel agents and to keep down staff costs.[34]

7. No connecting services, thus avoiding delays to outgoing flights through waiting for connecting passengers.

8. Minimal onboard catering and other services (this principle normally includes unassigned seating and may exclude services such as frequent flyer programs and even free provision for the disabled).[35]

9. Lower staff salaries and a higher proportion of staff assigned to flying duties than at euromajors.[36]

10. No carriage of cargo, thus cutting turn-round times and ground handling.

This strategy has enabled low-cost airlines to offer fares frequently as low as 40 per cent below those charged by network airlines and has caused substantial growth of traffic when a low-cost airline has entered a route. For example, traffic on the Dublin–Brussels route rose from 170 000 in 1997 (when Ryanair started flights to Charleroi) to 355 000 in 1999.[37] Such an increase involves both winning traffic from surface transport modes and prompting people to take trips that they would not otherwise take. The response of incumbent airlines, which is normally to offer some comparable fares, may inadvertently help the low-fare carriers.[38]

As Table 3.2 indicates, this strategy has enabled the low-cost airlines to attract traffic that is now greater than that of some of the smaller flag carriers and to achieve higher productivity than many network carriers. But the important question is how far the 'no-frills' are actually comparable to and in competition with the network carriers. To start with, comparisons of productivity as given above are undermined by differences in markets. For example, the long-haul flights operated by the euromajors (and by independents such as Virgin Atlantic) require higher staffing levels than short flights, if only to provide catering, as well as less crowded seating. By the same token, the higher fares paid by business travelers are to some extent justified by the additional services the network airline has to provide (such as last-minute changes in flights, refunding of fares, frequent flyer programs and guaranteed connections between flights on a 'seamless' network of domestic and international services). Beyond that, the business customer has to decide whether more comfortable accommodation and on-board catering justify paying a higher fare.

American experience suggests that business travelers (or, more exactly, their employers) will abandon full-service carriers if the low-cost airline becomes a serious competitor in terms of frequency of service and reliabil-

Table 3.2   Productivity of selected European low-fare and full-service airlines, 2000

Airline	(1) Passengers (000s)	(2) Employees	(3) Aircraft	Productivity	
				Passengers/ Employee	Passengers/ aircraft
Sabena	10 932	11 294	78	968	140 153
Finnair	7 438	10 985	58	677	128 241
AirLiberté/AOM	7 263	4 250	77	1 708	94 324
Ryanair	7 136	1 400	36	5 097	198 222
BMI British Midland	7 098	6 320	43	1 123	165 069
Olympic	6 691	7 030	32	916	209 093
Aer Lingus	6 639	5 635	40	1 178	165 975
EasyJet	5 996	1 400	21	4 282	285 523
TAP Air Portugal	5 291	6 826	33	755	160 333
Virgin Express	3 815	1 212	22	3 147	173 409
KLM UK	3 706	2 000	26	1 853	142 538
Deutsche BA	3 273	820	17	3 991	192 529
Go	2 646	550	14	4 810	189 000
Icelandair	1 479	1 600	12	924	123 250
Luxair	1 113	2 045	15	544	74 200

Note: Bold type indicates full-service airlines.

Source: Calculated from figures in *Air Transport World* (2001).

ity.[39] The European low-cost carriers seem to have understood that fairly high frequency is essential to establishing visibility and to attracting business passengers: on some British domestic routes such passengers now represent as much as 40 per cent of all traffic (and 20 per cent on some international flights). In particular, the availability of lower fares has stimulated travel by the staff of smaller businesses and the self-employed.[40]

A second front for low-cost carriers is competition with charter airlines.[41] This sector has historically controlled a large part of the European air transport industry, largely by offering inclusive tour packages to holiday resorts.[42] With liberalization, the regulatory distinction between the charter airlines (such as Monarch and Britannia in the UK and LTU in Germany) and the scheduled airlines disappeared, enabling the charter companies to move into scheduled services. This opportunity tempted some charter carriers, since the low costs and high productivity of this sector gave them an advantage over the network carriers. But several such transitions were spectacular failures, owing to the increased costs involved in scheduled services, the need for a more varied fleet of aircraft and the carriers' lack of recognition by passengers.

Charter carriers have therefore tended to stay in their traditional niche, while creating stronger, vertically integrated travel businesses and expanding their fleets to serve destinations in the Americas and Asia. However, competition between them and the low-cost airlines does occur because the latter include a substantial number of Mediterranean resorts among their destinations. Holiday passengers can now choose between, on the one hand, the convenience of a package tour and, on the other, the possibility of buying cheap air tickets on a low-fare carrier and making their own arrangements for accommodation (Mason *et al.*, 2000, p. 89).

CONCLUSION

Liberalization of the air transport industry in Europe has neither met all the expectations of its supporters nor confirmed the worst fears of its critics. It has not produced head-to-head competition on many routes (notably domestic routes) that were traditionally the preserve of flag carriers. It has led to the opening up of new international routes (especially between provincial cities); but on many of these routes traffic is too thin to support more than one carrier. It has not, as yet, produced a serious challenge to the duopolies exercised by the flag carriers on trunk routes between EU capitals, especially in the market for business travel, where there is little price competition in fully flexible business-class fares.

Further, the development of alliance systems, encouraged by the reliance of European airlines on long-haul routes, has led to the reinforcement of hub-and-spoke systems at major airports which are typically congested, thus creating serious barriers to entry for would-be new entrants. It has also accelerated the process (seen earlier in the USA) by which regional airlines and some start-up carriers lose their independence, becoming 'feeders' for the network airlines and their alliance partners. Finally, these network carriers, which form the European component of the alliances, have used their considerable political clout to resist attempts by the European Commission to remove structural barriers to competition within the single market, notably those presented by control of runway slots.

But the consolidation of the industry into two or three 'mega-carriers' – perennially predicted by commentators and widely feared by critics – has not happened, and may never happen.[43] In this respect, while alliances have great market power, the European airline industry has not followed the precedent of the American industry after deregulation. Paradoxically, a major reason for this divergence is the persistence of an international regulatory regime that, through bilateral agreements, requires 'substantial ownership and effective control' of airlines to be vested in nationals. This regime stands in the way of consolidation, since mergers and acquisitions would raise questions about corporate nationality and thus put international traffic rights at risk.

Ironically, then, a regulatory regime based on exclusive nationality provisions that is stringently (and logically) opposed by the European Commission has actually helped to prevent the consolidation, American-style, that many in Brussels feared would follow liberalization. National prestige has also helped to sustain carriers (and in the cases of Sabena and Swissair has inspired efforts to replace them).

European flag carriers seem to be as unsinkable as rubber ducks. But will low-cost carriers still be able to torpedo them? American experience is, again, an uncertain guide. Airlines such as EasyJet and Ryanair have consciously followed the example of Southwest in the USA and have flourished by doing so. They have now successfully entered the capital market and they plan to expand capacity at a rate of up to 25 per cent annually. They control some 3 per cent of traffic on routes within the EU and may achieve a share as high as 12–15 per cent by 2010.[44] EasyJet and Ryanair have already obtained the crucial status of being the dominant carrier on certain routes and have now set out to create hubs on the European mainland.[45]

But here they face serious obstacles. Whether because of loyalty to national carriers or because of high 'social' costs, low-cost carriers comparable to EasyJet and Ryanair have until very recently not been established in continental member states – or, when they have, they have been coopted by the national carriers.[46] The dramatic expansion of low-costs in Germany in 2002 may presage a new tide of competition for the flag carriers. But the low-cost airlines face very serious competition from continental railways which typically offer fares lower than those charged by their British counterparts and are in the process of upgrading to TGV level on major inter-city routes. These airlines, most of whose current routes cross water, will lose the 'traditional' advantage of European air transport as they expand operations from their chosen mainland hubs (Charleroi and Hahn for Ryanair and Amsterdam and Paris for EasyJet). Finally, their planned rate of expansion is considerably greater than that of Southwest in its early years and they may risk meeting the fate that has overtaken other low-fare airlines both in Europe and in the USA that overexpanded.[47]

The current situation of all European airlines is exceptionally challenging and will test severely the strategies and the resources of both the network carriers and their rivals. It will also present serious problems for those in Brussels and elsewhere who are dedicated both to realizing the competitive potential of the Single Market for consumers and to sustaining the efforts of European airlines to participate in and profit from the globalization of the air transport industry.

NOTES

1. In 2000, BA was ahead of Air France in terms of revenue-passenger-kilometers flown but behind Lufthansa and Air France in terms of passengers carried.
2. This tension was evident in statements of EU officials in the wake of the 11 September incidents, when US carriers had been given support by the US government. On 11 October, the EU transport commissioner, Loyola de Palacio, referred to complaints about the possibility of EU national airlines getting subsidies when she declared: 'The question is not maintaining a level playing field within the EU. The main difficulty at this moment is guaranteeing a level playing field with our competitors, the American airlines, especially in the transatlantic market' (quoted in Dombey, 2001).
3. The major exception was Lufthansa.
4. Thus by 1930 a traveler could fly by scheduled air service from London to India but not from London to any British provincial city.
5. One of the more printable renderings of the initials of the British long-haul state carrier, BOAC, was 'Bringing Over American Cash' (its imperial mission was also reflected in the inventive if disenchanted 'Better Off on A Camel').
6. By 1984, the number of passengers flying on charter flights from the UK exceeded the number flying on scheduled services.
7. On this process, see Kassim (1996), Lawton (1999), O'Reilly and Stone Sweet (1998), Williams (1993), pp. 75–85.
8. Commission of the European Communities, 'Civil aviation memorandum No. 2. Progress towards the development of a Community air transport policy', COM (84) 72, i, p. 27 (quoted in O'Reilly and Stone Sweet, 1998, p. 457).
9. In 1985, the Delors–Cockfield white paper proposing more rapid integration had criticized the European air transport industry, calling for changes in fares and limits on 'the rights of Governments to restrict capacity and access to the market'(Commission of the European Communities, 1985, p. 30). O'Reilly and Stone Sweet (1998, p. 464) note that integration itself had contributed to complaints about the cost of air travel between member states: 'As cross-border exchanges (trade, passengers and freight traffic) grew, so did the costs of a rigid, inefficient and necessarily patchwork regulatory system for those (major business users, private consumers, cargo shippers and ultimately governments) who bore them.'
10. 'Domestic' here refers to services flown within member states. In 1993, the British Civil Aviation Authority reported that long-haul routes were responsible for 31.1 per cent of the passengers carried by British Airways, for 60 per cent of its turnover and for 90 per cent of its profits (CAA, 1993, p. 75). On its routes to Africa, the Middle East and South Asia, BA had a profit rate of 22.5 per cent and one of 10 per cent on its routes to the Far East and Australasia – interestingly, routes typically governed by fairly restrictive bilaterals (Shifrin, 1994, p. 31).
11. Based on figures in *Airline Business* (1997).
12. Based on figures in *Air Transport World* (1997).
13. In 1991, BA actually obtained authority from the USA to fly from Paris to certain US cities as part of a deal which allowed American and United to fly into Heathrow. Though such flights would be permissible under the single market legislation, they have never been exercised because flights from Paris to the USA continue to be governed by the France–USA bilateral. The French government, not surprisingly, is reluctant to designate BA as a carrier under this agreement and can, correctly, point to BA's lack of French 'citizenship' in denying authorization.
14. Despite their connotations, 'open skies' agreements are simply liberalized bilaterals. Each allows all airlines of the two countries concerned freedom to fly between any points in those countries, with similar freedom in pricing and capacity. But they limit the benefits of liberalization to the carriers and passengers of the two signatory countries, though passengers from other countries may take advantage of them by making air or land connections through airports in the signatory countries.

15. 'Codesharing' is the practice of advertising a service flown by one airline as flown by another, thus allowing the partners to seem to offer a direct service within their own networks. For example, some flights between London and Paris, advertised as Qantas flights, are in fact operated by BA but they appear on computer systems as part of the Qantas network. This practice is now subject to strict regulation.

16. Despite the Spanish reference, Iberia was apparently not considered as a potential member. With combined traffic of some 32 million passengers a year, the Alcazar alliance would have had roughly 270 aircraft, over 80 000 staff and a network of four or more fairly well-dispersed hubs (Betts, 1993, p. 15).

17. Lord King, the chairman of BA, said that the takeover would create 'a British airline capable of taking on the world' (quoted in Thomson, 1990, p. 537).

18. BA went on to take over another independent airline, Dan Air. A former senior official of BA pointed out that, while the independents often complained about the privileges of state-owned airlines, they were actually in greater danger from a privatized state airline which was not accountable to government and which could not be required to give up routes. With privatization, wrote Roy Watts, BA became 'a natural predator': 'the natural processes of the market [emerged], namely, the aim to eliminate competition, not promote it, something governments frequently do not understand' (Watts, 1995, p. 99).

19. Attali frequently criticized what he called 'the feebleness of Europe confronted with the imperialism of other continents' and warned that within 10 years the European market would be 'under the domination of US carriers' (Attali, 1994, p. 11; Betts, 1992).

20. Referring to the third liberalization package, Heinz Ruhnau, chairman of Lufthansa, asked in May 1990: 'What must we do to prepare for 1 January 1993? We must occupy market positions in time. We must try to complete our fleet modernization by the end of 1992. The others will still have this before them' (quoted in Lehrer and Webber, 1997, p. 6). The authors comment that 'much of Lufthansa's strategy was political: to defuse the threat of deregulation of air transport in Germany and Europe' (ibid., p. 4).

21. Examples of such equity purchase include Air France's purchase of 37.5 per cent of Sabena (later sold), BA's purchase of 49.9 per cent of TAT in France, Lufthansa's purchase of 39.7 per cent of Lauda Air (in Austria) and SAS's purchase of 40 per cent of British Midland.

22. Of the US international carriers, only USAirways and Continental are outside the alliance system.

23. Between 1993 and 1998, the proportion of all flights offered by alliance partners at their major hubs rose from 77 per cent to 85 per cent (CAA, 1998).

24. On this trend, see Feldman (1997). In Belgium, Virgin Express took over flights between Brussels and London from Sabena, in Italy, Air One (a serious challenger on the Milan–Rome route) reached an agreement with Alitalia, and in Spain and Portugal Air Europa and Portugalia made deals with Iberia and TAP, respectively. Even the management of the stridently independent British/Swiss airline EasyJet reportedly held talks with BA about the possibility of its becoming an affiliate of the flag carrier (Feldman, 1998).

25. However, Deutsche BA subsequently announced that it would henceforth operate only German domestic services.

26. For example, in February 1998, competition commissioner Van Miert clashed with Jürgen Weber over the slots issue. Weber argued that the Commission's proposal to reduce the market power of alliances by requiring them to give up slots at European hubs amounted to 'expropriation'. According to United Airlines, this and other proposals to limit frequencies on specified routes would 'destroy alliances' (Leonhardt and Echikson, 1998).

27. CAA (1998, p. 12), Kinnock (1999). For earlier figures, see CAA (1993; 1995).

28. The aggregate share of traffic carried by the network airlines on the densest intra-European routes declined from 92 per cent in December 1992 to 83 per cent in December 1997. But this average was skewed by BA's lower level of market share (about 69 per cent): Air France, Alitalia, Iberia and Lufthansa held on to over 90 per cent of traffic on the densest intra-European routes serving their countries. Similarly, while the aggregate

share of traffic on major domestic routes controlled by the flag carriers went down from 75 per cent to 62 per cent, Air France, Iberia and Alitalia kept about 70 per cent of their domestic markets and BA's relatively low share of UK domestic traffic (by 1997, roughly 57 per cent) again skewed the average (CAA, 1998,pp. 4–6).

29. Donne (1998, p. 28), Commission of the European Communities (1997, p. 78). Neil Kinnock, then transport commissioner, claimed (Kinnock, 1999) that fares had fallen overall by between 10 per cent and 24 per cent between 1993 and 1999. Between 1988 and 1995, business fares rose by roughly 2 per cent. The Commission conceded that, in relation to business travelers, 'the EU [liberalization] measures have not produced the desired effect'.

30. CAA (1998, p. 181). This report points out that these figure may be misleading in that they do not reflect the considerable outsourcing that some firms undertook.

31. Commission of the European Communities (1997, pp. 75–6). The airline with the consistently lowest unit cost was KLM (at \$0.50 per ATK in 1993). European costs were still above those of the major American carriers.

32. For good accounts of the strategy of these airlines, see Mason *et al.* (2000) and Doganis (2001). The new airlines have suffered a high casualty rate: between 1992 and 1996 alone, 51 airlines suspended operations. Nevertheless, the total number of airlines operating within the EU rose from 127 in 1987 to 189 in 1999 (Vivier, 1999).

33. They may, however, include some hubs as destinations (as, for example, EasyJet does in flying to Amsterdam and Ryanair in serving Frankfurt).

34. By 2001, 90 per cent of EasyJet's reservations were being made online. However, this strategy entails much higher publicity costs than network airlines incur.

35. Ryanair, notably, has insisted on charging for the handling of disabled passengers, leading to complaints by advocacy groups and action by the European Commission (see Frost, 2001).

36. In 1998, 87 per cent of EasyJet's staff were involved in flying duties, compared to 33 per cent at BA (Mason *et al.*, 2000, p. 11). Comparative figures for salaries are not available.

37. Doganis (2001, p. 63). When EasyJet entered the London–Glasgow route in August 1997, the growth rate of traffic on the route jumped to 20 per cent and in many subsequent months traffic was double the monthly average (CAA, 1998, pp. 131–2).

38. As well as attracting passengers from the upstart, an incumbent may generate new demand which it does not satisfy either because of conditions it attaches to its own lower fares or because it offers too few seats, 'in an effort to avoid undue yield dilution': the disappointed passengers then go to the new carrier (CAA, 1998, p. 132).

39   The National Business Travel Association in the USA found that between November 1997 and March 1998, 54 per cent of corporations had booked their employees on low-cost airlines (Whirter, 1998, p 102).

40. See Cohen (2000): the author notes that the expansion of hi-technology businesses in the Cambridge area may have been helped by the availability of low-cost services from Stansted.

41. This section is largely based on Mason *et al.* (2000), pp. 1–7, Commission of the European Communities (1997, pp. 2, 42–4) and CAA (1998, pp. 111–23).

42. For example, in the early 1990s, 80 per cent of all traffic between Germany and Spain and 70 per cent of all traffic between the UK and Spain was carried by charter carriers (Verchère, 1994, p. 12). In the USA, the domestic holiday business has never been as clearly separated from the scheduled sector as it has in Europe.

43. Neither has the loss of service to smaller cities that occurred following deregulation in the USA.

44. Mason *et al.* (2000, p. 91). The share of US low-cost carriers is variously estimated at between 15 per cent and 22 per cent of the market: see Doganis (2001, p. 63) and *Economist* (2001).

45. Ryanair has long been the dominant carrier on many routes between the UK and Ireland and has now become the dominant carrier on two routes to Italy. EasyJet has replaced BA as second carrier on the London–Nice route (Doganis, 2001, p. 65).

46. The more successful survivors, such as Deutsche BA in Germany and Maersk in

Denmark, have for most of their existence not been 'low-cost' airlines on the Southwest model but rather cheaper full-service carriers like British Midland. Virgin Express, based in Brussels, was for a time a partner of Sabena on certain routes.
47. Doganis (2001, p. 64). Both EasyJet and Ryanair have enjoyed access to considerable private capital – the first from the Greek shipping interests of its founder, the second from the GPA aircraft leasing organization.

REFERENCES

AEA (1996), *Yearbook 1996*, Brussels: Association of European Airlines.
Air Transport World (1997), 'Trends', April, 1.
Air Transport World (2001), 'World Airline Traffic Statistics – 2000', July, 76–81.
Airline Business (1997), 'Data', August, 58.
Attali, Jacques (1994), *Les guerres du ciel*, Paris: Fayard.
Baker, Colin (2000), 'British Airways calls off KLM merger', *Airline Business*, October, 9.
Baker, Colin (2001), 'The global groupings', *Airline Business*, July, 42–5.
Betts, Paul (1992), 'Air France draws up the lines for battle', *Financial Times*, 9 July, 16.
Betts, Paul (1993), 'Co-operating to survive in a global market', *Financial Times*, 29 March, 15.
CAA (1993), *Airline Competition in the Single European Market*, London: Civil Aviation Authority, CAP 623.
CAA (1995), *The Single European Aviation Market: Progress So Far*, London: Civil Aviation Authority, CAP 654.
CAA (1998), *The Single European Aviation Market: The First Five Years*, London: Civil Aviation Authority, CAP685.
Cohen, Amon (2000), 'A big leap for smaller companies', *Financial Times*, 19 December, 14.
Commission of the European Communities (1985), *Completing the Internal Market*, COM(85) 310 final, Brussels.
Commission of the European Communities (1997), *Impact on Services: Air Transport*, Single Market Review, Subseries II, vol.2, Brussels: Kogan Page/Earthscan/Office for Official Publications of the European Communities/Cranfield University.
Cowell, Alan (2001), 'Turmoil hits large players and shakes second tier', *New York Times*, 21 September, W1.
Doganis, Rigas (1991), *Flying Off Course. The Economics of International Airlines*, 2nd edn, London: Routledge.
Doganis, Rigas (2001), 'Survival lessons', *Airline Business*, 62–5.
Dombey, Daniel (2001), 'Brussels may relax airline aid stance', *Financial Times*, 12 October, 4.
Dombey, Daniel and Birgit Jennen (2001), 'EU plans air "slot" change', *Financial Times*, 23 May, 8.
Donne, Michael (1998), *The Future of Air Passenger Transport. Towards the New Millennium*, London: F.T.Business Ltd.
Economist (2001), 'The squeeze on Europe's air fares', 26 May, 58.
Feldman, Joan (1997), 'Still waiting for contention', *Air Transport World*, September, 35–8.

Feldman, Joan (1998), 'Lovers, not fighters', *Air Transport World*, May, 32–3.

Frost, Laurence (2001), 'Under-fire airline targeted by Union plans for disabled', *European Voice*, 6–12 September, 2.

Kassim, Hussein (1996), 'Air transport', in Hussein Kassim and Anand Menon (eds), *The European Union and national industrial policy*, London and New York: Routledge, pp. 106–31.

Kinnock, Neil (1999), 'European air transport policy', in *European Civil Aviation and Airport Trends*, World Market Series, Business Briefing, 30, London.

Lawton, Thomas (1999), 'Governing the skies: conditions for the Europeanization of airline policy', *Journal of Public Policy*, 19 (1), January–April, 91–112.

Lehmann Brothers (1993), *European Airlines: A Turbulent Decade*, New York: Lehmann Brothers, 14 September.

Lehrer, Mark and Douglas Webber (1997), 'Re-organizing and privatizing German state enterprises. Case A', case no.198–001–1, INSEAD, Fontainebleau.

Leonhardt, David and William Echikson (1998), 'Taking a whack at airline alliances', *Business Week*, 16 March, 106.

Lyth, Peter (1998), 'Chosen Instruments: the Evolution of British Airways', in Hans-Liudger Dienel and Peter Lyth (eds), *Flying the Flag. European Commercial Air Transport since 1945*, Basingstoke: Macmillan and New York: St Martin's, pp. 50–86.

Mason, Keith, Conor Whelan and George Williams (2000), 'Europe's Low Cost Airlines. An analysis of the economic and operating characteristics of Europe's charter and low cost scheduled carriers', Research Report no.7, Air Transport Research Group, Cranfield University.

O'Reilly, Dolores and Alec Stone Sweet (1998), 'The liberalization and re-regulation of air transport', *Journal of European Public Policy*, 5 (3), September, 447–66.

Shifrin, Carole A. (1994), 'BA maintains profitable edge', *Aviation Week and Space Technology*, 13 June, 28–31.

Shifrin, Carole A and Pierre Sparaco (1993), 'European carriers regroup as Alcazar hopes fizzle', *Aviation Week and Space Technology*, 29 November, 29.

Thomson, Adam (1990), *High Risk. The Politics of the Air*, London: Sidgwick and Jackson.

Verchère, Ian (1994), *The air transport industry in crisis. Solving over-capacity and financing new equipment*, London: Economist Intelligence Unit.

Vivier, Jean-François (1999), 'Current trends and development within European civil aviation', in *European Civil Aviation and Airport Trends*, World Market Series, Business Briefing, 18, London.

Watts, Jean (ed.) (1995), *Roy Watts: a memoir*, Malvern Wells, UK: Images.

Whirter, Alex (1998), 'How low can you go?', *World Trade*, November, 102–4.

Williams, George (1993), *The airline industry and the impact of deregulation*, Aldershot: Ashgate.

4. The governance of telecommunications in the European Union

Kjell A. Eliassen, Catherine B. Monsen and Nick Sitter

Over the last two decades Western Europe has seen a shift from regulation of telecommunications by way of nationalized utilities and ministerial control to regulation of privatized operators through competition policy and independent regulators. This has taken place in the context of the revival of European integration with the Single European Market (SEM) and Economic and Monetary Union (EMU) projects. Like these two projects it has been based on a relatively free market-oriented approach to economic policy, or governance, that combines liberalization with Europeanization. The liberalization process has opened telecoms markets to competition, to a greater extent than in other utilities sectors such as energy, but it has also raised a series of questions about regulation of competitive markets. These have much in common with other sectors subject to special regulation, notably banking and financial services, where regulation is at one and the same time necessary to guarantee competition and a potential tool for protection. In the context of this volume the central question is whether this development of 'EMU governance' has generated 'a fully-fledged open market economy' or whether the liberalization process has provided continuing shelter for telecoms operators against the pressures of globalization.

The shift from a telecoms sector dominated by single state-owned self-regulating national players (traditional European telecoms *government*) to a competitive multi-player scene (*governance* in the shadow of EMU – or 'EMU governance') has raised three sets of questions. These concern (a) the extent of liberalization, or how fast and to what extent liberalization and cross-border competition should be introduced, (b) the extent of Europeanization, or whether the regime should be primarily supranational or intergovernmental, and (c) the balance between sector regulation and general competition policy. These questions were not answered at the same time, let alone consistently, in the telecoms sector or energy and financial markets regulation. Some still remain open.

PUBLIC POLICY REFORM IN THE EU: EMU, GOVERNANCE AND TELECOMS

The SEM and EMU projects entailed major reform of public policy as well as liberalization and deeper European integration. The agreement to establish full free movement of goods, services, capital and labor, and not to discriminate on the basis of nationality, removed some of the EU member states' central policy tools. To be sure, the effectiveness of the interventionist (or *dirigiste*) form of public policy associates with traditional West European government, and different degrees of corporatism, had been under fire for some time by the time the Single European Act was agreed in 1986, and this is widely seen as having contributed to agreement (Taylor, 1989; Sandholtz and Zysman, 1989; Moravcsik, 1991, 1998). But, as the debates over liberalization of telecoms and energy would show, and the limits to competition in the bank sector illustrate, this tilt toward the free market remains somewhat controversial. The 'New Right' schools of public policy have not established complete dominance in the reform debate, let alone in actual public sector change (Hood, 1998; Pollitt and Bouckaert, 2000). Although the EU member states all embarked on public sector reforms, these differ not only in their point of departure and political context, but also in direction and magnitude. The central common factors have been a degree of privatization of utilities, usually with a view to opening up to quasi-market mechanisms or actual competition. However, across sectors and states this has been found to require new regulation, and New Public Management mechanisms have not proved immune to policy failures (Dunleavy, 1995). The result has been a wide range of changes to public policy in EU states, driven by a range of factors related to domestic politics and developments beyond the EU, but developed in EU member states within the framework negotiated with the Single European Act and Maastricht Treaty. To this extent, 'EMU governance' means public policy in a context of liberalization and European economic and monetary integration.

The *governance* aspect of 'EMU governance' draws attention to the privatization and liberalization element in new policies on utilities. Drawing on the UK reforms, the term 'governance' refers to a new approach to public policy that includes privatization and liberalization but is defined in somewhat wider terms that center on non-hierarchical government, the blurring of public–private borderlines, 'arm's-length' administration and oversight by independent regulatory authorities or agencies. In other words, governance goes beyond the government associated with the unitary, centralized or interventionist state and corporatism (Pierre and Stoker, 2000). It draws on institutions beyond the state and blurs the borders between the public and private sector, thus featuring a degree of dependence between the organizations involved and elements of self-government or more market-oriented public policy. The government's success in achieving its goals therefore depends on successful management and leadership more than its authority or powers to command (Stoker, 1998). This can be considered a response to failures of the state and/or the market, and therefore a compromise 'second-best' solution with neither political nor economic legitimacy (Schmitter, 2001). Alternatively, using the same starting point, it may be considered a way to enhance the legitimacy of public policy in the light of 'ungovernability' problems (Kooiman, 1993).

In this sense we suggest that the EU reforms in the telecoms sector have indeed produced a system of 'governance' of the sector in Europe (both member and applicant states). The privatization and introduction of competition in some utilities sectors removed telecoms and energy from the traditional domains of government, and brought them closer to other regulated sectors such as banking and financial services (see Table 4.1). This holds even if the stricter 'network governance' models of EU politics associated with the Mannheim school (Kohler-Koch and Eising, 1999; see also Kohler-Koch, 1996; Marks *et al.*, 1996; Jachtenfuchs, 1995; Wessels, 1997) are rejected (Hix, 1998) or questioned with respect to specific sectors (Dyson, 1999; Sedelmeier, 2001). But regulatory change, especially in the context of European integration, raises a series of questions about the link between Europeanization, liberalization, competition and regulation (Scharpf, 1999, Majone, 1998). Given the greater extent of supranationalism in the banking and telecoms sectors compared to energy (Dufey, 1993; Schmidt, 1998; Levi-Faur, 1999), the central question pertaining to governance of the telecoms sector increasingly resembles that of banking and financial services as much as energy (see Table 4.2).

Table 4.1   Public utility and regulatory models

	Ownership	Primary objective	Regulator
Public utility model	State-owned national monopoly	Public service	Ministry (not subject to competition policy)
Regulatory model	Multiple (some cross-border) firms	Profit	Sector regulator and competition authority

Table 4.2 EU governance in three sectors

	Pre-SEM	Post-SEM	Central questions as of 2001
Banks	National governance	Supranational governance	EU/state balance: some unresolved Degree of liberalization: largely resolved Comp. policy v. sector regulation: open
Telecom	National government	Supranational governance	EU/state balance: largely resolved Degree of liberalization: resolved Comp. policy v. sector regulation: open
Energy	National government	Inter-governmental governance	EU/state balance: some unresolved Degree of liberalization: unresolved Comp. policy v. sector regulation: open

While the question of the balance between member state and EU competencies has largely been resolved, as has the extent of formal liberalization, the relationship between sector regulation and competition policy remains open. As in banking and financial services (but not yet energy, where even implementation is difficult) full liberalization has been established in principle and this established the divisions of competences between the EU and member state levels. If anything, the banking sector features greater scope for, and is more prone to, protectionism by way of national regulation than telecoms (Molyneux, 1996, 1999). The drivers behind and the path towards this process of liberalization are addressed in the next two sections, before we return to the current situation and questions about the relative weight of competition policy and sector regulation. After all, the regulator established for the first of Europe's liberalized telecoms market, the British regulator OFTEL, was merely intended as a temporary measure.

TO LIBERALIZE OR TO PROTECT? THE CHANGING BALANCE OF POWER IN THE EU TELECOMS SECTOR

The process of completing the Single European Market and liberalizing protected sectors has been anything but even or uniform, whether evaluated across the last two decades or comparing the relevant sectors. In the telecoms case it has involved the full range of actors found in EU public policy making: the Court of Justice upholding the Commission's widening of its powers, the member states and parliament championing and attempting to derail liberalization, utilities clamoring for protection and industry supporting liberalization. As for the Commission's role, the sector has been invoked as evidence of its leadership and autonomy (Sandholtz, 1993; Héretier, 1999); in support of networks (Schneider *et al.*, 1994) or multi-level governance analysis (Schmidt, 1997; 1998) where the Commission plays a conditional central role; and as evidence that it does little more than accommodate national preferences and industry interest (Davies, 1994; Esser and Noppe, 1996). And this despite telecoms being the first case in which the Commission used its powers under Article 86 (ex 90) unilaterally to issue directives breaking up member state monopolies. Although these conclusions are drawn from different theoretical approaches to liberalization, and are therefore to some extent incompatible, they reflect the plural-ist nature of the liberalization process in the telecoms sector. The Commission may have constituted the driving force behind telecoms liber-alization, but it did so through a gradual process that involved building up support from other actors and accommodating a considerable degree of member state diversity (Thatcher, 1997; Eyre and Sitter, 1999). This involved invoking and responding to pressures from four different levels: domestic developments in the member states, sector-specific change (driven by technology), the EU-level context of completing the single market, and competitive pressure and examples from the world outside the EU. The pressure for reform, the balance of pro- and anti-liberalizers, and the capacity of the Commission to promote its preferred reform program have varied considerably over time.

The central characteristic of West European telecoms markets before lib-eralization was the state-owned monopoly operator. This was broadly jus-tified in terms of remedying market failures and constituting natural monopolies, though their history generally reflected the states' concerns to appropriate monopoly profits (dating back to pre-industrial postal monop-olies). These single national vertically integrated monopolies, charged with fulfilling public policy objectives rather than pursuit of profit, provided for-midable lobbyists against liberalization. Even the privatization of British Telecom involved the government dropping plans to break up the company in the light of management and workforce opposition (Lawson, 1992). Inasmuch as technical equipment was supplied by a select group of privi-leged contractors, these added a third element to the protectionist cartel. Yet an 'electronic alliance' of large corporate users, multinational compa-nies and IT equipment suppliers was increasing in importance and pro-vided a central ally for the Commission (Davies, 1994). Come 1980, the member states and the Commission thus found themselves under growing pressure to investigate avenues for liberalization, from both domestic and multinational actors, despite the utilities' objections.

Technological change increased the potential benefits from liberalizing the sector far more than in comparable sectors such as energy (let alone banking), and the United States was beginning to provide an example of this. The combination of the high (or uncertain) costs associated with state-owned utilities and the elaboration of 'New Right' economic theories associated with the USA and the Austrian school (Dunleavy and O'Leary, 1987) prompted debates at national, OECD and EU level in the light of the US agenda. The initial focus on liberalization of telecoms under Commissioner Davignon in 1979 almost coincided with Thatcher's call for telecoms liberalization in opposition in 1978. By the mid-1980s, this was affecting the balance of power in favor of privatization and deregulation. Davignon's calls for liberalization were echoed by the Council of Ministers' non-binding recommendation in 1984. By 1987, in the wake of the Single European Act, the Commission issued a green paper that set the scenes for partial liberalization. This attracted broad support from the member state governments in principle, even if its specific directives would attract some opposition.

Moreover, the combination of globalization and technological change began to affect the balance among private interests. The French and German utilities reoriented their focus towards the potential benefits to be reaped from engaging in competition abroad (Bartle, 1999). Convergence of the IT and telecoms equipment industry, driven by digitalization, weakened their links with established privileged distributors (Davies, 1994). Hence Sandholtz's suggestion that the Commission's potential to exercise leadership is considerably greater in a period of adaptation and that the late 1980s were precisely such a period as far as telecoms were concerned (Sandholtz, 1993). Much the same could be said for the bank sector, which saw sector-specific developments in the shape of the Exchange Rate Mechanism and the move towards EMU, and these were linked to liberalization of financial markets. It was no coincidence that telecoms became a flagship for liberalization, whether in the UK or the EU. Compared to the energy sector, the benefits of liberalization were considerable in terms of quality improvement and new services, whereas the consequences of network failure were less severe (Levi-Faur, 1999). In addition, the UK government sought to guarantee success for its privatization program by starting with a well-known company that most people used (Lawson, 1992).

During the early 1990s, broad agreement developed in the Council on complete opening of the market, which has been attributed to the gradual impact of EU telecoms reform on domestic structures in key states like Germany, France and Italy. Here the proponents of liberalization were able to employ EU regulations to their advantage in the domestic policy game (Thatcher, 1999). States that liberalized at home in anticipation of EU liberalization, such as Sweden (which joined the EU in 1995), strengthened the pro-liberal camp. Similar patterns characterized the energy sector. Since the EU telecoms markets were opened in 1998, the cleavage between opponents and proponents of liberalization has given way to divisions over forms of regulation that pit incumbents against new entrants. More specifically, where the incumbents favor regulating the sector by way of competition policy, their competitions tend to favor sector-based regulation that constrains the incumbents more.

Although the Commission has maintained and developed a consistent approach to telecoms liberalization, its scope for action has depended on the context. Technological change and international pressure (anticipating globalization) played considerable roles in setting the scene for change in the late 1970s (Sandholtz, 1993), but so did the New Right public policy debate and rightwards shifts in economic policy in the UK, Germany and France in the 1980s (Moravcsik, 1998). By the second half of the 1980s, the Commission's gradualist strategy and efforts to build support through consultation were beginning to pay off, allowing the logic of completion of the Single Market to become a more salient factor. Come the early 2000s, however, technological developments (further convergence between telecoms and IT into the 'communications sector') and global change (World Trade Organization (WTO) arrangements) may be setting the scene for another period of adaptation and change in which the Commission may drive liberalization further. Before we address this question, the path toward liberalization is assessed.

REGULATING TELECOMS IN THE EU: THE PATH TOWARD LIBERALIZATION

In contrast to the banking sector, telecoms and energy liberalization entailed gradual progress toward liberalization starting from national monopolies. In the early 1980s, the Commission was the driving force in the early liberalization process (Eliassen and Sjøvaag, 2001). Its first initiative after Davignon's initial reports came with the 'six lines of action' proposed to the Council at the beginning of 1983. This formed the basis for a telecommunications action plan, approved by the Council in 1984. With this, the member states signaled their readiness to reform and indicated support for future measures. The initial strategy was, however, not to use legislation to regulate the sector, but to encourage harmonization of networks and equipment through the European standardization institutions, promote R&D cooperation through national and EU research programs and build networks of support for liberalization and its invoking international pressure for change (Héretier, 1999). This laid down the basis for liberalization of the market for terminal equipment. EU standards were to become the

norm for this equipment, a prerequisite for introducing Europe-wide offer-
ings of contracts for telecommunications equipment. The Commission
thus invoked technological change to pursue gradual regulation of slices of
the industry one at a time.

At the same time, some member states took their first tentative steps
toward privatization and liberalization. The Thatcher government in the
UK was the first to privatize and liberalize, splitting off the telecommunications wing of the General Post Office as British Telecom in 1981, and privatizing it gradually from 1984 (Thatcher, 1994). Meaningful liberalization
came only slowly, and weak regulation and a long period of transition from
monopoly to competition meant that BT was able to maintain its dominant
status for a long time (Marsh, 1991; Thatcher, 1999). This was therefore
first a case of change from a public to a private monopoly, and only later
did the regulator (Oftel) introduce a competitive regulatory regime. This
experience showed the need for sector-specific regulation in a liberalized
market, a lesson that was not missed by the European Commission.
Elsewhere, the German Witte Commission suggested that the telecommunications branch should be administratively separated from the postal
service and with greater autonomy from governmental control, but that it
be allowed to retain its monopoly on the basic network and on the totally
dominant voice telephony. This was indicative of many European states'
initial antipathy towards 'true' liberalization, as they preferred to retain
some privileges for the national carrier. As late as 1991, the French government reaffirmed France Telecom's monopoly over the basic telecommunications services. These rather reluctant moves towards increased
liberalization have much in common with the very negative stance on financial service liberalization adopted by many governments that feared takeovers from foreign banks.

The Commission's 1987 green paper on telecommunications became the
basis for all subsequent reform. It marked the point of departure for the liberalization and for systematic EU legislation, even if voice services were
exempted. It marked an important step in the Commission's drive to make
member states aware of the benefits of and need for liberalization. However,
it was not so much a strategy for advancing and improving the telecommunications sector as a doctrinaire application of EU competition policy
(which application to the sector had been confirmed by the Court of Justice
in 1985). It called for minimal changes to the status of the PTTs, which were
separated from regulators but could remain as public bodies and retain their
monopoly on basic telephone networks and infrastructure. This was in
accordance with views of almost all the member state policy review bodies,
and demonstrated that the states were not yet ready to surrender the monop-
olistic position on basic services, or to be bounced into the kind of privat-

ization measures introduced in Britain and the USA. Its most far-reaching and influential provisions are related to Open Network Provision (ONP), which lays down rules for network access. This remains the bedrock of liberalization. It was designed to prevent public network operators from frustrating competition by limiting access to the networks. The second crucial requirement for this new regime was the separation of market regulation and service provision, to ensure transparency. The 1997 ONP directive (97/51/EC) therefore demanded the establishment of a National Regulatory Authority (NRA) independent of the industry, which in most cases (with the exception of Italy) has resulted in an independent agency.

The Commission therefore sought to open the market to competition in all but 'reserved services' (effectively voice transmissions). Two directives followed, on terminal equipment in 1988 (88/301/EEC) and on value-added network services (90/388/EEC) in 1990, both issued unilaterally by the Commission under Article 86(ex 90). This was the first time this competition policy measure, which empowers the Commission to issue directives without the approval of the Council or Parliament, was used, and it was bound to be controversial. During this period the principal opposition to the Commission's drive for liberalization came from the more protectionist or interventionist member states, led by France and Spain, with Italy, Greece, Belgium and to a lesser extent Germany (Schmidt, 1998). The terminal equipment directive opened the market for terminal equipment, obliging the states to abolish all telecommunications operators' 'exclusive rights' regarding use and marketing of terminal equipment, to ensure that private suppliers could participate in the market and that users would have access to new public network termination points. Several states challenged the Commission's actions, resulting in a 30-month legal process that ended in the Commission's favor. The Value-Added Network Services (VANS) directive saw a similar fate, although in this case the opposition was somewhat misleading, given the Council's earlier acceptance of the principle of partial liberalization. Yet, from the mid-1990s, the member states would offer much more wholehearted support for liberalization, in contrast to more controversial sectors such as gas or electricity. Even the bank sector has seen considerably more indirect protection.

At the same time the Commission began to shift its focus from 'old' telecommunications policies to broader questions of regulation information and communication technologies (ICT). A green paper on satellite communications, designed to establish a more flexible regulatory system and foster the growth of these services, was adopted in 1990, and the directive followed four years later (94/46/EC). This offers a good example of the difficulties involved in separating regulation and operation of services in a sector with a multitude of actors. Regarding distribution of televised programs, the regulatory authority lies with the nation states, whereas access to the means of satellite communications was organized through international organizations such as Eutelsat, Intelsat and Inmarsat. This 'institutional confusion' resembles that later found with the convergence between IT services and telecommunications, where different providers, regulators and politicians which had been concentrating on their special segments (public broadcasting, newspapers, private one-to-one telecommunications) met in an attempt to form common policies. The shift in EU regulatory efforts from telecommunications policies to ICT policies brought many of the differences in the European regulatory regimes to the surface. A directive extending competition to alternative networks (including cable) followed in 1995 (95/51/EC). Regulation of mobile communications, in the form of the GSM (Global Systems for Mobile Communications) European technical standard from 1987, predated these moves. The 1996 Mobile Directive (96/2/EC) abolished the remaining exclusive rights within this market. It requires that mobile licenses be put out to competitive tender.

The partial liberalization evolved toward full opening of the markets (that is, including voice transmissions) with the Commission's 1993 Telecoms Review. This emphasized the EU context as the driver behind complete liberalization and a requirement for a fully functioning competitive internal market. The approach was to the energy and bank sector, although it found considerably more opposition in the former (Schmidt, 1997, 1998). The new regime was laid down in the ONP Interconnection Directive (97/33/EC), passed in 1997. This replaced the concept of the monopoly network operator with the idea of many competing public network operators. The Commission emphasized the rights and duties of these operators, citing unfettered market and network access and the obligation to guarantee universal service. Firms with 'significant market power' (SMP), defined as more than 25 per cent of the market share, have a 'general duty to supply'. Universal service means that every citizen has a right to access to a certain set of basic telecommunications services at 'affordable prices'. The exact content of the concept of 'basic services' is left to the member states to decide upon. For the time being, only the incumbent operators have sufficient market share to qualify for universal service obligations. There is, however, considerable political leverage in this question, as the question of 'affordable prices' is seen to entail a need of subsidies for some users. The final legal barriers to competition were lifted on 1 January 1998, but a debate on further measures such as local loop unbundling would soon follow (see below, and Figure 4.1).

It must be noted that, despite its long gestation period, this market opening was still ambitious in setting an absolute deadline for every member state to liberalize their telecommunications completely. Many states sought deroga-

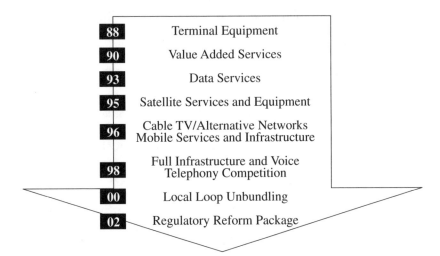

Source: The European Commission.

Figure 4.1 Evolution of policy: the road to the present

tions, claiming that their industries were simply not ready to liberalize. Some were granted. The most visible effect of liberalization has been the proliferation of new actors in the market. Small firms have been given the chance to compete with the previously dominant operators, and many are taking the opportunity to undercut the larger operators and offer new and innovative services such as combined entertainment–Internet–telephony applications. The mobile market in particular has seen an explosion in the number of companies bidding for licenses and providing services. Moreover, operators are expanding across borders, forming joint ventures and alliances abroad. There are therefore considerable similarities with the financial sector, although the governments' willingness to promote a free market and the technological capabilities to introduce it seems to be higher in the ICT sector. However, two questions remain. How European and unified is the single market (do future challenges warrant more or less flexibility?) and does this vary among the different parts of the converging communications industry?

THE EU TELECOMS REGIME: IS LIBERALIZATION TOO GOOD TO BE TRUE?

Compared to relatively similar utilities sectors such as gas and electricity, the Europeanization and liberalization in the telecoms sector is a success story inasmuch as the market has been fully opened. Yet, as in the financial services sector, this does not mean that a fully functioning Single Market has been established, even if a pan-European regime is starting to take shape and replace diverse traditional models. On one hand, the sector is a highly technical one that is prone to change, on the other it is dominated by strong incumbents, some of which enjoy close relations with governments. The new regulatory agency models entail unbundling (at least administrative separation) of the utilities' functions, the profit motive taking center stage (subject to regulation), separation of service provision and regulation, with NRAs sharing competence with competition authorities. This effectively divides operators into three categories (Cave and Larouche, 2001). Operators with 'significant market power' (SMP) are subject to the heaviest regulation by NRAs, including the ONP provisions; 'publicly available services' are subject to licensing but benefit from ONP provisions for network access; while the general regulatory framework applies to all provision of services and networks. The present trend is toward increasing use of competition policy rather than sector regulation, a move supported by the large operators inasmuch as it lightens the regulatory burden. Yet, despite formal market liberalization, significant evidence of increased competition and considerable pressure for further liberalization, there are several obstacles to the development of fully competitive markets. In the light of the first four years of open competition, several issues have come to constitute significant problems. Some of these emerged already in the Commission's 1999 Telecoms review (COM (2000) 814). These are addressed below, in the form of six topics, with a view to discussing the dynamics of reform in the subsequent section.

First, the incumbents still retain considerable market power, and this has generated pressure for further regulation. To be sure, the 1999 Review showed considerable annual market growth (9 per cent) as well as increasing choice for consumers in terms of both operators and services (an 80 per cent increase in voice telephony operators), and high mobile service penetration rates (as high as 70 per cent and not lower than 39 per cent). Prices are decreasing steadily, both for retail and leased line, and Internet usage is increasing, although penetration is still significantly below that of the USA. The old monopoly operators have been privatized (at least partly), face competition at home and engage in competition abroad by way of alliances and joint ventures. They have to satisfy clients that are increasingly sophisticated and demanding with regard both to quality and to price of old as well as new services, and have transformed (or are about to do so) their organizational structures in line with modern management principles. Yet they maintain a strong hold on the market in general, and competition in local markets has been limited. In this context, it is important for regulators to ensure that incumbents do not cross-subsidize tariffs, which should be cost-based. Moreover, regulators still have problems dealing with the lengthy delivery times of leased lines, which is becoming as significant a problem as price levels. At least, in Sweden, Belgium and Italy, this is the area in which new entrants have brought the most cases against the incumbents. The full range of carrier pre-selection services must be available, so that new entrants can reach end-customers in the same way as incumbents. Regulators must work even harder to ensure that new entrants can install their equipment at local exchanges for the provision of local access services. Call termination on mobile networks is still not competitively priced, and all calculations and charging of these tariffs need to be tackled.

Second, therefore, although the markets have been opened, supplementary legislation is required to make the Single Market fully competitive. A host of problems concern implementation and design. The 1999 Review identified problems in the field of licensing (onerous conditions, heavy fees), interconnection (cost-based pricing, delays) and consumer protection (disparities, lack of transparency), as well as high prices in the mobile market, especially for call termination, incomplete rebalancing of tariffs to prevent cross-subsidies, regulatory limits to carrier pre-selections, weak regulatory action against incumbents foreclosing competition in the local loop, high prices and delays for leased lines and considerable variations in terms and prices for new entrants in the Internet market. Interconnection, number portability, carrier selection and cost-based pricing were identified as the central problems for applicant states from East Central Europe seeking to catch up with the single market in telecoms.

Third, all member states feature NRAs, but there is a considerable national variation in their independence, power and resources. As regards the effective independence of telecoms regulators and competition authorities, it would be fair to state that the separation between regulation and politics is adequate. The exception is applicant states; for example, there is the supposedly independent Hungarian regulator that works out of the prime minister's office. However, several NRAs face limits in terms of lack of resources, power of enforcement and sanctions. Even though the drama of liberalization is over, Europe's regulators still have difficulties with the specifics of EU directives. Low salaries compared to the private sector exacerbate the problem. While competition is starting to flourish in some markets, in others it is moving at a slow crawl. Accelerating this process is a key task of the Commission and national regulators, but it is not proving easy. Findings both from the OECD and from the European Commission[1] show a two-tier system is emerging across Europe. While some member states struggle with the EU's initial regulatory package and directives, others formulate their own legislation to deal with areas not thoroughly addressed by EU legislation. The NRAs in Belgium, France, Germany, Luxembourg, Spain and Sweden have been criticized for their failure to intervene in interconnection disputes. Furthermore, new entrants have questioned the proactive role of the Greek NRA towards licensing. The EU also examined the intervention of the Dutch and Austrians regarding numbering. New entrants were concerned at the amount of time taken by the Belgian, Swedish and Italian NRAs to make decisions. On the more positive side, the powers of the NRA in Austria, Greece and Ireland have been increased, and Portugal's telecoms regulator was praised for its proactivity in dispute resolutions. The position of the regulator vis-à-vis the state has been questioned in some countries; again, this is a particular problem in applicant states. New entrants perceived the separation of powers between the Comisión del Mercado de las Telecomunicaciones and the Ministry of Development in Spain as ambiguous. Much the same holds for the overlap between Finland's NRA and its competition authority and the lack of clarity as to which functions have been transferred from the Ministry to the NRA in Italy.

Fourth, although it is more difficult to assess the extent of this problem, some states remain closely aligned with 'their' operators. Although the main elements of the government–regulator–incumbent trinity have been weakened with Europeanization and liberalization, the influence (and arrogance) of some incumbents is seen as a legacy of their past privileged position. No serious business would give up its dominant position without a fight. European operators may be privatized, but they behave monopolistically as long as they can. This is where regulators come in. In East Central Europe, price controls and the political costs imposing full market costs on customers add to the problem. Moreover, despite its being one of the most basic steps towards a fully liberalized market, even regulators in advanced markets find it difficult to ensure total separation from the government. On the one hand, member states argue that telecoms is very important and fully support the *e*Europe programme (to employ Internet technology), but at the same time they prevent the Commission from driving harmonization and fail both to put pressure on and to give resources to their independent regulators. Government intervention and protection of former utilities can still be seen, and the problem is not easily resolved. This situation will stay with us for a while.

Fifth, Europe's NRAs are struggling to keep up with the radical change in the market. While the first lessons about liberalization have been absorbed, few regulators are fully prepared for the next round. The Commission and independent regulatory bodies across the continent are all seeking ways to keep track of the new trends. While on the whole the 1999 Review held few surprises, the apparently simple principles for maintaining competition are continuing to pose tough challenges for Europe's regulators. As the timetable for the introduction of full competition was agreed in the mid-1990s, Europe's regulators were forced to prepare for full competition with unseemly haste. As a result, delays in implementing key legislation prompted accusations of bringing emergent free markets to a standstill and slowing the development of Europe's laggards. The greatest challenge that most NRAs currently face is that of adapting to rapid changes in the market place. The 1999 Review highlights these areas of change, but it only goes some way towards providing guidance for regulation of the next-generation services. With the Internet and mobile telephony, the ground rules for regulating the European telecoms market are changing even as they are being implemented. Increased competition means higher expectations of NRAs. As well as implementing existing regulation, they must strive to be forward-looking in all of their decisions. In short, convergence between telecoms, IT and the media (Figure 4.2) is raising new questions about regulation.

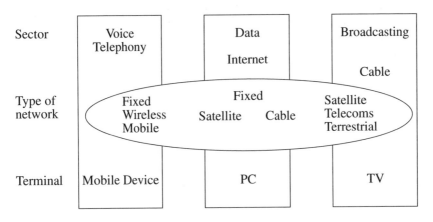

Source: Commissioner Erkki Liikanen, The European Commission.

Figure 4.2 Convergence removes sector boundaries

Sixth, and finally, in parallel with the current difficulties of the regulatory authorities, some regulators are already preparing for the next generation of services. Even Europe's most advanced markets face considerable challenges. Difficult issues such as the pricing of access to mobile networks and flat-rate Internet access have arisen over the last year. Introducing regulation into the previously unregulated cellular market is a difficult task for regulators. Regulating fixed-line markets also throws up significant new challenges. Aside from the usual and continuing disputes regarding interconnection and local-loop unbundling (i.e. opening the last section of the phone line into the household to competition), complex new areas such as the field of broadband must be tackled. These challenges, coupled with an uncertain future, means that Europe's NRAs face difficult decisions. While most would favor 'light-handed' regulation, many find that they must become more interventionist in order to drive telecoms policy forward. However, all NRAs are forced to look towards the Commission for guidance. All NRAs have had to struggle with complex and in some cases contentious issues such as the rollout of wireless local loop, the costing of number portability and carrier pre-selection, and the licensing of third-generation mobile networks. Over the past couple of years, several of Europe's regulators have tried to innovate within the existing regulatory framework, with varying degrees of success. A relevant example is the award of 3G licenses, which represented numerous surprises, although apparently following EU procedures. The much-debated 3G auctions across Europe can only be described as scandals characterized by high overbidding for a third-generation mobile network of great uncertainty. Could this be explained by too much regulation (from the NRAs)? Following the Commission's recommendations for the future path towards 3G (of March 2001), some regulators have already started to take control of infrastructure-sharing agreements in their markets, for instance allowing operators to make their own agreements (Sweden), and drawing up infrastructure sharing principles for operators (Germany). However, following the Commission's logic of less regulation within the future telecoms market, most NRAs will be cautious about intervening unnecessarily in agreements between operators.

All these issues should be seen in the light of the Commission's original aim not to use legislation to regulate and liberalize the sector, and its increasing focus on competition policy. As in the UK, sector regulation was intended as a temporary tool of governance in the transition to a fully competitive market. Moreover, the EU regulatory regime features few detailed requirements concerning state structures, which means great flexibility for government, NRAs and operators. This has enabled national policy makers to tailor reforms to national circumstances, which resulted in degrees and forms of privatization varying considerably. Likewise, differences in the structure of the new regulatory authorities, variations in number and methods of nomination and scrutiny of regulators (often to satisfy members of national parliaments) still set national markets apart from each other (Thatcher, 1999). These challenges prompted a new regulatory package on governance of telecoms in the 2000s.

THE GOVERNANCE OF TELECOMS IN THE 2000s: FROM REGULATION TO COMPETITION?

In July 2000, the European Commission adopted a package of legislative proposals designed to strengthen competition in the electronic communications markets in the EU for the benefit of consumers and the European economy. On 14 February 2002, the European Council formally adopted the set of four directives and a decision on regulation of electronic communications (COM (2000) 384, 385, 386, 392, 393), which is to be implemented within 15 months of publication. The adoption of such new legislative proposals was driven by three main concerns, which reflect the questions discussed in the section above: (a) the development of competition in local markets has been limited; (b) the Commission's strategy is not to use legislation to regulate the sector; and (c) convergence between telecoms, information technology and the media is changing the relevant markets. The central aim is therefore to drive forward the liberalization of telecommunications markets by adapting regulation to the requirements of the Information Society and the digital revolution. The convergence process means that a service can be delivered across a range of platforms and received via different terminals. The reforms are therefore geared toward providing the best conditions for a dynamic and competitive industry across the ICT sector; that is, for all electronic communication services in a rapidly changing technological environment where only fierce and fair competition will yield lower prices, better quality and innovative services. The package therefore includes the following:

- liberalization of the 'last mile' of telecommunications markets by unbundling access to the local loop. This will lead to cheaper and faster Internet access over local copper-wire networks;
- introduction of flexible mechanisms in the legislation to allow it to evolve with future technology and market changes and to roll back regulation when markets become competitive;
- establishing a level playing field across the EU by facilitating market entry through simplified rules and ensuring harmonized application through strong coordination mechanisms at the European level;
- adaptation of regulation to increasing competition by limiting most of market power-based regulation to dominant operators, as defined in EU competition law;
- maintenance of the universal service obligations in order to avoid exclusion from the Information Society;
- protection of the right to privacy on the Internet.

In this context, current developments center on three main themes: simplification of the regulatory framework, a shift towards increasing use of competition law to regulate the sector, and the question of whether an EU-level regulator is required.

First, on the topic of simplification, the Commission is moving in the direction of less, but improved regulation. '*Less regulation, easier market entry and a level playing field across EU are pre-requisites for development of world class telecommunications and Internet services in Europe*' (Liikanen, 2000, italics in original). However, for a combination of reasons related to incumbent market power and incomplete legislation (see above), simplification also means new and better regulation. The new regulatory framework reduces the number of legal measures from 28 to eight (Figure 4.3). Alongside a new consolidated and simplified Liberalization Directive, the new regulatory framework consists of a Framework Directive (replacing the ONP Framework Directive) and four specific directives (authorization, access and interconnection, universal service and user rights, and data protection in telecommunications services), a regulation on the unbundling of

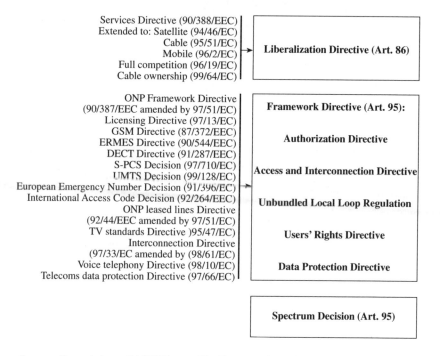

Source: Commissioner Erkki Liikanen, The European Commission.

Figure 4.3   Simplification and clarification

the local loop, and a decision on radio spectrum policy. This is presented as a cornerstone in ensuring Europe's transition to a new knowledge-based economy, as envisaged in the conclusions of the Lisbon European Council of 23–4 March 2000.

Experts in the field and community institutions[2] applaud this new regime as representing clear progress in simplifying and clarifying the existing regulatory framework. The broad approach taken in the new regime on pre-emptive regulation makes it less vulnerable to technological change, and thus makes it flexible enough to accommodate evolutionary market developments. However, two aspects especially have been criticized (Cave and Larouche, 2001). The first is an alleged lack of concern for internal market objectives on the part of the EU institutions, inasmuch as there is no internal market for electronic communications and the new framework does not make it much more likely that it will be achieved soon. Although clear improvements are expected, one could claim that the new regulatory framework is outdated before it is agreed, let alone implemented. It does not take into account problems linked to the overlap between closely related regulatory schemes based on different principles, such as the Television Without Frontiers Directive and the E-commerce Directive. Both adhere to the member state control principle, in contrast to the regulation of electronic communications at a common EU level. Second, there is a clear distinction between electronic services and content, which might be too strong given the actual and obvious links between the two. As Cave and Larouche point out, the Community should not hide behind these conceptual distinctions to avoid presenting a coherent regulatory scheme that would advance the internal market in electronic communications.

Second, the Commission envisages a gradual shift from ONP to competition law. The new regulatory regime is intended to operate as a *sui generis* form of competition policy, and is therefore an important step towards normal competition governed by generic competition law. The end goal is a sector governed by competition law, and the Commission therefore proposes to move away from the rather arbitrary approach in the current regulatory framework, towards something more consistent with competition law. However, competition law is to be applied in a pre-emptive ex ante form, not in a responsive ex post fashion. Therefore this new regime is dependent on a definition of relevant markets, an identification of dominance and formulation of remedies. This means that, within the uniform framework necessary for the internal market, but permitting flexibility and variable pace, the NRAs can define relevant markets, dominance and remedies. In line with the Commission's proposed model, 'relevant markets' will no longer be defined in directives (under the current regime, the relevant market is defined in the specific ONP directives on interconnection, voice telephony and leased lines). Under the New Framework Directive (Article 14), the Commission will be required to publish a decision on relevant product and service markets, to be defined along competition policy lines. This decision will list those markets within the communications sector whose characteristics may justify the imposition of ex ante regulatory obligations. In addition, the Commission will publish guidelines on market analysis and the calculation of dominance, or SMP. However, NRAs may depart from the decisions with respect to geographical market definitions if they believe this is appropriate in regard to their own circumstances.

In terms of their effect on the intrusiveness and effectiveness of regulation, market definitions cut both ways. A narrow, precise definition increases the prospect of firms falling into the SMP category, but it confines the scope of regulation to the product or service covered. A broad, more ambiguous, definition that does not distinguish between types of products or services reduces any firm's 'market share' by broadening the 'relevant market', but thereby permits the NRA to intervene across a wider sector when SMP is determined (Cave and Larouche, 2001). The risk is that this approach could lead to market fragmentation and legal uncertainty because the significant freedom of the NRAs to depart from the principles of competition law could result in divergence of regulatory decision making across the EU (Nikolinakos, 2001). Furthermore, dominance (or SMP) can be exercised by a single firm, or collectively, or leveraged into a vertically related market. This creates further uncertainty about the regulatory outcome. It is difficult for firms to forecast how widely NRAs or the bodies to which their decisions can be appealed will define dominance. Finally, in regard to remedies, the NRAs have to do something when confronted by SMP, but, because of their flexibility, application is highly unpredictable and can result in considerable differences among the member states. In this respect, instead of a development going from ONP regulation to competition law, the New European Regulatory Regime for Electronic Communications might better be described as a development from ONP to an extended ONP regulation.

Third, and finally, this raises questions as to the need for a pan-Europe regulatory body. Despite policy innovations such as broadband initiatives in different member states, all NRAs are forced to look towards the Commission for guidance. The relationship between the Commission and Europe's NRAs has naturally come under scrutiny from all angles, giving rise to the same question as in a range of EU sectors. Is there a need for a pan-Europe regulatory authority? The long-running and complex debate on possibility of creating a pan-Europe regulatory body has been discussed among EU institutions, NRAs, member states and telecoms operators since before the implementation of the directives on liberalization. However, it is worth emphasizing a few central points. Most actors do not, at least at this point, believe that a pan-Europe regulatory authority is the solution to current challenges. This includes the member states, the NRAs and even the Commission. However, both the NRAs and the Commission see increased communication as crucial to a better understanding of European regulation. As a result, a number of Europe's regulators set up the Independent Regulators' Group (IRG), which gathers every six months to discuss common concerns and compare experiences of implementing EU directives. Indeed, the IRG has been functioning so well that the Commission and the European regulators are considering upgrading the group to a more formal standing. How much time it may take to establish a pan-Europe international body is another matter.

There is no easy solution, but most parties agree that such a body would need to work in close cooperation with the NRAs. With most NRAs being novices in this game and the creation of a pan-Europe regulatory body likely to be a slow process, Europe's regulatory landscape appears unlikely to change in the near future. The Commission will keep on seeking greater powers to intervene in the implementation of EU directives by NRAs, but by and large the choice as to how to follow EU guidelines remains with the NRAs. While this may prove frustrating for many new entrants, it is the best offer available for now. The Commission has put forward a proposal to increase the transparency and consultation with and among NRAs to make the application of EU law more coherent and harmonized. This might help address some of the concerns surrounding the performance of the NRAs, but is not a solution that can solve the immediate issues such as the lack of a proper platform for communicating amongst NRAs and with the Commission with regard to individual decisions taken by regulators. The result has been a tendency towards fragmentation and differing applications and interpretation of EU law. A Commission working plan includes developing a better framework for such cooperation (COM (2000) 393). Whether adding a further layer of bureaucracy will strengthen the position of the NRAs remains an open question. However, some of the largest pan-Europe network operators argue that there is a clear demand for the Commission to take a more interventionist role. Commission action has not yet been triggered, because it only acts on the evidence put before it. As long as the aim is to attain a single market in telecoms one could argue that the Commission requires more power to stop member states fragmenting it.

CONCLUSION

Returning to the central question regarding the emergence of governance in the shadow of EMU – or 'EMU governance' – and the extent to which this has generated a fully-fledged open market economy, the answers are to a large extent positive; that is, there has been a shift from 'government' at the national level to supranational 'governance' and this has entailed a considerable degree of liberalization. The Commission has to a large extent driven developments in the EU telecoms governance regime, albeit within the parameters that member state preferences delimit. The power and influence of industry, governments, regulators and the Commission have changed over time, producing a 'governance' regime characterized by negotiation, compromise and so on, in line with the notion of 'EMU governance'. However, this is not to say that a fully-fledged open market has been established. The balance between sector regulation and competition remains open, and the sector is set to undergo further technologically driven change.

Given the variations in national regulatory regimes, the single market is not yet fully functional. The remaining different balance between intervention and free market across states reflects the three compromises inherent in EU governance (state/market, EU/member state and open market/protection). As the international scope of the market increases, the relationship between different national regulatory structures, and the relationship between national and supranational regulatory structures, become much more important. The current European telecommunications industry could be described as consisting of national regulation and global competition. Although direct state intervention should have been eliminated, the new regulatory framework is established in order to secure prices, standards and so on, and to prevent the market from destroying itself. In a regulatory regime based on flexibility, some states fulfill regulations better than others and these states often represent a more liberalized and competitive market place. This is also the case in Europe, and we can therefore not talk about *a* European telecommunications market. There is no single market in telecoms (yet), but rather as many markets as there are nation states. Even with globalization, or at least multinational operation, the vast majority of services are still produced and consumed within individual national boundaries (Barnes, 1998).

In this context, and in the light of technological developments, the balance between sector regulation and open competition has emerged as the central question regarding completion of the single market for communications. The new framework indicates that the Commission is increasingly oriented toward replacing sector regulation with competition instruments where possible. However, how to define relevant markets remains controversial, as does harmonization. The current system of telecom regulation is not equipped to handle new markets, and market definitions should probably therefore be as wide as possible. Technical development and market changes are always a challenge and could change the basis for regulation. Harmonization of SMP is important in order to secure a coherent framework in Europe. This issue is still controversial, and the Council of Ministers will not allow the Commission too much power through harmonization. Some kind of a compromise is in the pipeline with the idea of establishing a European Regulatory Group. Moreover, the present combination of technological change and globalization is generating conditions similar to those that the Commission exploited to shape and accelerate integration in the 1980s. Further convergence between telecoms and IT into the 'communications sector' and change through global organizations as the WTO may be setting the scene for another period of adaptation and change in which the Commission may drive liberalization further.

In most competitive telecom markets regulation is the linchpin. Much of the talk of 'deregulation' refers to nothing of the sort. Instead, competition is encouraged and policed by means of an industry regulator armed with a variety of powers and numerous rules. Although many governments would like to aim for an unregulated free market in telecoms in the long run, most begin their march in that direction with heavy reregulation of the sector. This creates a veritable regulatory industry with problems of its own, not least the suspicion that such bodies will never be prepared to regulate themselves out of existence. To be sure, there are legitimate requirements for regulation in markets newly opened to competition and dominated by a former monopoly, but most new regulatory bodies go further and impose regulations on every aspect of the market until it can be demonstrated that regulations are no longer required. These issues are as relevant for the banking sector as for telecoms, and they are prompting further regulatory debate and reform. Competition in the years to come is likely to be far more unpredictable than it was during the 1980s and 1990s, while the emergence of multi-media networks and services adds to the complexity of the market.

NOTES

1. In the sixth report on implementation of the EU regulatory measures (December 2000), the European Commission (EC) charted the regulatory progress made by each NRA.
2. Interviews, DG INFSO, Telenor Brussels, DG COM, in Brussels, 12 November 2001.

REFERENCES

Barnes, F. (1998), 'Regulating Telecommunications', in Dieter Helm and Tim Jenkinson (eds), *Competition in Regulated Industries*, New York: Oxford University Press.

Bartle, I. (1999), 'Transnational Interests in the European Union: Globalisation and the Changing Organisation in Telecommunications and Electricity', *Journal of Common Market Studies*, 37(3): 363–83.

Cave, M. and P. Larouche (2001), 'European Communications at the Crossroads', Report of a CEPS Working Party, Centre for European Policy Studies, Brussels, October.

Davies, A. (1994), *Telecommunications and Politics: The Decentralised Alternative*, London: Pinter.

Dufey, G. (1993), 'Banking in the EC after 1992', in W.J. Adams (ed.), *Singular Europe: Economy and Polity of the European Community after 1992*, Ann Arbor: University of Michigan Press.

Dunleavy, P. and B. O'Leary (1987), *Theories of the State: The Politics of Liberal Democracy*, London: Macmillan.

Dunleavy, P. (1995), 'Policy Disasters: Explaining the UK's Record', *Public Administration*, 10(2), 52–70.

Dyson, K. (1999), 'Economic and Monetary Union in Europe: A Transformation of Governance', in B. Kohler-Koch and R. Eising (eds), *The Transformation of Governance in the European Union*, London: Routledge.

Eliassen, K.A. and M. Sjøvaag (eds) (1999), *European Telecommunications Liberalisation: Too Good to be True?*, London: Routledge.

Eliassen, K.A. and M. Sjøvaag (2001), 'Telecommunications Policy: Interest Convergence and Globalization', in S.S. Andersen and K.A. Eliassen (eds), *Making Policy in Europe*, London: Sage.

Esser, J. and R. Noppe (1996), 'Private Muddling through as a Political Programme? The Role of the European Commission in the Telecommunications Sector in the 1980s', *West European Politics*, 19(3): 547–62.

Eyre, S. and N. Sitter (1999), 'From PTT to NRA: Towards a New Regulatory Regime', in K.A. Eliassen and M. Sjøvaag (eds), *European Telecommunications Liberalisation: Too Good to be True?*, London: Routledge.

Héretier, A. (1999), *Policy-Making and Diversity in Europe: Escape from Deadlock*, Cambridge: Cambridge University Press.

Hix, S. (1998), 'The Study of the European Union II: The "New Governance" Agenda and Its Rival', *Journal of European Public Policy*, 5(1): 38–65.

Hood, C. (1998), *The Art of the State: Culture, Rhetoric and Public Management*, Oxford: Clarendon Press.

Jachtenfuchs, M.J. (1995), 'Theoretical Perspectives on European Governance', *European Law Journal*, 1(2): 115–33.

Kohler-Koch, B. (1996), 'Catching up with the Change: The Transformation of Governance in the European Union', *Journal of European Public Policy*, 3(3): 359–80.

Kohler-Koch, B. and R. Eising (eds) (1999), *The Transformation of Governance in the European Union*, London: Routledge.

Kooiman, J. (ed.) (1993), *Modern Governance New Government–Society Interactions*, London: Sage.

Lawson, N. (1992), *The View from No. 11*, London: Bantam Press.

Levi-Faur, D. (1999), 'The Governance of Competition: The Interplay of Technology, Economics and Politics in European Union Electricity and Telecom Regimes', *Journal of Public Policy*, 19(2): 175–208.

Liikanen, E. (2000), 'Commissioner for Enterprise and the Information Society', Press Release 12 July.

Majone, G. (1998), 'State, Market and Regulatory Competition in the European Union: Lessons for Integrating the World Economy', in A. Moravcsik (ed.), *Centralization or Fragmentation? Europe Facing the Challenges of Deepening, Diversity, and Democracy*, New York: Council of Foreign Relations.

Marks, G., F.W. Scharpf, P.C. Schmitter and W. Streeck (eds) (1996), *Governance in the European Union*, London: Sage.

Marsh, D. (1991), 'Privatization under Mrs Thatcher: A Review of the Literature', *Public Administration*, 69, 459–80.

Molyneux, P. (1996), 'Banking and Financial Services', in H. Kassim and A. Menon (eds), *The European Union and National Industrial Policy*, London: Routledge.

Molyneux, P. (1999), 'Increasing Concentration and Competition in European Banking: The End of Anti-Trust', *European Investment Bank Cahiers Papers*, 4(1): 127–36.

Moravcsik, A. (1991), 'Negotiating the Single European Act: National Interests and Conventional Statecraft in the European Community', *International Organization*, 45(1): 19–56.

Moravcsik, A. (1998), *The Choice for Europe: Social Purpose & State Power from Messina to Maastricht*, Ithaca: Cornell University Press.

Nikolinakos, N.T. (2001), 'The New European Regulatory Regime for Electronic Communications Networks and Associated Services: The Proposed Framework and Access/Interconnection Directives', *European Competition Law Review (ECLR)*, 22(3): March.

Pierre, J. and G. Stoker (2000), 'Towards Multi-Level Governance', in P. Dunleavy, A. Gamble, R. Heffernan, I. Holiday and G. Peele (eds), *Developments in British Politics*, vol. 6, London: Macmillan.

Pollitt, C. and Bouckaert, G. (2000), *Public Management Reform, a Comparative Analysis*, Oxford: Oxford University Press.

Sandholtz, W. (1993), 'Institutions and Collective Action: The New Telecommunications in Western Europe', *World Politics*, 45, 242–70.

Sandholtz, W. and J. Zysman (1989), '1992: Recasting the European Bargain', *World Politics*, 41(1): 95–128.

Scharpf, F.W. (1999), *Governing in Europe: Effective and Democratic?*, Oxford: Oxford University Press.

Schmidt, S.K. (1997), 'Sterile Debates and Dubious Generalisations: European Integration Theory Tested by Telecommunications and Electricity', *Journal of Public Policy*, 16(3): 233–71.

Schmidt, S.K. (1998), 'Commission Activism: Subsuming Telecommunications and Electricity under European Competition Law', *Journal of European Public Policy*, 5(1): 169–84.

Schmitter, P.C. (2001), 'What is there to Legitimize in the European Union . . . and how might this be Accomplished?', Jean Monnet Working Paper 14/01, New York University Law School.

Schneider, V., G. Dang-Nguyen and R. Werle (1994), 'Corporate Actor Networks in European Policy-Making: Harmonising Telecommunications Policy', *Journal of Common Market Studies*, 32(4): 473–98.

Sedelmeier, U. (2001), 'Comparative Politics, Policy Analysis and Governance – A European Contribution to the Study of the European Union?', *West European Politics*, 24(3): 173–82.

Stoker, G. (1998), 'Governance as Theory: Five Propositions', *International Social Science Journal*, 155, 17–28.

Taylor, P. (1989), 'The New Dynamics of EC Integration in the 1980s', in J. Lodge (ed.), *The European Community and the Challenge of the Future*, London: Pinter.

Thatcher, M. (1994), 'Regulatory Reform in Britain and France: Organizational Structure and the Extension of Competition', *Journal of European Public Policy*, 1(3): 4441–64.

Thatcher, M. (1997), 'The Development of Regulatory Frameworks: The Expansion of European Community Policy-Making in Telecommunications', in S. Stavridis, E. Mossialos, R. Moran and H. Machin (eds), *New Challenges to the European Union: Policies and Policy-Making*, Aldershot: Dartmouth.

Thatcher, M. (1999), 'The Europeanisation of Regulation: The Case of Telecommunications', Working Paper RSC 99/12, European University Institute.

Wessels, W. (1997) 'An Ever Closer Fusion? A Dynamic Macropolitical View on Integration Processes', *Journal of Common Market Studies*, 35(2): 267–99.

5. The new framework of transatlantic economic governance: strategic trade management and regulatory conflict in a multilateral global economy

Chad Damro and Alberta Sbragia

INTRODUCTION

Transatlantic economic relations have been gradually reshaped as the accomplishments of the liberal trading system negotiated during the postwar period have taken hold. Tariff barriers to transatlantic trade, while still inflammatory at times, are no longer the primary concern of the European Union (EU) and the United States of America (USA). Rather non-tariff barriers have achieved such prominence that the EU–USA economic relationship should be conceptualized in terms of both tariff and non-tariff barriers.[1] In addition to non-tariff barriers, highly developed regulatory regimes are increasingly creating important 'behind-the-border' barriers to trade for both economic and political reasons. Such regimes include so-called 'economic regulation', which focuses on the activity of firms as well as tax codes, and 'social regulation', which addresses issues related to public health and environmental protection. While these regulatory regimes have been constructed for the purposes of domestic public policy, they now reduce market access for foreign goods. In the case of transatlantic economic relations, therefore, the increasingly important barriers that inhibit trade are domestic regulations rather than simply tariff and non-tariff barriers.

Given the initial political dynamics which led to the creation of such regulatory systems, it is perhaps not surprising that EU–US conflicts over regulatory differences are particularly intractable, politically salient and difficult to resolve. Regulatory policy is often adopted after a considerable amount of domestic political conflict so that the ultimate compromise reflects a complex set of bargains among numerous private and public actors that are not easily changed. To be successful, international negotiations over such policy necessarily would require reshaping such bargains within the domestic arena, a politically difficult and costly exercise.

As the EU and the USA, two 'regulatory states', confront each other over a myriad of differences rooted in their respective domestic regulatory regimes, they are faced with the problem of how to resolve such conflicts.[2] In the arena of tariff barriers to trade, the World Trade Organization (WTO) serves as a key referent and arbiter. To prevent economic disputes from escalating into destabilizing trade wars, the EU and the USA are increasingly managing their disagreements through the rule-based system of the WTO. Management of economic disputes within this mutually agreed system does not prevent retaliation, but it does increase certainty for policy makers and industries. At the same time, the EU and the USA are able to use the WTO's built-in time lag in a strategic fashion to accrue domestic gains before adjusting offending trade measures. Such a multilateral approach to strategic trade dispute management works well for resolving traditional trade disputes related to tariff and non-tariff barriers, and it moves transatlantic economic relations away from a bilateral to a multilateral approach.

In the case of regulatory conflict, however, the multilateral framework so important for settling traditional trade disputes becomes far more problematic. Compliance with WTO decisions that involve adjusting domestic regulatory regimes is far more difficult for governments than when those decisions address the removal of traditional tariff and non-tariff barriers. In fact the intractable nature of transatlantic regulatory conflict has encouraged the development of new mechanisms specifically designed to facilitate regulatory cooperation.

This chapter argues that, to the extent that transatlantic economic relations involve traditional tariff and non-tariff barriers to trade rather than regulatory conflicts, the more likely it is that the WTO's dispute settlement mechanism will prove effective in resolving such economic disagreements. While this multilateral mechanism works relatively well at *dispute resolution* in trade conflicts, as disputes over regulations become more prominent in the transatlantic market place, a new framework for transatlantic economic governance is needed. This new framework will continue to rely on the WTO system for dispute resolution in traditional trade conflicts. However, a system of transatlantic economic governance that emphasizes *dispute prevention* seems better suited for managing transatlantic regulatory conflicts. Such a system of governance will require complementary bilateral and multilateral approaches to regulatory dispute prevention, such as maintaining and expanding bilateral Mutual Recognition Agreements and multilateral recommendations, codes and standards.

We therefore argue that a useful analytical distinction can be made between transatlantic disputes over traditional tariff and non-tariff barriers to trade and disputes arising from different regulatory approaches. While traditional trade and regulatory issues often overlap, transatlantic relations are best conceptualized as two different streams that prompt different levels of economic conflict and cooperation. The interaction of domestic EU and US politics with the multilateral rules of the WTO helps to explain the likelihood of this transatlantic conflict and cooperation over trade and regulatory issues.

This chapter assesses the state of transatlantic economic relations in the following manner. First, we briefly detail the central importance of the transatlantic relationship for the global economy, focusing primarily on the private and public sources of trade and investment flows, and investigate the bilateral and multilateral dimensions of EU–US economic relations. Secondly we develop an analytical approach for understanding current and future levels of conflict and cooperation in transatlantic economic relations. This approach emphasizes the interaction of the WTO system and domestic politics and the differentiation between trade and regulatory issues Finally, we apply our analytical approach to four recent disputes in transatlantic economic relations (the EU's banana regime and ban on hormone-treated beef, and the USA's steel tariffs and foreign sales corporations) to illustrate how and why significant transatlantic trade and regulatory disputes emerge and can (or cannot) be resolved. Our conclusion discusses the implications for transatlantic governance of reshaping the transatlantic economic relationship.

THE NEW 'PRIVATE' AND 'PUBLIC' SPHERES IN THE TRANSATLANTIC ECONOMIC RELATIONSHIP

Private and public sector actors both play important roles in the transatlantic economic relationship. As a result, one analyst has pointed out that 'transatlantic relations now are composed of both a 'private sphere' and a 'public sphere'' (Sbragia, 1998, p. 148). Whereas the transatlantic economic relationship as traditionally conceptualized was principally composed of exporters and importers, the new private sphere has expanded the role of the business community. In particular, European and American multinational corporations have become far more important than they were previously as foreign direct investment (FDI) has flourished. The nature of the public sphere has also changed as new transatlantic institutional relationships have been created and new bilateral agreements forged. As a result, the EU and the USA now deal with each other in a multiplicity of bilateral relationships as well as within the multilateral framework of the World Trade Organization. This section details those changes that have occurred

in the 1990s in both the private and public spheres of the transatlantic economic relationship.

The Private Sphere: the Transatlantic Twins of Trade and Investment

Global economic growth depends heavily on a vibrant transatlantic market
place because it represents the largest and most important bilateral economic relationship today.[3] The EU and the USA are the world's largest
industrialized economies, collectively accounting for roughly 56 per cent of
global gross domestic product. This figure is particularly striking considering that the combined population of the EU and the USA constitutes only
10 per cent of the world's total (Burghardt, 2001, p. 21). The twin indicators of trade and FDI reflect the growing size and interdependence of the
transatlantic market place. In fact, EU–US economic relations account for
the world's largest bilateral economic relationship, generating around
$1 billion of trade and investment per day (European Commission, 2002a).

Transatlantic economic relations are typically thought of in terms of
trade flows. Such an emphasis is understandable considering how vital
international trade is to economic growth in both the USA and the EU. In
the USA, exports accounted for over one-quarter of economic growth
during the 1990s. For the EU, exports accounted for an estimated 45 per
cent of economic growth over the last decade (Zoellick, 2001a, p. 4). Such
dependence on trade underlies the priority placed by the EU and the USA
on liberalizing international trade. Both parties are very active international traders, responsible for 40 per cent of world trade (European
Commission, 2002a). Bilaterally, the EU and the USA are each other's
largest single trading partners, accounting for approximately one-fifth of
each other's total trade in goods and one-third of total trade in services
(Burghardt, 2001, p. 21). Tables 5.1 and 5.2 show the increasing volume of
EU–US trade in goods and services.

Trade relations, however, account for only one – albeit a very important
one – dimension of transatlantic economic relations. Foreign direct investment, which has been called 'the neglected twin of trade', has become
increasingly important in transatlantic economic relations (Julius, 1991). In
addition to becoming more interdependent in trade relations, the EU and
the USA are major sources of and destinations for each other's FDI.
Reflecting a general trend in the global economy, transatlantic FDI activity has increased considerably over the last two decades. Table 5.3 demonstrates the flows of transatlantic FDI from 1995 to 1999.

It is worth noting that the growth of European FDI in the USA has not
been accompanied by institutional changes within the political structure of
the EU. While the EU has become the key player in European trade policy,

Table 5.1   Bilateral EU–US trade in goods (billion ECU/Euro)

	1995	1996	1997	1998	1999	2000
EU exports to the USA						
Value	103	114	141	161	183	232
Change year on year (%)	−0.4	10.7	23.5	14	13.6	26.5
EU imports from the USA						
Value	104	113	138	152	161	196
Change year on year (%)	3.6	8.9	21.6	10.3	5.6	22.1

Source: Eurostat, reproduced from European Commission (2002a).

Table 5.2   Bilateral EU–US trade in services (billion ECU/Euro)

	1995	1996	1997	1998	1999
EU exports to the USA					
Value	60	64	78	77	85
Change year on year (%)	−6.9	7.2	17.9	−1.3	9.4
EU Imports from the USA					
Value	58	63	73	77	91
Change year from year (%)	−2.5	8.4	13.6	5.2	15.3

Source: Eurostat, reproduced from European Commission (2002a).

Table 5.3   Flows of transatlantic foreign direct investment (billion ECU/Euro)

	1995	1996	1997	1998	1999	Average 1994–9
USA FDI into the EU						
Value	24	20	21	61	75	40
As % of FDI into the EU	65	63	54	57	65	61
EU FDI into the USA						
Value	25	17	48	133	197	84
As % of EU FDI abroad	54	36	44	60	66	52

Source: Eurostat, reproduced from European Commission (2002a).

competency over investment remains largely in the hands of national governments (Atlantic Council, 2001, p. 13). Thus FDI plays a much greater role in the private sphere of EU–US relations than in the public sphere, where trade policy remains dominant.

Similar to the volume of transatlantic trade flows, EU–US FDI accounts for the largest flow of global foreign direct investment. To place EU and US FDI in the context of the global economy, Tables 5.4 and 5.5 provide comparisons of the FDI flows and stock values for the US, the EU and the world as a whole.

Table 5.4   FDI flows ($billions)

	1985–95 annual average	1997	1998	1999	2000
US inward	44.4	103.4	174.4	295.0	281.1
US outward	41.0	95.8	131.0	142.6	139.3
EU inward	64.5	127.6	261.1	467.2	617.3
EU outward	93.4	220.4	454.3	720.1	772.9
Rest of world inward	180.3	477.9	692.5	1075.0	1270.8
Rest of world outward	199.5	466.0	711.9	1005.8	1149.9

Source: UNCTAD (2001).

Table 5.5 FDI stocks as a percentage of GDP

	1985	1990	1995	1999
US inward	4.6	7.1	7.6	11.1
US outward	6.2	7.8	9.9	13.0
EU inward	8.3	11.0	13.4	22.2
EU outward	10.3	11.7	15.5	29.6
Rest of world inward	7.8	9.2	10.3	17.3
Rest of world outward	6.4	8.6	10.2	16.7

Source: UNCTAD (2001).

The Public Sphere: Bilateral and Multilateral Dimensions of Transatlantic Economic Relations

While traditional tariff and non-tariff barriers to trade have not been eliminated, regulatory differences are increasingly becoming behind-the-border obstacles to transatlantic commerce. This transition is apparent in the bilateral and multilateral dimensions of the transatlantic market place. Bilaterally, the EU and the USA have institutionalized their economic relations via three formal agreements signed during the 1990s: the Transatlantic Declaration, the New Transatlantic Agenda and the Transatlantic Economic Partnership. Multilaterally, the EU and the USA have committed themselves to co-managing economic disputes within the WTO system. This commitment to the multilateral system was most recently witnessed in the EU–US cooperation that preceded the successful launch of the Doha Round of trade talks.

Bilateral institutionalization

The current state of transatlantic relations can be traced through a series of formal bilateral agreements signed during the 1990s. Through these agreements, EU–US relations have moved from consultation to joint action and early warning. Most importantly for the current chapter, these agreements have recognized the EU (rather than its individual member states) as a single interlocutor for the USA, increasingly focused on the economic dimension of transatlantic relations, and committed both the EU and the USA to working within the WTO system.

The landmark Transatlantic Declaration (TAD) was signed in November 1990. The TAD reflected the desire of Europe and the USA to renew and redefine their commitment to the transatlantic relationship in the wake of the Cold War.[4] The TAD is significant as the first example of the USA formally engaging the EU instead of relying on bilateral agreements and relations with the individual member states of the Union.[5] As such, the TAD indicates Washington's perception of the EU as an emergent and important international economic actor. This perception was enhanced by the development of the EU's competence in foreign economic policy and the pending completion of the Single European Market through the 1992 program.[6] With the goal of increasing EU–US cooperation through consultation, the TAD was the first step in a process of institutionalizing transatlantic economic relations.

The TAD specified three major objectives: economic cooperation; education, scientific and cultural cooperation; and responding to transnational challenges (for example, combating terrorism, drug-trafficking, money laundering, international crime, weapons proliferation and missile technology). On economic cooperation, the TAD highlighted the need to strengthen the multilateral trading system. This strengthening would require further steps towards liberalization, transparency, and the implementation of principles promoted in the General Agreement on Tariffs and Trade (GATT) and the Organization for Economic Cooperation and Development (OECD). Such steps were to address trade in goods and services and investment. Reflecting changes in the international trading system, the TAD also promised a dialogue on 'technical and non-tariff barriers to industrial and agricultural trade, services, competition policy, transportation policy, standards, telecommunications, high technology and other relevant areas'.

The TAD regularized transatlantic contacts by establishing biannual summit meetings. These high-level summits were supplemented by regular meetings among European ministers, the European Commission and the US secretary of state; ad hoc presidency 'Troika' meetings with the US secretary of state; and biannual consultations between the Commission and the US government at the cabinet level. Although the TAD did not provide a comprehensive operational plan, the consultation scheme established a framework for increasing cooperation and solidifying the bilateral relationship.

The next major EU–US agreement, the New Transatlantic Agenda (NTA) of 1995, moved the transatlantic relationship from simple consultation to joint action.[7] The NTA was seen as necessary to alleviate perceptions of transatlantic drift and to realize the goals stated in the TAD.[8] The NTA comprises four chapters outlining objectives for transatlantic relations. The first chapter addressed the promotion of peace and stability, democracy and development around the world. The second chapter focused on global challenges, such as environmental and public health protection and law enforcement issues.

The third chapter called for the expansion of world trade and closer economic relations. Specifically, the chapter declared, 'We have a special responsibility to strengthen the multilateral trading system, to support the World Trade Organisation and to lead the way in opening markets to trade and investment.' This economic chapter also called for strengthening regulatory cooperation, creating a New Transatlantic Marketplace by 'progressively reducing or eliminating barriers that hinder the flow of goods, services and capital,' concluding a customs cooperation and mutual assistance agreement, creating a Transatlantic Information Society, and establishing a joint working group on employment and labor-related issues.

The fourth chapter of the NTA encouraged 'building bridges across the Atlantic'. These bridges would provide new mechanisms for transatlantic governance of the bilateral relationship and management of the global economy. In particular, the chapter notes the need for input from civil society through various dialogues, such as the Transatlantic Labour Dialogue, the Transatlantic Consumer Dialogue, the Transatlantic Environmental Dialogue and the Transatlantic Legislators' Dialogue.[9] These dialogues represent new and variably successful 'private–public sphere interfaces' through which different segments of civil society generate recommendations and influence the agenda of transatlantic economic relations.

As a private–public sphere interface, the Transatlantic Business Dialogue (TABD) is particularly notable for shaping the transatlantic economic relationship through its policy recommendations (Green Cowles, 2001a, 2001b). For example, the TABD, which launched its inaugural conference in Seville, Spain in 1995, has consistently produced recommendations urging EU–US regulatory cooperation and has been instrumental in calling for and expanding the Mutual Recognition Agreement.[10] In addition, the TABD lent its explicit support to the EU–US commitment to the WTO system when it called for 'full support for the rules and principles of the World Trade Organisation (WTO) and other relevant institutions' in its overall conclusions at the Seville Conference.

The NTA also expanded the regular consultations that had been instituted under the TAD. For example the NTA gave the Senior Level Group the task of reviewing progress and submitting reports to and setting the agenda for the biannual summit meetings that originated under the TAD. The implementation of the agreement was mandated to an NTA task force made up of representatives from the EU's presidency and directorates-general and the US Department of State. In addition, provisions were made for a variety of standing consultative and working groups to address specific issues. The so-called 'NTA' process that followed generated a number of transatlantic economic accomplishments. Table 5.6 lists some of the policy outputs, or 'deliverables,' attributed to this closer cooperation.[11]

The final major EU–US agreement focused primarily on transatlantic economic relations. Agreed at the London Summit in May 1998, the Transatlantic Economic Partnership (TEP) divides its agenda into bilateral

Table 5.6 Deliverables emerging from the NTA process

Agreement	Date	Substance
Agreement on customs cooperation and mutual assistance in customs matters	May 1997	Outlines cooperation between EU and US customs authorities
Science and technology agreement	December 1997	Encourages cooperation between EU scientific institutions and US government research agencies
EU–US agreement on the application of positive comity principles	June 1998	Clarifies implementation of positive comity in competition policy cooperation
Mutual recognition agreement	December 1998	Covers standards for goods, including telecom equipment, pharmaceuticals, medical devices, electromagnetic compatibility, electric safety and recreational craft
EU–US veterinary equivalence agreement	July 1999	Facilitates trade in live animals and animal products

and multilateral relations.[12] Bilaterally, the TEP covers non-tariff barriers to trade in goods and services, intellectual property rights, mutual recognition, agriculture and government procurement, among others. Multilaterally, the TEP encourages the pursuit of further trade liberalization and reaffirms the transatlantic commitment to the WTO.[13] Table 5.7 lists the shared bilateral and multilateral priorities identified in the TEP.

Table 5.7   Bilateral and multilateral priorities of TEP

Bilateral	Multilateral
Technical (regulatory) barriers to trade in goods	Implementation of WTO commitments and respect for dispute settlement obligations
Trade in services	Liberalization of services in WTO negotiations
Agriculture (scientific cooperation and regulatory cooperation in human, plant and animal health issues, including biotechnology)	Multilateral negotiations in agriculture
	WTO forward-looking work on trade facilitation
	Reduction of industrial tariffs
Government procurement	Intellectual property rights
Intellectual property rights	Common approaches on investment, competition, public procurement and trade and environment
	Accession of new members and better integration of least developed countries in multilateral trading system
	Electronic commerce in WTO and keeping electronic transmissions duty-free
	Internationally recognized core labor standards, agreement on ILO declaration, and rejection of labor standards as protectionist measures
	Combat corruption

Finally, the TEP expands the mechanisms for transatlantic economic governance. To enhance economic policy making, the TEP calls for an extension of the various transatlantic dialogues launched as part of the NTA process. The TEP also adds to the institutional structure of transatlantic economic relations by establishing the official level TEP steering group within the institutional structure of the NTA. This group informs the senior level group and ministers of progress on implementing the TEP. Assisted by ad hoc and specialized working groups, the Steering Group (a) monitors and reports on the realization of TEP objectives; (b) monitors implementation of agreements reached under the TEP; (c) identifies and reviews cooperative objectives on a continuing basis; (d) provides a forum for recommendations by business, environment, consumer and labor dialogues; and (e) provides a forum for bilateral consultation and early warning with a view to preventing conflicts and resolving trade disputes.

This final provision for an early warning system is particularly significant in the construction of the new framework of transatlantic economic governance. The early warning system 'is designed to give officials on both sides a "heads-up" (alert) when potentially sensitive legislation is being considered that might have negative impacts on bilateral trade' (Burghardt, 2001, p. 23). This new mechanism of dispute prevention reflects a forward-looking TEP process that has moved the EU–US economic relationship from consultation to joint action and early warning.

The end of the Cold War challenged the EU and the USA to redefine the transatlantic relationship. Notably, the USA signed the TAD with the EU instead of pursuing bilateral agreements with the Union's individual member states. The TAD and subsequent agreements established a variety of mechanisms for transatlantic governance of economic relations. In particular, the institutionalization of regular consultation, joint action and early warning reflects the importance that each party attaches to the relationship. While strengthening the bilateral relationship, the EU and the USA also made an explicit commitment to the WTO and to cooperating in shaping and managing the multilateral trading system.

Co-management in the multilateral system

As reflected in their bilateral agreements of the 1990s, the EU and the USA put a premium on cooperating when it comes to shaping the multilateral trading system. In fact that system relies very heavily on cooperation between the 'two biggest elephants' in the global economy (Lamy and Zoellick, 2001).[14] Today's multilateral trading system has been created through a series of trade talks, or 'rounds', that have produced a number of treaties on international trade liberalization. This process began with the General Agreement on Tariffs and Trade (GATT) in 1947. In 1994, the international trading system changed considerably with the agreement to create the WTO. The traditional process of trade liberalization continues to occur through successive rounds of talks designed to negotiate treaties.[15] Although it is not sufficient for the USA and the EU to agree on key issues before a new round of trade talks can be officially opened, it is certainly necessary.

Most recently, EU–US cooperation was crucial to the successful launch of a new round of trade talks at the WTO's Fourth Ministerial Conference in Doha, Qatar, in November 2001. In addition to addressing the inevitable EU–US disagreements over current bilateral disputes and the inclusion of certain agenda items, the new round, to be successfully launched, had to address the demands of developing countries and grass-roots opposition to further trade liberalization. A growing number of influential developing countries were expressing concerns that they were not benefiting from the agreements struck at previous trade rounds.[16] While the vocal grass-roots opposition – which included a broad array of labor, environmental and other groups – did not speak with one voice, it had been a factor in the earlier failure to open a new round of trade talks at the WTO's Third Ministerial Conference (1999) in Seattle, Washington. Given these obstacles, it is instructive that an agreement to initiate the Doha Round was reached at all.[17]

The agenda that emerged from Doha provides general insights into the future direction of the international trading system. Table 5.8 summarizes the range of subjects currently under negotiation in the Doha Round and highlights the increasing attention being paid to non-traditional trade issues. The WTO's Fifth Ministerial Conference, scheduled for 2003 in Mexico, will assess the continuing negotiations and prepare for the round's planned conclusion in 2005.

Table 5.8   Doha Round work program

Implementation-related issues	Subsidies
Agriculture	Regional agreements
Services	Dispute settlement understanding
Market access for non-agricultural products	Trade and environment
	Electronic commerce
Intellectual property rights	Small economies
Trade and investment	Trade, debt and finance
Trade and competition	Trade and technology transfer
Government procurement	Technical cooperation and capacity building
Trade facilitation	Least developed countries
Anti-dumping	Special and differentiated treatment

Source: WTO web page (*www.wto.org*), 2002.

The compromises made by the EU and the USA reflect the shared interests and urgency they (and other WTO members) displayed regarding continued trade liberalization and launching the new round. Failure to agree to a new Doha Round would have been viewed by many as a vote of no confidence in further trade liberalization. Such a perception would have threatened the prospects for growth in a global economy that was already showing signs of recession (Zoellick, 2001b, p. 5).[18] Worse yet, according to US Trade Representative (USTR) Robert B. Zoellick, failure in Doha could have threatened the momentum of trade liberalization: 'The bicycle theory of trade is again in force: If the trade liberalization process does not move forward, it will, like a bicycle, be pulled down by the political gravity of special interests' (ibid., p. 4). Again the political influence of domestic interests is cited for the potentially important role they can play in limiting liberalization or even increasing protectionism.

This new round was also viewed as an endorsement of the WTO's rule-based system of trade agreements and recourse to its multilateral dispute settlement mechanism. The EU and the USA's commitment to managing transatlantic disputes within the WTO regime became particularly evident in the run-up to the Doha Round when EU Trade Commissioner Pascal Lamy and USTR Zoellick (Lamy and Zoellick, 2001) asserted, 'we will continue to manage our differences through reason, negotiation, respect for each other's political constraints, and particularly by compliance with WTO rules'. Because of this transatlantic commitment to a multilateral, rule-based system of dispute resolution, EU–US economic relations can no longer be understood in simple bilateral terms. Rather, an understanding of the WTO system and the domestic politics at work in individual cases of cooperation and conflict is required. The next section lays out an analytic framework for understanding the interaction of the WTO system and domestic politics.

THE DOMESTIC POLITICS OF TRANSATLANTIC ECONOMIC DISPUTE MANAGEMENT

This section introduces an analytical approach to understanding transatlantic economic relations. The framework incorporates two different but related factors to help explain variance in the levels of economic cooperation and conflict: (a) the interaction of the WTO system and domestic politics and, (b) the different pressures created by trade and regulatory issues. While economic disputes are inevitable in a relationship as intensive and extensive as the transatlantic relationship, the EU and the USA still share the same basic interest in an open, rule-based, international trading system. From this follows an important commitment to managing economic disputes through the WTO's multilateral trade rules and dispute settlement mechanism. However, owing to domestic politics, the extent and durability of this commitment to the multilateral system varies between traditional disputes over tariff and non-tariff barriers to trade and disputes arising from regulatory differences. While this analytical approach focuses on the WTO, it should not be taken to imply that other multilateral fora are insignificant. Rather, the WTO is seen as the most important forum for *dispute resolution*, while other international organizations (for example, the

Organization for Economic Cooperation and Development, and the International Standards Organization) largely aim at *dispute prevention* through multilateral recommendations, codes and standards that encourage mutual recognition and/or harmonization.

In bilateral trade relations, the likelihood and uncertainty of destabilizing trade wars has been reduced considerably because of the EU and US decision and commitment to manage their trade disputes within the WTO's dispute settlement mechanism – a legalistic and rule-based procedure for resolving disagreements among member states.[19] The WTO has established specific but flexible deadlines for this mechanism. Once a case is brought before the WTO, the proceedings typically take one year or longer. During the proceedings, parties to a dispute can, and are encouraged to, negotiate a resolution at any time. At the conclusion of these proceedings, one party is typically authorized to retaliate against trade barriers by suspending previously agreed tariff concessions. If a party appeals a final WTO ruling, the dispute settlement proceedings are extended for another three months.[20] Owing to different domestic costs, this time lag appears to play a larger role in cases of traditional trade disputes than in cases that derive from 'behind-the-border' regulatory differences.[21]

Within this multilateral framework, the cost of WTO-authorized retaliation frequently outweighs the political benefit of indefinitely maintaining offending trade measures. This is so because WTO-authorized retaliation allows the offended party to suspend concessions on products across various sectors that are unrelated to the original case. The particular products are typically selected for retaliation because of their political salience. Thus the decision to change an offending trade measure becomes a domestic battle between exporters and interests in multiple sectors versus those exporters and interests in the single sector that benefit from the offending measure.[22]

The strategic use of the WTO time lag allows the EU and the USA (and other members) to delay the costs of WTO-authorized retaliation. The time lag provides a cushion of at least one year in which a government can accrue the domestic political gains often associated with protectionist trade measures. As the conclusion of the WTO proceedings draws closer, the EU and the USA can negotiate a settlement before the offender suffers the domestic costs of WTO-authorized retaliation. Thus what previously could have escalated into a destabilizing trade war and significantly increased uncertainty for industries and policy makers is now managed through a mutually agreed set of rules. These rules provide the basis for strategic trade dispute management. In particular they create a time lag in which an offending party can accrue domestic political gains before deciding to change the offending trade measure to avoid WTO-authorized retaliation.

Alternatively, the likelihood of resolving EU–US disputes over regulatory issues appears to be much lower. Indeed, regulatory disputes have already become a serious source of transatlantic trade tensions (Vogel, 1997). As the transatlantic trade agenda treats regulatory differences as technical barriers to trade, the disputes that emerge are likely to be less tractable because different regulatory approaches often reflect different domestic regulatory regimes and consumer preferences.[23] As a result of these ingrained institutional and social differences and general public support for their maintenance, the costs of changing offending regulatory measures frequently outweigh the costs of WTO-authorized retaliation.

In disputes over regulatory differences, the WTO's time lag plays a less significant role in the process of dispute resolution. While the WTO system does offer a multilateral option for resolving regulatory disputes related to trade, the EU and the USA are often unwilling or unable, because of high domestic costs, to negotiate changes to their offending regulations. This reluctance to negotiate changes exists despite the costs associated with WTO-authorized retaliation. Again the excessive costs of changing domestic regulations reflect the comparative political sensitivity of adjusting regulatory approaches based on long-held and deeply ingrained beliefs about the best practices for guaranteeing and managing risks to public health and safety.

To illustrate this analytical distinction, the last section investigates four cases of transatlantic economic conflict: traditional trade disputes over bananas and steel and regulatory disputes over hormone-treated beef and foreign sales corporations. Table 5.9 summarizes the simple domestic costs of changing or not changing the offending trade or regulatory measure in each case. The costs are calculated by comparing domestic gains and losses. When the domestic gains of an offending measure outweigh the domestic losses of WTO-authorized retaliation, the cost of changing the measure (C_1) is greater than the cost of not changing the measure (C_2). Likewise, when the domestic losses of WTO-authorized retaliation outweigh the domestic gains of an offending measure, the cost of changing the measure (C_1) is less than the cost of not changing the measure (C_2).

Table 5.9 Domestic costs of changing trade and regulatory measures

Case	Cost calculation
Bananas (tariff and non-tariff barriers)	$C_1 < C_2$
Hormone-treated beef (public health regulation)	$C_1 > C_2$
Steel tariffs (tariff barrier)	$C_1 < C_2$
Foreign sales corporations (economic regulation)	$C_1 > C_2$

In traditional trade disputes (those arising from tariff and non-tariff barriers), the costs of changing an offending measure (C_1) are frequently less than the costs of not changing the measure (C_2). This is increasingly the case as the EU and the USA use the WTO's time lag as a strategic delaying tactic to reduce further the costs of changing a measure. However in disputes arising from regulatory differences, the costs of changing a measure (C_1) generally exceed the costs of not changing a measure (C_2). In these cases, the WTO time lag does not reduce the costs of changing the measure and dispute resolution is more elusive.

TRANSATLANTIC TRADE AND REGULATORY DISPUTES

The intent of this section is not to provide a comprehensive, descriptive overview of all transatlantic economic disputes. Rather, this section investigates four recent and current disputes: the EU banana regime and hormone-treated beef and the US steel tariffs and foreign sales corporations. For the purposes of the current study, the banana and steel cases are employed as examples of traditional trade disputes over tariff and non-tariff barriers, while the hormone-treated beef and foreign sales corporation cases reveal the particularly intractable nature of regulatory disputes. The cases are selected to illustrate how and why significant transatlantic trade and regulatory disputes emerge and can be resolved.

While this section focuses on economic disputes between the EU and the USA, it is worth pointing out that significant levels of cooperation do occur in transatlantic economic relations. Indeed, as EU Ambassador to the US Guenter Burghardt argues, 'over 98% of trade between the EU and the U.S. is completely dispute-free, with a little over 1% of transatlantic trade volumes subject to formal disputes' (Burghardt, 2001, p. 22). One such area of successful transatlantic cooperation is competition policy, where, notwithstanding the much-publicized disagreement in 2001 over the GE/Honeywell merger, cooperation continues to be the norm.[24]

In addition, the EU and the USA are devising ways to prevent regulatory differences from becoming disputes, such as through the Mutual Recognition Agreement process (see above). To reduce further the likelihood of regulatory disputes, the EU and the USA also signed Guidelines on Regulatory Cooperation and Transparency in April 2002, as part of the TEP process. These guidelines are non-binding, but designed to 'promote a more systematic dialogue' between EU and US regulators, especially during the early development of regulatory approaches. The guidelines also stress 'transparency and public participation as necessary elements to promote more effective regulatory cooperation, better quality regulation, and to help minimize possible regulatory-based trade disputes' (European Commission, 2002b). Finally, to enhance international regulatory cooperation, the EU and the USA also remain active in developing preventive recommendations, codes and standards through various multilateral fora, including the WTO and OECD, among others (Vogel, 1997; Green Cowles, 1997).

EU Banana Regime

The EU's banana case created a major transatlantic trade dispute in which two banana regimes were challenged successfully in the WTO. The dispute was finally resolved in 2001, after years of negotiation within the dispute settlement process that included US imposition of WTO-authorized retaliatory sanctions. Because the parties worked within the dispute settlement system, this long-running dispute ultimately provided the WTO with much-needed international credibility. The case is particularly useful in the current study as an example of the domestic costs of changing offending traditional trade measures.

Under the EU's Lomé Convention, individual countries within the Union imported bananas under an assortment of national practices.[25] For example Germany, with the world's highest per capita consumption of bananas, favored tariff-free banana imports; Spain relied on domestic bananas from the Canary Islands; France preferred banana imports from its Overseas Departments and former colonies; and other countries supported tariffs at a value of 20 per cent (Hanrahan, 1999, p. 2). While the transatlantic banana case is characterized as a traditional trade dispute,[26] the ingrained preferences of different European countries reflect the cultural and historical differences that frequently accompany regulatory disputes. For example, inexpensive, tropical bananas took on a symbolic value in Germany as a sign of prosperity, while other member states desired bananas specifically from their ex-colonies (Stevens, 1996, p. 332).

The varying national import practices for bananas were soon challenged by the requirements of European integration. As part of the 1992 Programme, the EU passed a banana regulation in 1993 that created a Union-wide banana regime and erected tariff and non-tariff barriers to trade. The new regime established a complex, multi-layered quota system. Preferential access was granted to bananas imported from Lomé countries, while banana imports from other countries were subject to variable tariff rates. The banana regime also included a licensing system through which quotas were allocated to banana distributors. Germany and Denmark initially opposed the specifics of the quota system because their consumers preferred less expensive bananas from Latin America. Thus, while this case originated from a domestic regulation, the trade dispute arose from the tariff and non-tariff components of the new banana regime.

The USA does not export bananas, but this new banana regime created problems for US firms growing bananas in Latin America. In particular, Chiquita faced significant losses in market share because its banana-producing facilities were located in Central and Latin American countries that were not accorded ACP preferential access by the EU.[27] In response, Chiquita launched an active campaign in the US Congress to challenge the EU banana regime (Peterson, 2001, p. 175). In particular, Chiquita enlisted the Senate majority leader Bob Dole (R-Kansas) to pressure the USTR to investigate the case (Gardner, 1997, p. 40).[28] In 1994, Chiquita filed a Section 301 petition.[29] The USTR threatened action under Section 301, but withdrew its unilateral threat in 1995 in lieu of pursuing the establishment of a WTO dispute panel in 1996.[30] The decision to pursue the banana dispute within the multilateral framework offered an opportunity for the WTO to increase significantly its international credibility.[31] For example, US agricultural interests and skeptical members of Congress saw the banana dispute as a proving ground for the WTO dispute settlement mechanism (Hanrahan, 1999, p. 5).

For its part the EU argued that a waiver granted under the Uruguay Round Agreement (1994) protected its banana regime. Nevertheless, in 1997, the WTO ruled that certain provisions of the banana regime (in particular, the non-tariff barrier created by the licensing agreements) were inconsistent with the EU's multilateral trade obligations. While the EU appealed the ruling, a subsequent Appellate Panel upheld the decision. Following an EU request for arbitration, the WTO gave the Union until 1 January 1999 to bring its banana regime into conformity with its multilateral obligations. Following domestic negotiations, the EU changed its licensing agreements within the allotted time frame and claimed WTO-compatibility for its revised banana regime. These internal Union negotiations again reflected the long-held and ingrained consumer preferences found in the EU member states mentioned above.

The USTR remained dissatisfied with the EU's changes and made public its intention to retaliate by raising import duties on a variety of exports from the Union. In particular, the retaliation would be aimed at notable products from influential EU member states – including Louis Vuitton plastic handbags from France, pecorino cheese from Italy and cashmere sweaters from the UK (Winestock and King, 2002, p. A2) – in an effort to encourage domestic European opposition to the banana regime. In April 1999, the USA imposed WTO-authorized retaliatory trade sanctions at a value of $191.4 million of EU exports. The value of these sanctions was the equivalent amount of damages that the EU's banana regime had caused to

US banana interests. This retaliation prompted the EU to open further bilateral negotiations with the USA on acceptable revisions to the banana regulation.

As a result of these negotiations, the EU and the USA announced an understanding to resolve the dispute in April 2001. The resolution included phased implementation steps to increase market access for US banana distributors. By July 2001, the EU had adopted a new licensing system and agreed to finalize a tariff-only regime for bananas to replace its offending multilayered quota system by 2006.[32] The USA suspended its retaliatory sanctions. However, the USTR will monitor EU compliance with the agreement; failure to comply may result in the USTR taking action under Section 301.

The banana case was one of the WTO's first real tests. The case also demonstrates how lengthy and complex the multilateral dispute settlement process can become.[33] Because the banana case included both tariff and non-tariff barriers, resolution of the dispute was more complicated than in those cases arising exclusively from tariff barriers to trade. Although the case is categorized for the purposes of the current study as a traditional trade dispute (due to the quota and tariff systems), it also combined elements of a regulatory case. Indeed, the high costs of changing a domestic EU regulation complicated and lengthened the resolution of this dispute beyond what would be expected in traditional trade disputes. The high costs of changing the offending trade measures in the EU banana regulation reflected the ingrained consumer preferences for bananas in some member states. However, throughout the almost decade-long case, the EU and the USA made the conscious decision to manage the trade dispute within the WTO system and conformed to the established rules for negotiating a settlement.

EU Hormone-treated Beef

The hormone-treated beef case reveals the domestic sources of intractable transatlantic regulatory disputes. The costs of WTO-authorized sanctions have not provided the incentive for the EU to adjust its offending domestic regulations. The EU position reflects the extremely high costs associated with changing domestic regulations that follow from an approach to risk management known as the 'precautionary principle.' This dispute foreshadows future transatlantic disputes over the domestic regulation of genetically modified organisms and the risks of biotechnology to public health and safety.

In the USA, various hormones are used to increase the rate of cattle growth and produce a leaner carcass. The US Food and Drug Administration

(FDA) and US Department of Agriculture (USDA) maintain that these hormones do not present a significant physiological risk to humans. However, the European Commission disagreed and, in 1985, enacted a ban on the production and importation of meat derived from animals treated with growth-promoting hormones. This ban was, at least in part, motivated by widespread press reports during the 1980s of sales of 'hormone cocktails' on the black market and reports of serious adverse health effects from consuming hormone-treated meat (Hanrahan, 2000, p. 1; Vogel, 1997, pp. 15–17).[34]

The USA challenged the EU's ban in the Committee on Technical Barriers to Trade under the Standards Code of the GATT. Despite the US challenge, the ban came into effect in January 1989. The Commission justified the ban as a measure to protect consumer health and safety from the illegal and unregulated use of hormones in livestock in some EU member states. The USA threatened retaliation by releasing a list of unrelated EU exports (for example, tomatoes, citrus fruit, pasta and hams) that would be saddled with $100 million worth of tariffs. Not wanting the transatlantic dispute to disrupt current and sensitive Uruguay Round negotiations, the EU and the USA established a bilateral task force to negotiate a solution to the issue within 75 days (Hanrahan, 2000, p. 2).

In May 1989, the bilateral task force reached an 'interim agreement' establishing a system to certify US producers who would be listed as hormone-free and, thus, permitted to export meat to the EU. The USDA's Food Safety and Inspection Service was enlisted to ensure that beef exports met the certification requirements of the system (ibid.). In the meantime both sides hoped that the Uruguay Round negotiations and the conclusion of an Agreement on the Application of Sanitary and Phytosanitary (SPS) Measures would provide a lasting solution to the dispute.

During the early 1990s, domestic events within the member states strengthened European opposition to hormone-treated beef, so that the domestic costs of changing the offending regulations increased significantly. For example, outbreaks of bovine spongiform encephalopathy (BSE) in British cattle herds increased health-related fears about US beef among EU consumers (Egan, 2001, p. 192). While BSE has no direct link to beef hormones, European beef producers are hesitant to do anything, such as using hormones, which would further discourage consumers from buying meat products (Hanrahan, 2000, p. 2).

In 1994, the SPS agreement was signed as part of the Uruguay Round of trade negotiations. While ensuring that domestic health and safety standards can be used to protect consumers (Pollack and Shaffer, 2001b), the agreement is not intended to promote the use of food safety and animal and plant health regulations as trade protectionism. In order to eliminate the use of standards as protectionism, the SPS agreement encourages members to base their sanitary and phytosanitary measures on existing international standards, guidelines and recommendations.[35] Members are allowed to maintain or introduce stricter standards based on 'scientific evidence' or appropriate risk assessments, as outlined in Article 5 of the agreement.

In April 1996, the US filed a WTO challenge to the EU ban on hormone-treated beef. At the same time, the European Parliament voted unanimously to maintain the ban, citing 'consumer worries, questions of animal welfare, meat quality, and the effects of hormones on the EU beef and milk sectors' (Hanrahan, 2000, p. 2). In addition, the EU agriculture ministers voted (by a margin of 14 to 1[36]) to maintain the hormone ban. This unified front was based on the EU's preference to regulate risks to public health and safety according to the 'precautionary principle'. The precautionary principle reflects the EU's lower level of acceptable risk in public health and safety and is expressed, under certain circumstances, in the SPS agreement:

> In cases where relevant scientific evidence is insufficient, a Member may provisionally adopt sanitary or phytosanitary measures on the basis of available pertinent information . . . In such circumstances, Members shall seek to obtain the additional information necessary for a more objective assessment of risk and review the sanitary or phytosanitary measure accordingly within a reasonable period of time. (Article 5.7)

Despite the SPS agreement and the EU's preference for the precautionary principle, the WTO ruled against the Union's hormone ban in August 1997. The WTO found that the EU ban was not based on appropriate risk assessments and that it arbitrarily discriminated against products based on different levels of hormones, such as those originating from the USA. This product discrimination was ruled to be lacking in scientific justification. In response, the EU appealed the WTO ruling. However, in 1998, the appeal failed as the WTO decided that the precautionary principle could not override the need for risk assessments outlined in the SPS agreement.[37]

Despite the WTO ruling, the European Commission voted unanimously to continue its beef hormone ban on 11 May 1999. As a result, the WTO authorized the USA, in July 1999, to suspend tariff concessions to the EU at the level of $116.8 million per year (USTR, 2002, p. 113). Further complicating the situation, on 24 May 2000, the Commission announced that it would ban indefinitely one disputed hormone and others provisionally, in accordance with Article 5.7 of the SPS agreement, while risk assessments were undertaken.

While the EU continues to try to convince the USA to lift or phase out its retaliatory sanctions, the USA has rejected the offers for compensation and adjustment of the ban. At the time of this writing the EU remains constrained by the domestic costs of changing the beef hormone regulation.

These costs are exceptionally high because of strong public opposition in many member states to lifting the ban and general support for a regulatory approach based on the precautionary principle. To address these costs, the EU continues to conduct risk assessments and evaluate scientific evidence. However the USTR remains unconvinced by the EU's efforts, arguing, 'Although the EU recently published a number of new studies that analyzed the use of hormones in beef production, none of these studies presented any new evidence to support the EU's hormone ban' (2002, p. 113).

The beef case foreshadows the intractable nature of current and future transatlantic disputes over genetically modified organisms (GMOs) and biotechnology.[38] The EU's reluctance to approve the release and marketing of new GMOs has imposed a de facto moratorium on new product approvals since 1998 (Pollack and Shaffer, 2001b, p. 154). For its part the USTR argues that 'Biotechnology continues to be more of a political than a scientific issue in Europe and prospects for improvement remain dim' (USTR, 2002, p. 111). As with the beef hormone ban, the USA has hinted that it may take these non-approvals and biotechnology regulations to the WTO's dispute settlement mechanism (US Mission, 2002h, pp. 5–6).

Disputes over GMOs and biotechnology may escalate into significant transatlantic conflicts owing to inherent difficulties in changing regulatory systems and traditions, especially the EU's preference for regulation based on the precautionary principle. Like the continuing dispute over hormone-treated beef, such regulatory disagreements are particularly intractable because of the higher costs of changing domestic regulations compared to the costs of changing offending measures in traditional trade disputes.

US Steel Tariffs Dispute

The current transatlantic dispute over US steel tariffs is classified as a traditional trade dispute. The US decision to erect tariffs reflects the ability of domestic politics to steer a, generally, pro-free trade government to erect protectionist trade barriers. At the same time the dispute illustrates the domestic gains that can follow from the time lag provided by the WTO dispute settlement mechanism. As a result, the pro-free trade Bush administration is able to accrue domestic gains from temporary protectionist measures while negotiating a settlement before suffering WTO-authorized retaliatory sanctions.

Feeling pressure from the restructuring US steel industry, accusations that foreign steel has benefited from years of government support, and global overcapacity,[39] the new Bush administration asked the US International Trade Commission (USITC) to investigate the impact of imports on the US steel industry.[40] The dispute escalated considerably on

10 December 2001, when the USITC recommended the imposition of tariffs on US steel imports.[41] On 5 March 2002, President Bush acted on the recommendation and imposed 20–30 per cent tariffs for three years on imported steel.[42] These safeguard measures, which are aimed at hot-rolled sheet, cold-rolled sheet and coated sheet steel, are notable for not applying to states currently in free trade agreements with the USA: Canada, Mexico, Israel and Jordan. In addition, the safeguard measures do not apply to most developing countries and emerging markets.[43]

As disagreements over the steel tariffs emerged within the pro-free trade Bush administration, it became clear that pressing domestic considerations were significant factors motivating the president's protectionist decision.[44] Most informative was the administration's declaration that the safeguard measures are 'temporary' and in conformity with WTO rules recognizing that because 'imports can cause such serious harm to domestic industries . . . temporary restraints are warranted' (US Mission, 2002a, p. 2). USTR Robert Zoellick adds, 'We'll also monitor and review how the industry uses this period of adjustment . . . And we can adjust the safeguards if conditions warrant.' He refers to this 'temporary' measure as 'breathing space' for the US domestic steel industry to restructure (US Mission, 2002b, p. 1).

The 'temporary' nature (three years) of these tariffs appears to be an important element of the US strategy: by the time the EU brings the case through the WTO's dispute settlement mechanism, the administration will be able to adjust the tariffs and negotiate a resolution.[45] Thus the USA intends to avoid WTO-authorized retaliation and provide temporary relief for the US steel industry to restructure.[46] At the same time, the administration has increased domestic support from the steel industry in important electoral states and support for trade-promotion authority[47] from key representatives and senators in those same states (King and Winestock, 2002, p.A3).[48] Finally, the tariffs also help Republican house members in crucial re-election bids in steel industry states.

The EU has been the most vocal opponent of the steel tariffs, claiming that the safeguard measures could result in annual losses of $2 billion in trade for European steel makers.[49] The EU and US legal arguments are based on different interpretations of the multilateral trade rules. The EU's threat of retaliation is based on multilateral trade rules allowing for compensation if safeguard measures are not initiated in response to an absolute increase in imports.[50] The European Commission argues that WTO jurisprudence 'requires a finding of an emergency situation caused by a recent, sharp and sudden rise in imports before safeguard action can be taken. These circumstances are clearly not present in this US case. For example, for the largest product category concerned, i.e. carbon and alloy flat products (55 to 60% of total) imports have continuously fallen since 1999 and particularly heavily in 2001' (European Commission, 2001, p. 1).[51] On the other side of the Atlantic, 'U.S. trade officials accused the Europeans of sleight of hand by focusing only on import figures after 1998, while the U.S. steel industry was most battered by imports during 1997 and 1998' (King and Winestock, 2002, p. A3). Thus, if a negotiated settlement cannot be agreed, a WTO panel ultimately will determine whose interpretation of the tariffs is consistent with the multilateral trading rules.

For its part the EU is shrewdly pursuing this case according to multilateral trade rules. In particular, the Union is trying to reduce the domestic gains that originally motivated the administration's decision. In drafting a list of retaliatory sanctions, the EU concentrated on products made in states that the Bush administration considers vital to its re-election bid and retaining Republican control of the House of Representatives in elections in November 2002: for example, Harley-Davidson motorcycles from Wisconsin, Tropicana orange juice from Florida, steel exports from Virginia and Pennsylvania, and textiles and apparel from North and South Carolina.[52] According to Pascal Lamy, these counter-measures, which will have to be authorized by the WTO in the absence of a negotiated settlement, are intended 'to leverage a change of decision . . . you have to do that in sectors and places where you can build a coalition' (Winestock and King, 2002, p.A2).[53] The assumption is that, by strategically threatening to reduce the domestic gains expected by the Bush administration, the EU can force the USA to change the offending measures.

Possibly the most significant and longer-term fallout of the US steel tariffs may be that the dispute could slow and complicate a variety of current negotiations on the Doha Round. Given the EU's announcement that future WTO-authorized sanctions will be levied against a variety of unrelated US exports, the domestic costs to the USA of not changing this offending measure are likely to outweigh the costs of continuing to protect the US steel industry in this way. However, these costs will not become manifest for the Bush administration until the EU's retaliatory sanctions are authorized through the WTO. Therefore, owing to the WTO's time lag, the Bush administration will be able to reap the short term domestic gains of this temporary trade measure before negotiating a final adjustment that will address the EU's concerns and conform to the multilateral trade rules. At the time of this writing the US strategy of review and adjustment is revealed by the fact that the administration has already revised the original measures by releasing three separate lists of steel products to be excluded from the tariffs.

US Foreign Sales Corporations

The current dispute over foreign sales corporations (FSCs) revolves around a program of US tax breaks to exporting corporations.[54] This case has the potential to escalate into a much larger transatlantic dispute. The FSC case has already generated two WTO decisions against the US legislation, including authorization of the largest retaliatory sanctions in the history of the multilateral dispute settlement mechanism. As an example of economic (tax) regulation, the case is particularly intractable owing to domestic politics in the USA.

The EU views the FSC tax breaks as unfair government support to large US firms. Partly in response to the USA's continued intransigence over the EU's banana regime and ban on hormone-treated beef, the EU decided to challenge the FSCs in the WTO (Winestock, 2002a, p.A18). The first challenge to the FSCs was a favorable finding for the EU that the tax arrangements violated US multilateral trade obligations. While the USA appealed the decision, in February 2000, the WTO Appellate Body upheld the initial panel ruling. In an attempt to remedy the offending measure, the US Congress enacted the FSC Repeal and Extraterritorial Income Exclusion Act (ETI Act) in November 2000. Still unsatisfied, the EU responded by challenging the ETI Act in the WTO.

In August 2001, a second WTO panel issued a report against the ETI Act. The USA reacted by again appealing the panel report to the WTO Appellate Body in October 2001. On 29 January 2002, the WTO Appellate Body ruled in favor of the EU, finding that the tax breaks in the ETI Act still constitute an export subsidy prohibited by the USA's WTO obligations. The EU was authorized to impose retaliatory trade sanctions against US imports equal to the level of injury EU business had incurred from FSCs.

According to EU Trade Commissioner Pascal Lamy, the EU has calculated its retaliatory sanctions at approximately $4 billion in compensation for the FSC export subsidies (King and Winestock, 2002, p. A8). This would be the largest sanctions bill in the history of the WTO (Denny, 2002). By contrast, the USTR has calculated the level of tariffs available to the EU at only $956 million annually (US Mission, 2002e, p. 1). Without a negotiated EU–US agreement on the exact value of the WTO-authorized retaliatory sanctions, the WTO is left to determine the level of retaliatory tariffs (US Mission, 2002f).

Sensing the potential domestic costs of these massive sanctions, the US Trade Representative Zoellick developed in early 2002 a plan that would require a congressional change to the US tax code. However, because of the domestic politics of US fiscal policy, such a change 'could take years to achieve', according to Senate Finance Committee Chairman Max Baucus

(D-Montana) (US Mission, 2002f). This potentially lengthy option would seriously test the EU's patience and increase the domestic US costs of not changing the offending measure if the EU did levy the retaliatory sanctions. There is no guarantee that Congress will act on this option because many members remain irritated at the WTO's rejection of the USA's earlier attempt at reconciliation through the ETI Act. However, recent business scandals in the USA do reduce the costs of changing the offending measure and may ultimately lead to a resolution acceptable to the EU.

On the European side, Pascal Lamy has said that the 'EU would hold out the threat of retaliation as leverage for possibly resolving the dispute more amicably' (US Mission, 2002g).[55] The EU would prefer the USA to draft a voluntary compensation program rather than forcing the Union to impose the retaliatory sanctions. One reason that the EU would like to avoid retaliatory sanctions is that 'Few member states have shown much enthusiasm over drawing up lists of US goods to target, fearing that America could retaliate by putting to test the legality of the EU's own agricultural export subsidy programmes at the WTO' (Denny, 2002).[56] In addition, such a voluntary compensation program could be negotiated with the administration, thus avoiding the lengthy and uncertain congressional procedures for changing the US tax code.

The FSC dispute has already generated two WTO panel decisions against the USA's offending measure. Unlike the US steel tariffs, congressional intransigence in the FSC case – a case of economic regulation – reflects the intractable nature of regulatory disputes embedded in domestic politics. In this case, the time lag provided by the WTO dispute settlement mechanism does not provide any significant domestic gains to the US administration. Rather, domestic gains (for both the US administration and Congress) accrue from the continued benefits of protecting large exporting corporations. The crucial calculation in this dispute is whether those domestic gains of protectionism will continue to outweigh the costs of the EU's pending WTO-authorized retaliatory sanctions. As with the steel tariffs case, the EU will likely aim its retaliation at those (unrelated) industries that hold the greatest potential for increasing the domestic political costs of not changing the FSCs measure. To avoid the potentially high domestic costs of retaliatory sanctions, and to circumvent congressional obstacles, the US administration must also weigh the option of negotiating a voluntary compensation program. However, this option may become less necessary as recent US corporate scandals reduce congressional and other obstacles to changing the FSCs measure.

CONCLUSIONS

The transatlantic market place has witnessed a number of significant changes in both the private and public spheres during the 1990s. Through a series of bilateral agreements, EU–US relations have moved from consultation to joint action and early warning. This institutionalization of transatlantic economic relations has been accompanied by a commitment to manage EU–US disputes within the multilateral framework of the WTO. While these developments will encourage future EU–US economic cooperation, intermittent conflicts are still very likely in the transatlantic market place. The likelihood of conflicts increases especially as the international trade agenda shifts to the problems of reconciling behind-the-border regulatory differences. The analytical approach employed in this chapter relies on an understanding of the different pressures created by traditional trade disputes and regulatory disputes as well as the dynamics of the WTO system and domestic political demands.

The EU and the USA are likely to continue using the multilateral rule-based system and lengthy procedures as a form of strategic trade dispute management. As shown in the banana and steel tariff cases, WTO authorization to retaliate with trade sanctions creates leverage for the offended party to effect change in the behavior of the offender. However, owing to the inherent time lag in the WTO dispute settlement mechanism, the offender can reap the domestic political gains that accrue from the original protectionist measure before suffering the actual retaliation. Thus the EU and the USA will likely continue using the mutually beneficial WTO system as a strategic means to provide at least temporary protection to domestic constituents before changing their offending trade measures.

Alternatively, the beef hormone and FSC cases suggest that regulatory disputes are less likely to be resolved through the multilateral system because domestic politics make them less tractable and the WTO's time lag does not provide similar domestic political gains. Because the costs of changing a regulatory measure often exceed the costs of not changing the measure, regulatory disputes will continue to create tensions in the transatlantic market place. In addition, these disputes are likely to continue because reducing the costs of changing regulatory measures often requires significant political resources and extended periods of time.

Traditional trade conflict therefore can be thought of as far more compartmentalized within the domestic polity than is regulatory conflict. For example, in the USA, the former concerns primarily producer groups (businesses and unions), the USTR's office and the Commerce Department. By contrast, regulatory conflict touches a far greater number of politically organized groups (businesses, unions, consumers and various other civil society advocacy groups) and government agencies. In the case of regulatory conflict, US regulatory agencies themselves can easily become important actors either facilitating or obstructing transatlantic regulatory cooperation. In the EU, the Commission functions as a significant regulatory actor determining the parameters of transatlantic regulatory cooperation and conflict. The WTO therefore seems most effective in dealing with those disputes falling under the rubric of traditional trade politics. It is less effective in disputes arising from divergences in regulatory structures. In short, tariff and non-tariff barriers are far more negotiable than regulatory policies.

To confront the inherent limitations of this system of bilateral and multilateral dispute management, the EU and the USA are pursuing alternative means to prevent such disputes from reaching a point at which they must be brought to the WTO. For example as stated above, they are enhancing dispute prevention by expanding the MRA process and the more general TEP process that has recently produced the Guidelines on Regulatory Cooperation and Transparency. These types of procedures will be seriously tested in the future as the prevention and resolution of transatlantic disputes turns to trade in services, intellectual property rights, investment, competition policy, public procurement and trade and the environment. Since such regulation is integral to public policy in both the EU and the USA, it is likely that conflicts over these issues will increase over time unless very concrete steps are taken on both sides to work toward further mutual recognition and/or harmonization.

Given the difficulties of settling regulatory conflicts within the WTO system, dispute prevention at the transatlantic level has become extremely important. The future of transatlantic economic governance therefore will depend on how skillfully bilateral mechanisms, such as mutual recognition agreements, and multilateral measures, such as international regulatory codes and standards, can be negotiated so as to prevent regulatory disputes from emerging or reaching a point at which they are brought to the WTO. Such economic governance may also require a willingness on both sides of the Atlantic not to bring cases based on regulatory divergence to the WTO. The challenge for the EU and the USA will be to demonstrate flexibility and innovation in the regulatory arena while maintaining compliance with WTO rulings in the traditional trade area. The new framework of transatlantic economic governance will therefore require strengthening bilateral and multilateral dispute prevention mechanisms, flexibility and restraint in regulatory dispute resolution, and a recognition that the expansion of the public sphere of transatlantic economic relations into the regulatory arena will link the domestic politics of the USA and the EU much more tightly than they have been hitherto.

NOTES

1. While there are many types of non-tariff barriers, common examples include quotas, trade prohibitions, import licensing requirements and voluntary export restraints. For a useful cross-national analysis of non-tariff barriers, see Mansfield and Busch (1995).
2. For useful discussions of the development and role of the 'regulatory state' in Europe and the United States, see Majone (1994, 1996) and Meier (1999).
3. The increasing importance of the EU–US economic relationship has encouraged a growing body of literature investigating the bilateral and multilateral management of transatlantic economic relations. For example, see Bermann *et al.* (2001), Philippart and Winand (2001), Pollack and Shaffer (2001a), Henning and Padoan (2000), Meunier (2000), Guay (1999), Eichengreen (1998), Hanson (1998), Vogel (1997) and Peterson (1996).
4. For a detailed discussion of the TAD, see Gardner (1997, 2001).
5. While the TAD was a significant landmark, Featherstone and Ginsberg note, 'In both US and EC official circles, though, the declaration was described as a "half-way" document, unable to meet more ambitious objectives owing to hesitations on both sides' (1996, p. 91).
6. On the development of the EU's foreign economic policy, see Young (2000, 2001) and Meunier and Nicolaïdis (1999). For useful discussions of the US perception of the Single European Market, see Hanson (1998) and Hocking and Smith (1997).
7. The NTA was accompanied by an EU–US Joint Action Plan, essentially an operational plan for implementing the NTA.
8. On the context and negotiations over the NTA, see Gardner (1997, 2001). For a recent evaluation of the NTA, see Pollack (2001).
9. On these dialogues, see Green Cowles (2001a, 2001b), Knauss and Trubek (2001) and Bignami and Charnovitz (2001). On the role of civil society in enacting domestic regulation in the EU and the USA, see Vogel (1995, 1997).
10. The Mutual Recognition Agreement (MRA) encourages the removal of regulatory barriers to trade by encouraging equivalency for standards and testing and certification requirements for EU and US firms producing certain products. The MRA is generally supported by business interests in sectors facing 'heterogeneous standards and duplicative regulatory burdens' (Egan, 1999, p. 22) and where exports are subject to product certification requirements, such as the pharmaceutical industry. Dispute prevention through the MRA process is limited as it currently covers only a small number of products and continues to encounter resistance from domestic regulators. For a more detailed discussion of the MRA process, see Egan (2001).
11. For a more comprehensive assessment of the outputs generated by the NTA, see Philippart and Winand (2001, pp. 431–63).
12. The TEP was signed after a more ambitious, Commission-led initiative to implement a 'New Transatlantic Marketplace' failed to gain sufficient support from within the Union (Pollack and Shaffer, 2001a, p. 16).
13. More specifically, the TEP declared,

    > In keeping with our leading role in the world trade system, we reaffirm our determination to maintain open markets, resist protectionism and sustain the momentum of liberalisation. The most effective means of maintaining open markets and promoting the expansion of trade is the continued development and strengthening of the multilateral system. The EU and US will give priority to pursuing their objectives together with other trading partners through the World Trade Organisation.

14. Of course, transatlantic economic relations are embedded in a broad and complex politico-security relationship. Both parties are capable of linking issues across the economic and politico-security realms to increase their negotiating leverage (for example, see Brittan, 2002). While these two realms are not separate, they are analytically separable.

Thus the current chapter does not assert a clear divide between economic and politico-security relations, but, rather, focuses on transatlantic economic relations for analytical simplification.

15. For more on the GATT and WTO systems, see Hoekman and Kostecki (1995).
16. For example, India, a leader of the developing countries, was reluctant to open its markets further owing to weak domestic prices and a flood of inexpensive imports from China (Pearl, 2001, p.A7).
17. Notably, the final Doha Declaration did include provisions specifically addressing the concerns of developing and least developed countries (paras 12, 36, 42–4) and environmental interests (paras 31–3).
18. The urgency of the trade round was also linked to the USA's war on terrorism (Zoellick, 2001c).
19. The WTO's rule-based system differs from previous results-oriented approaches, such as the management of trade through agreements on quotas and voluntary restrictions as well as agreements to stabilize and set prices and allocate market shares (Hoekman and Kostecki, 1995, p. 24).
20. For more on the dispute settlement mechanism and these deadlines, see the WTO website (*www.wto.org*).
21. It is useful to add that 'traditional trade disputes' do not include disputes over trade in services. While the WTO system remains relatively untested at settling disputes over trade in services, such disputes may actually conform more to the dynamics of regulatory disputes because of the inherently regulatory nature of services.
22. A large body of literature has investigated in great detail the relationship between domestic politics and trade policy. However, this literature does not directly compare its findings with the relationship between domestic politics and regulatory policy. For examples of the trade policy literature, see Mansfield *et al.* (2000), Meunier (2000), Destler and Balint (1999), Morrow *et al.* (1998), Hanson (1998), Frieden and Rogowski (1996), Alt *et al.* (1996), Garrett and Lange (1995), Destler (1995), Mansfield and Busch (1995), Goldstein (1993), Hayes (1993), Frieden (1991), Rogowski (1989), Milner (1988) and Destler and Odell (1987).
23. For example, on the institutional differences between US and European approaches to the regulation of biological products, see Kraus (2000). On the different preferences of European and American consumers over the regulation of food safety, see Pollack and Shaffer (2001b, pp. 154–60). On the different EU and US approaches to behind-the-border environmental regulation, see Sbragia with Damro (1999) and Vogel (1997, pp. 38–56). On the reasons why domestic preferences may diverge, see Green Cowles (1997).
24. See Damro (2001, 2002) and Devuyst (2001).
25. The Lomé Convention created a system of preferential access to the European market for numerous products from former European colonies in Africa, the Caribbean and Pacific (ACP).
26. Petersmann argues that 'The banana dispute was an old-style dispute about trade discrimination in favour of former colonial countries of EC member states' (2001, p. 86).
27. According to Gardner, 'Whereas the market share of Dole and Del Monte in the EU banana market rose from 11 per cent to 15 per cent and from 7.5 per cent to 8 per cent between 1991 to 1994, respectively, the market share of Chiquita dropped from 25 per cent to 18.5 per cent during the same time period' (1997, p. 51, n.50).
28. Shaffer notes that the controlling shareholder of Chiquita was among the top contributors to both the Democratic and the Republican parties in 1998 (2001, p. 99).
29. Section 301 refers to the US Trade Act of 1974, which requires the USTR to take action if 'an act, policy or practice of a foreign country . . . is unjustifiable and burdens or restricts United States commerce'.
30. The WTO complaint was supported by Honduras, Ecuador, Mexico and Guatemala.
31. At its inception in 1995, the extent of the WTO's practical utility and the enforceability of its authority were unclear: if the EU and the USA opted for unilateral retaliation instead of bringing disagreements before the dispute settlement mechanism, the organization would be seriously weakened.

32. For more details on the agreement, see USTR (2002, pp. 109–10).
33. According to Shaffer, the legal disputes in the banana case 'involved over a dozen claims under four WTO agreements', including the 1994 GATT, the General Agreement on Trade in Services, the agreement on Trade-Related Investment Measures and the Licensing Agreement (2001, p. 104).
34. In addition, domestic EU beef producers lobbied hard for the ban. EU beef producers had high surpluses thanks to CAP price supports and export subsidies in 1980s. Thus prices would be threatened by increasing inexpensive imports from the USA, as well as growing European consumer demand for diets low in fat and cholesterol (Hanrahan, 2000, p. 2).
35. For example, Article 3.4 states, 'in particular the Codex Alimentarius Commission, the International Office of Epizootics, and the international and regional organizations operating within the framework of the International Plant Protection Convention.'
36. Only the United Kingdom voted in opposition, arguing that the scientific basis for maintaining the ban was insufficient (Hanrahan, 2000, p. 2).
37. For a useful discussion of European efforts to base regulatory decision making on scientific evidence and risk assessments, see Joerges *et al.* (1997).
38. On GMOs and biotechnology, see Pollack and Shaffer (2000, 2001b), Vogel (1997, 2001) and Egan (1999).
39. According to the US Mission to the EU, 'A glut of cheap imports combined with world steel overcapacity caused steel prices to fall to the lowest levels in 20 years. As a result of falling profitability, the industry registered 30 bankruptcies and shed 20,000 jobs since 1997, according to press reports' (2002a, p. 1).
40. When US industries believe they have been injured or threatened by imports, they may seek relief under Section 201 of the 1974 Trade Act, which covers fairly traded goods, not dumping or other activity covered by unfair trade laws (US Mission, 2002a, p. 1).
41. The USITC decision was unanimous, but the six members disagreed on the precise remedies to be implemented. Two members actually recommended higher tariffs, up to 35–40 per cent (US Mission, 2002b, p. 3).
42. The three-year duration of the tariffs is within the periods provided under Article 7.1 of the WTO Agreement on Safeguards (1994).
43. See US Mission (2002c, p. 3) for a list of the countries.
44. It has also been argued that the USTR is 'working to build a pro-U.S. counterweight to Europe to further U.S. interests in other international trade issues, such as the promotion of genetically modified crops. The White House decision to exclude Canada, Mexico and dozens of developing countries from the steel tariffs forms part of that strategy' (King and Winestock, 2002, p. A3).
45. Another possible option available to the USA would be to compensate the EU by lowering tariffs on other goods.
46. Restructuring of the US steel industry could occur via mergers. However, the biggest obstacle to this restructuring is that traditional integrated mills (as opposed to minimills) are hesitant to merge because of 'legacy costs' like the very large and unpaid pension and health plans for laid off, retired and numerous soon-to-be-retired employees.
47. Trade-promotion authority (previously called fast-track authority) allows the administration to bring international trade agreements before Congress for approval – without amendments – within 90 days. Trade-promotion authority was a major objective for the USTR in 2002, particularly considering the upcoming negotiations on the Doha Round and the Free Trade Area of the Americas (US Mission, 2002d).
48. King and Winestock continue: 'In briefing congressional staffers, administration officials said they expected the steel rescue package would gain them at least six votes in favor of fast-track trade authority on the House side and a similar number among wavering steel-state senators' (2002, p. A8).
49. In addition to the Commission, British Prime Minister Tony Blair and German Chancellor Gerhard Schröder have denounced the US decision (King and Winestock, 2002, p. A3). See also Brittan (2002).

50. For example, see Article XIX of the GATT Agreement (1947) and the WTO Agreement on Safeguards (1994).
51. In addition, the EU argues that US steel imports have actually fallen by 33 per cent since 1998 (King and Winestock, 2002, p. A3).
52. The EU has drafted two separate lists of products for retaliation: a 'long list' for retaliation at the conclusion of the WTO process and a 'short list' (under Article 8.2 of the WTO Safeguards Agreement) for retaliation that could be applied much earlier.
53. This tactic resembles the Clinton administration's decision to retaliate against the EU's banana regulation by improving tariffs on unrelated notable products (see above).
54. See the Deficit Reduction Act of 1984 (US Code, Title 26/SubtitleA/Chapter 1/Subchapter N/Part III/Subpart C – Taxation of Foreign Sales Corporation) and the Domestic International Sales Corporations (DISC) Provisions of 1971 (US Code, Title 26/Subtitle A/Chapter 1/Subchapter N/Part IV/Subpart A).
55. Lamy claims to want to avoid linking the retaliatory FSC tariffs with the current steel dispute: '"The objective of sanctions isn't tit-for-tat," he said. "It's not a case of you sock me and I'll sock you." Mr. Lamy has pledged not to apply sanctions if he thinks the U.S. is serious about complying with the WTO's demands' (Winestock, 2002a, p. A18). On European steel makers' concerns over the possibility of retaliatory tariffs, see Winestock (2002b).
56. For an example of the complexity surrounding European and transatlantic agricultural relations, see Patterson (1997).

REFERENCES

Alt, James E., Jeffry Frieden, Michael J. Gilligan, Dani Rodrik and Ronald Rogowski (1996), 'The Political Economy of International Trade: Enduring Puzzles and an Agenda for Inquiry', *Comparative Political Studies*, 29(6): 689–717.
Atlantic Council of the United States (2001), 'Changing Terms of Trade: Managing the New Transatlantic Economy', policy paper (April), Washington, DC: Atlantic Council.
Bermann, George, Matthias Herdegen and Peter L. Lindseth (eds) (2001), *Transatlantic Regulatory Cooperation: Legal Problems and Political Prospects*, Oxford: Oxford University Press.
Bignami, Francesca and Steve Charnovitz (2001), 'Transatlantic Civil Society Dialogues', in Mark A. Pollack and Gregory Shaffer (eds), *Transatlantic Governance in the Global Economy*, Lanham, MD: Rowman & Littlefield Publishers, pp. 255–84.
Brittan, Leon (2002), 'No Way to Treat an Ally: George W. Bush's Decision to Impose Tariffs on Steel Will Undermine Wider Transatlantic Co-operation, Warns Leon Brittan' *Financial Times*, 19 March.
Burghardt, Guenter (2001), 'New Challenges for the Transatlantic Partnership', speech at The Economic Club of Memphis, Memphis, Tennessee, 14 November.
Damro, Chad (2001), 'Building an International Identity: The EU and Extraterritorial Competition Policy', *Journal of European Public Policy*, 8(2): 208–26.
Damro, Chad (2002), 'Economic Internationalization and Competition Policy: International and Domestic Sources of Transatlantic Cooperation', PhD dissertation, University of Pittsburgh, Pittsburgh, Pennsylvania.
Denny, Charlotte (2002), '$4bn US Subsidies Incur WTO's Wrath', *The Guardian*, 14 January.

Destler, I.M. (1995), *American Trade Politics*, 3rd edn, Washington, DC: Institute for International Economics.

Destler, I.M. and Peter J. Balint (1999), *The New Politics of American Trade: Trade, Labor, and the Environment*, Washington, DC: Institute for International Economics.

Destler, I.M. and John S. Odell (1987), *Anti-Protection: Changing Forces in U.S. Trade Politics*, Washington, DC: Institute for International Economics.

Devuyst, Youri (2001), 'Transatlantic Competition Relations', in Mark A. Pollack and Gregory Shaffer (eds), *Transatlantic Governance in the Global Economy*, Lanham, MD: Rowman & Littlefield Publishers, pp. 127–52.

Egan, Michelle (1999), *Conference Report: Creating a Transatlantic Marketplace – Government Policies and Business Strategies*, Washington, DC: American Institute for Contemporary German Studies, The Johns Hopkins University.

Egan, Michelle (2001), 'Mutual Recognition and Standard Setting: Public and Private Strategies for Governing Markets', in Mark A. Pollack and Gregory Shaffer (eds), *Transatlantic Governance in the Global Economy*, Lanham, MD: Rowman & Littlefield Publishers, pp. 179–209.

Eichengreen, Barry (ed.) (1998), *Transatlantic Economic Relations in the Post-Cold War Era*, New York: Council on Foreign Relations.

European Commission (2001), 'Press Release: US Steel: EU Expresses Concern Over US International Trade Commission Findings', 23 October (*europa.eu.int/comm./trade/goods/steel/pr_231001.htm*).

European Commission (2002a), 'The EU's relations with the United States of America – Overview', (*http://europa.eu.int/comm/external_relations/us/intro/index.htm*), 7 March.

European Commission (2002b), 'Press Release: United States and European Commission agree increased Regulatory Cooperation', IP/02/555, 12 April.

Featherstone, Kevin and Roy Ginsberg (1996), *The United States and the European Union in the 1990s: Partners in Transition*, 2nd edn, New York: St Martin's Press.

Frieden, Jeffry (1991), *Debt, Development and Democracy: Modern Political Economy and Latin America, 1965–1985*, Princeton, NJ: Princeton University Press.

Frieden, Jeffry and Ronald Rogowski (1996), 'The Impact of the International Economy on National Policies: An Analytical Overview', in Robert Keohane and Helen Milner (eds), *Internationalization and Domestic Politics*, New York: Cambridge University Press, pp. 25–47

Gardner, Anthony (2001), 'From the Transatlantic Declaration to the New Transatlantic Agenda: The Shaping of Institutional Mechanisms and Policy Objectives by National and Supranational Actors', in Éric Philippart and Pascaline Winand (eds), *Ever Closer Partnership: Policy-Making in US–EU Relations*, New York: P.I.E.-Peter Lang, pp. 83–106.

Gardner, Anthony Laurence (1997), *A New Era in US–EU Relations? The Clinton Administration and the New Transatlantic Agenda*, Brookfield, VT: Ashgate.

Garrett, Geoffrey and Peter Lange (1995), 'Internationalization, Institutions, and Political Change', *International Organization*, 49(4): 627–55.

Goldstein, Judith (1993), *Ideas, Interests, and American Trade Policy*, Ithaca, NY: Cornell University Press.

Green Cowles, Maria (1997), *Conference Report: The Limits of Liberalization: Regulatory Cooperation and the New Transatlantic Agenda*, Washington, DC: American Institute for Contemporary German Studies, The Johns Hopkins University.

Green Cowles, Maria (2001a), 'The Transatlantic Business Dialogue: Transforming the New Transatlantic Dialogue', in Mark A. Pollack and Gregory Shaffer (eds), *Transatlantic Governance in the Global Economy*, Lanham, MD: Rowman & Littlefield Publishers, pp. 213–34.

Green Cowles, Maria (2001b), 'Private Firms and US–EU Policy-Making: The Transatlantic Business Dialogue', in Éric Philippart and Pascaline Winand (eds), *Ever Closer Partnership: Policy-Making in US–EU Relations*, New York: P.I.E.-Peter Lang, pp. 229–66.

Guay, Terrance (1999), *The United States and the European Union: The Political Economy of a Relationship*, Sheffield, UK: Sheffield Academic Press.

Hanrahan, Charles E. (1999), 'The U.S.–European Union Banana Dispute', CRS Report for Congress, RS20130, 9 December.

Hanrahan, Charles E. (2000), 'The European Union's Ban on Hormone-Treated Meat', CRS Report for Congress, RS20142, 19 December.

Hanson, Brian T. (1998), 'What Happened to Fortress Europe? External Trade Policy Liberalization in the European Union', *International Organization*, 52(1): 55–85.

Hayes, J.P. (1993), *Making Trade Policy in the European Community*, New York: St Martin's Press.

Henning, C. Randall and Pier Carlo Padoan (2000), *Transatlantic Perspectives on the Euro*, Pittsburgh, Pennsylvania: European Community Studies Association and Washington, DC: Brookings Institution Press.

Hocking, Brian and Michael Smith (1997), *Beyond Foreign Economic Policy: The United States, the Single European Market and the Changing World Economy*, Washington, DC: Pinter.

Hoekman, Bernard and Michel Kostecki (1995), *The Political Economy of the World Trading System: From GATT to WTO*, New York: Oxford University Press.

Joerges, Christian, Karl-Heinz Ladeur and Ellen Vos (eds) (1997), *Integrating Scientific Expertise into Regulatory Decision-Making*, Baden-Baden: Nomos.

Julius, DeAnne (1991), 'Foreign Direct Investment: The Neglected Twin of Trade', occasional paper 33, Group of Thirty, Washington, DC.

King, Neil Jr. and Geoff Winestock (2002), 'Plan to Rescue Steel Industry Draws Fire', *The Wall Street Journal*, 7 March, A3 and A6.

Knauss, Jody and David Trubek (2001), 'The Transatlantic Labor Dialogue: Minimal Action in a Weak Structure', in Mark A. Pollack and Gregory Shaffer (eds), *Transatlantic Governance in the Global Economy*, Lanham, MD: Rowman & Littlefield Publishers, pp. 235–54.

Kraus, Martine (2000), 'Licensing Biologics in Europe and the United States', in Robert A. Kagan and Lee Axelrad (eds), *Regulatory Encounters: Multinational Corporations and American Adversarial Legalism*, Berkeley, CA: University of California Press, pp. 313–40.

Lamy, Pascal and Robert B. Zoellick (2001), 'In the Next Round', *The Washington Post*, 17 July, A17.

Majone, Giandomenico (1994), 'The Rise of the Regulatory State in Europe', *West European Politics*, 17(3): 77–101.

Majone, Giandomenico (1996), 'A European Regulatory State?', in Jeremy Richardson (ed.), *European Union: Power and Policy-Making*, New York: Routledge, pp. 261–77.

Mansfield, Edward D. and Marc L. Busch (1995), 'The Political Economy of

Nontariff Barriers: A Cross-National Analysis', *International Organization*, 49: 723–49.

Mansfield, Edward D., Helen V. Milner and B. Peter Rosendorff (2000), 'Free to Trade: Democracies, Autocracies, and International Trade', *American Political Science Review*, 94 (June): 305–21.

Meier, Kenneth J. (1999), *Politics and the Bureaucracy: Policy Making in the Fourth Branch of Government*, 4th edn, New York: Harcourt Brace College Publishers.

Meunier, Sophie (2000), 'What Single Voice? European Institutions and EU–U.S. Trade Negotiations', *International Organization*, 54(1): 103–35.

Meunier, Sophie and Kalypso Nicolaïdis (1999), 'Who Speaks for Europe? The Delegation of Trade Authority in the EU', *Journal of Common Market Studies*, 37(3): 477–501.

Milner, Helen (1988), *Resisting Protection: Global Industries and the Politics of International Trade*, Princeton, NJ: Princeton University Press.

Morrow, James D., Randolph M. Siverson and Tressa E. Tabares (1998), 'The Political Determinants of International Trade: The Major Powers, 1907–1990', *American Political Science Review*, 92 (September): 649–61.

Patterson, Lee Ann (1997), 'Agricultural Policy Reform in the European Community: A Three-Level Game Analysis', *International Organization*, 51(1): 135–66.

Pearl, Daniel (2001), 'U.S. Urges a Reluctant India to Support New Global Trade Talks', *The Wall Street Journal*, 10 August, A7.

Petersmann, Ernst-Ulrich (2001), 'Dispute Prevention and Dispute Settlement in the EU–US Transatlantic Partnership', in Mark A. Pollack and Gregory Shaffer (eds), *Transatlantic Governance in the Global Economy*, Lanham, MD: Rowman & Littlefield Publishers, pp. 73–95.

Peterson, John (1996), *Europe and America: The Prospects for Partnership*, 2nd edn, London: Routledge.

Peterson, John (2001), 'Shaping, Not Making – The Impact of the American Congress on US–EU Relations', in Éric Philippart and Pascaline Winand (eds), *Ever Closer Partnership: Policy-Making in US–EU Relations*, New York: P.I.E.-Peter Lang, pp. 155–86.

Philippart, Éric and Pascaline Winand (eds) (2001), *Ever Closer Partnership: Policy-Making in US–EU Relations,* New York: P.I.E.-Peter Lang.

Pollack, Mark A. (2001), *The New Transatlantic Agenda at Five: A Critical Assessment, Conference Report*, Florence: European University Institute.

Pollack, Mark A. and Gregory C. Shaffer (2000), 'Biotechnology: The Next Transatlantic Trade War?' *The Washington Quarterly*, 23(4): 41–54.

Pollack, Mark A. and Gregory C. Shaffer (eds) (2001a), *Transatlantic Governance in the Global Economy*, Lanham, MD: Rowman & Littlefield Publishers.

Pollack, Mark A. and Gregory C. Shaffer (2001b), 'The Challenge of Reconciling Regulatory Differences: Food Safety and GMOs in the Transatlantic Relationship', in Mark A. Pollack and Gregory Shaffer (eds), *Transatlantic Governance in the Global Economy*, Lanham, MD: Rowman & Littlefield Publishers, pp. 153–78.

Rogowski, Ronald (1989), *Commerce and Coalitions: How Trade Affects Domestic Political Alignments*, Princeton, NJ: Princeton University Press.

Sbragia, Alberta M. (1998), 'The Transatlantic Relationship: A Case of Deepening and Broadening', in Carolyn Rhodes (ed.), *The European Union in the World Community*, Boulder, CO: Lynne Rienner, 147–64.

Sbragia, Alberta M. with Chad Damro (1999), 'The Changing Role of the European Union in International Environmental Politics: Institution Building and the Politics of Climate Change', *Environment and Planning C: Government and Policy*, 17: 53–68.

Shaffer, Gregory C. (2001), 'The Blurring of the Intergovernmental: Public–Private Partnerships behind US and EC Trade Claims', in Mark A. Pollack and Gregory Shaffer (eds), *Transatlantic Governance in the Global Economy*, Lanham, MD: Rowman & Littlefield Publishers, pp. 97–123.

Stevens, Christopher (1996), 'EU Policy for the Banana Market: The External Impact of Internal Policies', in Helen Wallace and William Wallace (eds), *Policy-Making in the European Union*, 3rd edn, New York: Oxford University Press, pp. 325–51.

UNCTAD (2001), *World Investment Report 2001: Promoting Linkages*, United States Country Fact Sheet, Geneva: UNCTAD.

United States Trade Representative (2002), *National Trade Estimate Report on Foreign Trade Barriers*, Washington, DC: USTR.

US Mission to the European Union (2002a), 'Press Release: President Bush Imposes Safeguards on Steel Imports', 5 March (*www.useu.be/Categories/Trade/Steel/Mar0502BushSteelDecisionTafiffs.html*).

US Mission to the European Union (2002b), 'Press Release: USTR's Zoellick Says Steel Tariffs a Safeguard Step', 5 March (*www.useu.be/Categories/Trade/Steel/Mar0502ZoellickSteelTariffs.html*).

US Mission to the European Union (2002c), 'Press Release: U.S. Officials Defend Temporary Relief for Steel Industry', 6 March (*www.useu.be/Categories/Trade/Steel/Mar0602USTRAllgeierSteel.html*).

US Mission to the European Union (2002d), 'Press Release: USTR Zoellick Outlines Trade Objectives for 2002', 6 February (*www.useu.be/Categories/WTO/Feb0602ZoellickTradeObjectives.html*).

US Mission to the European Union (2002e), 'Dossier: Foreign Sales Corporation', 7 March (*www.useu.be/Categories/FSC/Index.htm*).

US Mission to the European Union (2002f), 'Press Release: Senate Chairman Plays Down Tax Deal in Resolving FSC Dispute with EU', 6 February (*www.useu.be/Categories/FSC/Feb0602FSCSenatorBaucus.html*).

US Mission to the European Union (2002g), 'Press Release: USTR Challenges EU Sanctions Claim in FSC Case', 14 February (*www.useu.be/Categories/FSC/Feb1402USTRSanctionsFSC.html*).

US Mission to the European Union (2002h), 'Press Release: U.S. Needs Trade Authority, Agriculture's Veneman Says', 25 February (*www.useu.be/Categories/Trade/Feb2602VenemanTPA.html*).

Vogel, David (1995), *Trading Up: Consumer and Environmental Regulation in a Global Economy*, Cambridge, MA: Harvard University Press.

Vogel, David (1997), *Barriers or Benefits? Regulation in Transatlantic Trade*, Washington, DC: Brookings Institution Press.

Vogel, David (2001), 'Ships Passing in the Night: The Changing Politics of Risk Regulation in Europe and the United States', working paper, RSC No. 2001/16, Florence: European University Institute.

Winestock, Geoff (2002a), 'How One Trade Dispute Fuels Another', *The Wall Street Journal*, 12 March, A18.

Winestock, Geoff (2002b), 'European Steel Maker Is Wary of a Trade War', *The Wall Street Journal*, 15 March, A6.

Winestock, Geoff and Neil King, Jr. (2002), 'EU Aims at White House in Retaliation to Steel Tariffs', *The Wall Street Journal*, 22 March, A2.

Young, Alasdair R. (2000), 'The Adaptation of European Foreign Economic Policy: From Rome to Seattle', *Journal of Common Market Studies*, 38(1): 93–116.

Young, Alasdair R. (2001), 'Extending European Cooperation: The European Union and the "New" International Trade Agenda', working paper, RSC No. 2001/12, Florence: European University Institute.

Zoellick, Robert B. (2001a), 'The United States, Europe and the World Trading System', speech to The Kangaroo Group, Strasbourg, France, 15 May.

Zoellick, Robert B. (2001b), 'The WTO and New Global Trade Negotiations: What's at Stake', speech to the Council on Foreign Relations, Washington, DC, 30 October.

Zoellick, Robert B. (2001c), 'Countering Terror with Trade', *The Washington Post*, 20 September, A35.

6. Does the monetary dialogue with the European Parliament influence the European Central Bank?

Sylvester C.W. Eijffinger and Edin Mujagic

INTRODUCTION

Starting from 1 January 1999, the European Central Bank (ECB) took over the conduct of monetary policy in the Euro area. Its founding fathers have given it a high degree of independence owing to the well-known fact that an independent central bank has many advantages, such as avoiding the time-inconsistency problem (Kydland and Prescott, 1977). It has been suggested by some that the ECB is probably the most independent central bank in the world. Although independent, a central bank must give account for its actions. In the Euro area, the ECB is held accountable by the European Parliament.

In this chapter we take a closer look at the most important part of the relation between the ECB and the European Parliament, namely the quarterly monetary dialogues between the Committee on Economic and Monetary Affairs (ECON) and the ECB. This monetary dialogue is based on Article 113 (3) of the Treaty on European Union, which states that 'The President of the ECB and the other members of the Executive Board may, at the request of the European Parliament or on their own initiative, be heard by the competent committees of the European Parliament.' The ECON and the ECB agreed, on the basis of this article, that the President of the ECB would appear every quarter before the ECON to discuss monetary policy and the activities of the ECB and the ESCB (European System of Central Banks).

We investigate whether this monetary dialogue influences the ECB with regard to its procedures and arrangements by comparing the issues raised by the ECON and its panel of experts and the changes in ECB's procedures and arrangements. The contribution of the panel of experts is twofold: first of all, each quarter members of this panel present briefing papers to the ECON and, secondly, they appear before the ECON a week later, discussing the subjects raised with the members of the ECON, preparing them even more for their dialogue with the ECB. On the basis of this research, we conclude that the ECB is to a significant degree responsive to the ECON. This response of the ECB can be divided into two parts. We distinguish between immediate response (comments by Duisenberg – the President of the ECB – during monetary dialogue) and delayed response (the degree to which the ECB incorporates points raised during the dialogue in its policy).

The remainder of this chapter is built up as follows. After describing the methodology used, we take a look at the contribution of the panel of experts by analysing the briefing papers it has provided for the ECON up to July 2002. We use these to construct a list of subjects the panel has raised. In the following section we do the same for the ECON by analysing the transcripts of the question-and-answer sessions between the ECON and the president of the ECB. To complete the analysis we have sifted through all press conferences and press releases of the ECB to make a list similar to those mentioned. Finally, we compared them in order to provide an answer to the question whether these monetary dialogues matter. In addition we have included a short section comparing monetary dialogue with the Humphrey–Hawkins testimonies of the Federal Reserve.

METHODOLOGY

Doing research on this or a similar subject involves certain difficulties, as the data used are not quantitative but rather qualitative in nature. In order to be able to present a list of subjects mentioned in the monetary dialogue certain steps were followed.[1] First we constructed a framework to be able to determine when a mention of a subject had to be included in the aforementioned list. One possibility was to include only those subjects where it has been *clearly suggested* that the ECB take action with regard to the subject in question. This approach, however, has two negative side-effects. First, it is necessary that there be an explicit suggestion. Second, this approach would not account for the frequency of each subject. With regard to the former, it is very possible that the words used *imply* that a suggestion is being made but this would have to be left out because an *explicit* suggestion, using the actual definition of the phrase, is not made. To control for this handicap one could decide to include those implicit suggestions, but then another difficulty would immediately crop up: what to include and what to exclude would be a highly subjective choice. Furthermore, as this choice would have to be made on a case-by-case basis, the probability is high that it would either, unintentionally, be inconsistent or would be perceived as such. In turn, as subjectivity would only be increased and a certain 'choice bias' would emerge, this procedure clearly would not satisfy the desire to make the process of the analysis as clear and as transparent as possible. Therefore we opted for the second option, namely to include those subjects *mentioned* (instead of suggested) in the monetary dialogue.

The next step is to make a clear distinction between subjects related to transparency (including communication) and accountability, and those related to other tasks of the ESCB.[2] In selecting what subjects are to be included in this thesis the following rule was used: only those subjects that would affect one or more aspects of monetary policy (as defined above) in a profoundly changing manner have been selected. 'Profoundly changing manner' is defined as potentially having a clear impact on transparency, accountability or communication or, put differently, potentially forming a breach in the policy of the ECB in those areas. The criteria we used for defining subjects affecting transparency, accountability and communication, and including them in the analysis, are[3] as follows:

- formal objectives of monetary policy (goals as defined in the Maastricht Treaty) and the definition of price stability;
- the explanation how information is used and analysed for monetary policy purposes (for example, publication of macroeconomic models and forecasts);
- the stability-oriented monetary policy strategy and the openness regarding it; and
- accountability with regard to the target.

Admittedly, these rules, definitions and the entire procedure are subjective, but it has to be recognized that subjectivity, try as we may, cannot be fully eliminated. It is even more important to note that it is not the rules and definitions used that are of the utmost importance here. Subjective as they are, they can be challenged by others. Subjectivity with regard to the definitions, rules and followed procedure is not a problem as such. It is the subjectivity in the analysis that should be eliminated. What is of the utmost importance is that an independent observer can be enabled to follow the procedure and reproduce the analysis. This can be done by clearly defining the rules, definitions and procedure and then applying them properly and consistently.

SUBJECTS RAISED BY THE PANEL OF EXPERTS AND THE ECON

The ECON has formed a panel of experts to help it prepare itself for its quarterly monetary dialogue with the ECB. This panel provides members of the ECON on a quarterly basis with briefing papers on various subjects, helping them to raise topics concerning monetary policy in the Euro area; to put it more bluntly, it provides them with academic-style ammunition for their confrontation with the monetary policy maker. After the analysis of the briefing papers provided to the ECON by the panel of experts, we have been able to put together a list of subjects that have frequently received attention (see Table 6.1).

Table 6.1   Subjects mentioned by the panel of experts

Subject	Frequency[a]
The stability-oriented monetary policy strategy	11
The secondary objective as described in Article 105 of the treaty	11
The definition of price stability as defined by the ECB	11
Publication of the minutes of meetings of the governing council of the ECB	6
Publication of (inflation) forecasts	7
Improvement of published (inflation) projections	5

Note: [a] Frequency relates to the number of papers (up to May 2002) in which these subjects have been mentioned.

Other subjects have on occasion also surfaced in one or more papers, such as the enlargement of the Euro area and restructuring of the governing council of the ECB in order to cope with this change, the inability of the governing council to speak with one voice, the role of asset prices in monetary policy, tactics with regard to the interest rate instrument (interest rate stepping versus interest rate smoothing) and the exchange rate of the Euro, but largely not in the context as defined above. When this was the case they were of course included under the appropriate heading.

Overall, one can say that the points of critique give a good representation of the academic view on the matters related to monetary policy. It should also be mentioned that, while the panel of experts strongly criticizes the ECB on a number of issues, most of the panel members also highly praise its monetary policy actions that have been taken so far. It can be stated that the way the policy actions were taken and communicated to the outside world have been criticized, but not the actions themselves. Using the transcripts of the question-and-answer sessions we constructed a similar list for subjects raised by the ECON (up to the monetary dialogue of May 2002). See Table 6.2.

Some points have to be presented here with regard to the table. The last criterion, accountability, does not include comments on the weak exchange rate of the Euro. Although this point was mentioned very regularly, from the legal point of view, as the ECB does not have an exchange rate target, it is not possible to hold the ECB accountable for it. Furthermore, comments regarding the secondary objective as defined in Article 105 of the Maastricht Treaty were included not, in the last criterion, but in the second one. The reason is similar to the one given with regard to the exchange rate. The ECB has price stability as its primary and overriding goal. Therefore, in order to assess the ECB's performance on its secondary objective, it is imperative it fulfilled the first one over the medium term. Despite the fact that the ECB has not clearly defined 'medium term', it can safely be assumed that it should not be measured in months but rather in years (see also Hämäläinen, 2001). The ECB can be held accountable only for the price stability and nothing else, including the exchange rate. However, when the Euro exchange rate was mentioned in relation to the communications of the ECB (concerning, for example, the second pillar of the stability-oriented monetary policy strategy), it has been included in Table 6.2.

Table 6.2   Subjects from monetary dialogues

Criterion	Frequency
The stability-oriented monetary policy strategy and communication	46
Primary and secondary objectives, including the definition of price stability	42
Forecasts	22
Accountability	1

The one occasion when the ECB's track record was attacked is the perfect example of how some members of the ECON still do not understand or do not want to understand what the ECB's task is and on what it should be judged. In May 2001, one of the members, William Abitbol made it very clear that, in his opinion, the ECB had failed as 'inflation was high and was shooting up, growth slowed down and capital was fleeing the Euro area'. Only the first argument from May 2001 is legitimate when we look at the treaty and the statute of the ECB, and even then it can only be used after some time has elapsed to allow the actions of the ECB to come into effect. The fact that the economic growth has slowed down can hardly be blamed on the monetary policy and the same applies to Abitbol's remark that capital was fleeing the Euro area. Both can to a large extent explained by referring to the global slowdown and the (expectations of) relatively better performance of the US economy.

Summarizing, the last criterion includes only statements directly concerning the performance on the price stability objective. Because the ECB has not been operating for a long time and because the other three criteria have a wide span, the frequency given to this criterion should not be taken at face value.

Stability-oriented Monetary Policy Strategy and Communication

In the 14 monetary dialogues considered here,[4] issues relating to the stability-oriented monetary policy strategy and communication with regard to this policy strategy surfaced regularly (for more on ECB's strategy, see ECB, 2001). Attention was focused on two main features: publication of minutes and votes of the meetings of the governing council of the ECB and the two pillars of the aforementioned strategy, especially the relevance of the first pillar. The binding element, not just between these two subjects but also between the other criteria specified above, is the notion that the ECB cannot be read well and is not understood by the public and the financial markets. This unclear communication in turn leads to relative high uncertainty and lack of confidence in the ECB with all its negative consequences, such as rendering its actions less effective. It is this line of thought that is used as the argument for pressing for publication of minutes and, in combination with some other arguments, for the abolishment of the first pillar of the stability-oriented monetary policy strategy.

Minutes of the meetings

Apart from the view that publishing minutes increases transparency and accountability, it also has the benefit of increasing the understanding of the arguments presented, both in favor of and against a certain decision. The fact that even experts have trouble reading and understanding the ECB strengthens this view of ECON. Finally, publication of minutes in some form would make it possible to get an indication of likely policy actions in the future. Ever since the ECB took over the conduct of monetary policy in the Euro area, there have been occasions that seem to justify ECON's case. Some of them have been mentioned both by the members of ECON and by the panel of experts, such as the now famous interest rate decrease of 10 May 2001. Another example is the intentional severe undersubscription by commercial banks in weekly tenders (in February, April and October 2001) as they were convinced that they had read the ECB's intentions and expected that they could compensate for the liquidity shortage by borrowing more, at a lower interest rate, in the following week. Finally, one of the most recent examples dates from September 2001. On 12 September, Duisenberg, replying to the concerns expressed regarding the impact of

11 September in New York on real economy and the wish that the ECB help to alleviate these effects, stated, 'it is far too early to judge what these consequences are going to be and I think a quick move . . . would have inspired a reaction of panic rather than one of stability and calm'. However, on 17 September, the ECB lowered its key interest rates by 50 base points. It is highly questionable, to say the least, that 'far too early to judge' no longer applied, only five days after the remark was made.

The panel of experts has somewhat different view on this particular issue than the ECON. Although Eijffinger (2001a) argues that the transparency of monetary policy increases if minutes of the meetings and/or the decisions including all arguments presented (in favor and against) are published, he recognizes that the importance is unclear as the ECB essentially does this by means of press conferences that follow immediately after the relevant meeting of the governing council. In his view the minutes should contain an analysis of environment in the Euro area, an estimation of the risks to price stability and a consistent and logical explanation of decisions based on the first two reasons given, but not the voting behavior of the members of the governing council. Regarding calls for publication of voting behavior, some argue that this would in essence do more harm than good as it could be interpreted along national lines, although all members of the governing council share a collective responsibility (see also Issing, 1999b). This, in turn, could result in pressure being put on separate members of the council. Because of this Wyplosz (2001a) argues that, 'as long as interpretation along national lines is likely to occur, minutes of the meetings should not be published'.

These views do not support calls from ECON on the ECB to publish minutes. However, there is also another line of argument that goes as follows. The ECB is seen by some observers as lacking transparency and accountability. These shortcomings can only be solved via institutional reform, but these changes could and should be anticipated by some modest reform, as proposed by Mazier (2000). One of these proposed changes is the 'full publication of internal debates and votes of the ECB and a much richer dialogue with the European Parliament'. Finally, it has been argued that, if minutes were published, conspiracy theories, such as the suggestion that the ECB sometimes has delayed taking a certain action in order to show that it is indeed independent and cannot be influenced, would vanish (Gros, 1999a). Despite these different views, ECON seems determined in its calls for the publication of minutes and votes, as can be concluded from, among others, the frequency of the discussions on this subject.

Communicating with the general public is very important to the ECB. This point has been made over and over again by the ECB. Its enormous communications efforts should be seen in this light. However, publication of minutes has been held back, on two grounds. First, as after every meeting of the governing council of the ECB when monetary policy is discussed its decisions and reasoning are published, it is not clear, as Duisenberg stated, 'that publishing a discussion itself without even mentioning the names would add anything to what we already publish' (monetary dialogue, April 1999). Giving a full account of discussions would 'create more confusion as in the discussion attitudes and opinions are adjustable' (monetary dialogue, November 1999). Furthermore, by calling for any publication of minutes including the voting pattern, it is assumed that decisions are indeed taken by vote. According to Duisenberg, however, 'it rarely occurs' that the governing council even takes a vote (monetary dialogue, May 2001).

Second, making public how individual members have voted (in cases where a decision was taken by vote) could expose them to pressure and make internal debate on monetary policy issues not as free as it is at the moment. In this case, arguments presented by individual members would become well-prepared and carefully edited written documents that every individual member would read out in the meeting, de facto 'killing' discussion within the governing council. The notion that the strategy of the ECB is unclear is strongly rejected by the ECB by referring to the simple fact that the ECB is the only central bank that even has a strategy and goes out of its way to explain it.

The two-pillar strategy
Views on the usefulness of the first pillar in the monetary strategy of the ECB are much more similar between ECON and the panel of experts than those on the previous issue.

The two-pillar strategy, and the first pillar in particular, is attacked on two accounts: first, it is said to be confusing and to mislead people and, second, it is attacked on the prevailing view that the connection between money growth and inflation is not so evident. The academic world has not been as kind to the ECB as it has been with regard to the publication of minutes. The first pillar of the ECB's monetary strategy has been criticized by virtually almost everyone. A recent paper by Begg *et al.* (2002) described it as 'flawed beyond repair' and looking 'extremely ridiculous, giving perverse signals that the ECB probably ignores', a view shared by the panel of experts.

The first pillar of the stability-oriented monetary policy strategy is said to be confusing to the public as the growth rate of M3 monetary aggregate is regularly higher than the reference value, but the ECB does not react to this. ECON has also suggested that it is also confusing because it looks as if the ECB follows one pillar only, while officially there are two pillars. The argument is that it would react to the danger of high inflation but not necessarily to overshooting of its reference value for monetary growth. Begg *et al.* (2002) show that the correlation between the money growth indicator used by the ECB and its interest rates decisions is not even equal to zero but rather it has the wrong sign; that is, in times when monetary growth was higher than the reference value, the ECB actually lowered interest rates. Therefore, as the ECB will react to a rise in expected inflation but not to abundant money growth, it seems already to act as having one pillar only. To end confusion regarding its strategy, it should officially declare this.

Another source of confusion is the strategy itself. The ECB is said to pretend that both pillars point in the same direction (Gros, 2001). It can therefore revert to either of the two pillars to justify interest rate changes (see also Eijffinger, 2001b). While one of its predecessors, the Bundesbank, had enough credibility to regularly ignore the data on monetary growth, the ECB has not (yet). Ignoring monetary growth or justifying it in an inconsistent way only increases confusion and uncertainty (Mazier, 2001). Finally, potential conflict between the two pillars exists as the one could point towards increasing inflationary pressure while the other could point in the other direction (Bofinger, 1999). As it is not clear what weights are given to the two pillars, this only adds to the confusion that already exists. In this case nobody has even the faintest idea what pillar the ECB will let prevail. It is clear that this increases the degree of uncertainty already associated with the ECB by many observers. On another note, it is questionable whether the M3 is a good indicator at all (see, for example, De La Dehesa, 2001, Mazier, 2001).[5]

Svensson (2000) has suggested that experience from a majority of countries shows that shifts in the money demand function in the long run are not uncommon and therefore may occur again any time, although he admits that there is some evidence that the long-run money demand for the Euro area is stable. Even without these shifts the existing correlation between money growth and inflation is often misunderstood, according to Svensson (2002), because, as the two variables are endogenous variables, nothing can be said about the direction of causality. Even if one was to allow for inclusion of some monetary target, the ECB is said to be using the wrong one, as it has been shown by Svensson (2000, 2002) that the real money gap is the target to use instead of the currently used nominal money-growth indicator.[6] The ECB seems to have taken note of these results (Issing, 1999a) but does not appear to act on it.[7] Finally there has also been confusion about how to interpret the M3 growth figures (Mazier, 2001). This confusion makes statistical corrections like the one on 10 May 2001, no matter how justifiable they may be, nullify the very reason why the first pillar exists, namely its transparency (Gros, 2001).

Members of the panel of experts and of ECON are unanimous in presenting the solution: a combination of the first and second pillar in one pillar only, de facto abolishing the first pillar.[8] This would make monetary policy decisions less confusing and easier to explain and would therefore enhance credibility of the ECB. A nominal anchor should not be monetary growth but flexible inflation forecast targeting[9] (Svensson, 2000). Monetary growth would then be reduced to *an* indicator instead of being *the* indicator, as monetary growth does contain relevant information, but it is questionable whether it deserves such a prominent role (Bofinger, 1999). Svensson (2000) rejects the argument that this change, or any change in monetary policy strategy of a central bank for that matter, would negatively affect credibility. On the contrary, it would, in his view, most likely improve it.

Finally, the monetary policy strategy of the ECB is still seen as the combination of monetary targeting and inflation targeting, whereby the first pillar is marked as being a monetary target and the second as an inflation target. This is illustrated by views from both ECON and the panel of experts. Bean (1999), for example, has described the second pillar as 'not a million miles away from a formal inflation target', while one of the members of ECON, Giorgos Katiforis, referred to it as 'a lot of words for an inflation target'. The ECB sticks to its line that the stability-oriented monetary policy strategy is 'neither monetary nor inflation targeting, not even a mixture of these two approaches well known to observers' (Issing, 1999a). Duisenberg has on several occasions during past monetary dialogues stated that the fact that inflation is ultimately, in the long run, a monetary phenomenon is one of the reasons why money should have, and in case of the ECB does have, a prominent role in monetary policy strategy, even with those central banks that officially have adopted inflation targeting, i.e. targeting a certain range of inflation as their strategy. Moreover, assigning this prominent role to money growth is not the same as monetary targeting. Monetary targeting involves some target rate for the growth of a certain monetary aggregate. The ECB, however, does not have a *target* growth rate for M3 but rather a *reference value*, meaning that it compares the money growth of M3 with the reference value and tries to explain the possible deviation in order to check whether that deviation constitutes any danger for price stability. It analyses the deviation to see whether there is any danger to price stability, then does the same within its second pillar, cross-checks the results and then takes a decision whether or not to change its short-term interest rates. So far, the ECB has rejected calls that it should adopt inflation targeting (see Issing, 2002).

Primary and Secondary Objective and the Definition of Price Stability

Although price stability is the primary objective of the ECB, its very name implies that there is also a secondary objective to be observed. Even before the start of the analysis of the monetary dialogues one expects ECON, being a political body, to show a special interest in the secondary objective of the ECB because, as Wyplosz (2000) stated, 'price stability is highly desirable, but so is economic growth and full employment'. Therefore it is not surprising that this issue was raised in every monetary dialogue, with an absolute peak on 12 September 2001, a day after the terrorist attacks on New York. In this monetary dialogue the attention was almost exclusively concentrated on the immediate effect on the economy and the role of, among others, the monetary authority.

The ECB has from the beginning defined its primary objective but has failed, in the view of ECON, to do the same for its secondary objective. This in turn is said to have diminished transparency and made it even harder for the markets and the public to read the ECB. Furthermore, the ECB is seen to be too hawkish on inflation. On one occasion it has even been suggested that the general view in Europe is that the ECB causes lower growth and higher unemployment, as interest rates are said to be too high, hindering investment in the Euro area. Finally, the very definition of price stability is said to be too rigid, focusing too much on inflation and making it virtually impossible for the central bank to pursue its secondary objective. This definition of price stability could hurt employment because a rise in output is likely to lead to inflation pressures, which in turn would mean that interest rates will rise, leading to lower output and eventually lower employment. Apart from the view that having such a narrow band makes it difficult to achieve price stability, at the same time it prevents the ECB from lowering its interest rates in times when economic growth slows and more expansionary monetary policy is needed (Fitoussi, 2001).

The ECB rejects the criticism that is has not defined its secondary objective, pointing to its regular statements that the best monetary policy can do to support growth and employment is to achieve and maintain price stability. This definition is rejected on the grounds that monetary policy does have an effect on real variables in the short term, of which fact the Fed is a good example (see, for example, Horn, 2001; Gros, 1999b; Bofinger, 1999). In practice it is found that the ECB is not overly concerned by the fact that it has missed its target in its first years of existence (Wyplosz, 2001b). It also appears to accommodate temporary shocks, as can be derived from the fact that interest rates do not differ from the levels that would result if the Taylor rule was used,[10] meaning in fact that its monetary policy in practice is much more in line with the Maastricht Treaty than what would be expected from its conceptual framework (Bofinger, 1999). It is not hard to see that this, although it might be welcomed, negatively affects the credibility of the ECB, as it in fact means that the ECB does not do what it says it will do; that is, its deeds do not match its words.

Forecasts

The third most often mentioned subject in monetary dialogues concerns the publication of forecasts prepared by the ECB that are used in the decision-making process. ECON has called for publication of these forecasts because it would help to understand monetary policy of the ECB properly and because it would give a clearer picture of the strategy and the horizon of monetary policy. As Bean (1999) describes it, the problem with the ECB is that it does not reveal in a transparent manner how all the various indicators that it looks at are implicitly aggregated together in reaching a final decision.

The ECB refused to publish forecasts based on a number of arguments, the main one of which is that publishing an inflation forecast would send the message that a complex, thorough and comprehensive analysis of various indicators carried out by the governing council can be summarized in a single number. Furthermore, the general public might misinterpret this figure and see it as the target, implying that it would expect the ECB to react mechanistically,[11] which in turn would not be consistent with the ECB's principle of clarity as eventually it would 'obscure rather than clarify what the Governing Council is actually doing' (Duisenberg, 1998).

CHANGES AT THE ECB AND THE ANALYSIS

We have used ECB press releases and press conferences to find out what changes the ECB had implemented in previous years (up to 31 July 2002). In chronological order, they include, first, further enhancement of the transparency policy. On 13 April 1999 the governing council announced that,

> with a view to further enhancing the ECB's transparency policy, the Governing Council has today decided to publish all non-confidential legal instruments governing the relationship between the ECB and the euro area national central banks in the *Official Journal of the European Communities* . . . The members of the Governing Council regard the transparency of the decision-making process as an appropriate means by which to strengthen the democratic nature of the institution and to increase the public's confidence in its administration.

Second, there were changes regarding communication strategy. Up to 15 July 1999, the ECB had somewhat modified its communication strategy, reacting to the criticism that the message conveyed by members of the governing council could be and has been interpreted in various ways, making it difficult to read the central bank. As a reaction, the ECB increasingly started speaking with one voice, trying as hard as possible to communicate one message, even if through many mouths – despite the obvious linguistic problems, for example. Furthermore, it agreed, and communicated this very strongly, that when changes in monetary policy were apparent the markets should listen only to the president. Moreover the ECB, according to the president and the vice president, 'changed the tone of the assessment and its presentation' starting from 15 July 1999.

Third, there was the replacement of fixed rate tenders with variable rate tenders. On 8 June 2000, the governing council decided to conduct the main refinancing operations of the Eurosystem by using variable rate tender, applying the multiple rate auction procedure.

Fourth, the ECB published staff economic projections. In June 2000 it was announced that, starting from December 2000, the ECB would publish its staff economic projections for, among others, real GDP growth and HICP (Harmonized Index of Consumer Prices). Finally, the decision was made to assess monetary policy once a month instead of twice a month. In November 2001, the governing council of the ECB decided effectively to halve the number of meetings in which it assesses monetary policy. This decision was induced by the impression the council had that a relatively high frequency (compared to the Fed, for example) amplified speculation in the markets and led to higher volatility in interest rates and exchange rates. By assessing monetary policy stance once a month, the ECB also enabled itself to devote its second meeting each month to other tasks and responsibilities of the ESCB, such as supervision.

The next question to examine is, given these changes, how did ECON perform in past years? We will examine this by relating the changes listed above to the changes ECON requested. Some of these requested changes were outlined in the European Parliament's resolution on the annual report for 1998 of the European Central Bank, adopted on 27 October 1999, based on the report of the ECON (Report A5–0035/1999). In this report the Committee called on the ECB:[12]

1. to publish a summary of minutes taken at the meetings of the ECB governing council,
2. to publish macroeconomic forecasts on a six-monthly basis,
3. to publish a regular overall report of economic developments in each of the participating Euro area countries,
4. to make publicly available on an annual basis econometric models of the Euro area economy and the global economy used at the ECB, and
5. to make clear how monetary policy is intended, as long as the objective of price stability is maintained, to contribute to a balanced and appropriate policy mix, with a view to promoting sustainable growth and employment.

In addition, two other criteria will be included, based on the outcomes of the analysis of the papers from the panel of experts and the monetary dialogues:

6. to abolish the first pillar of the stability-oriented monetary policy strategy and adopt inflation targeting. For an in depth discussion of this monetary policy strategy see Svensson (1999).
7. to relax the existing definition of price stability.

After relating changes that have been implemented to the seven criteria above, we derive two seemingly contradictory conclusions. First, the ECB has fulfilled three out of the seven criteria, namely criteria 2, 4 and 5. The second conclusion that we can derive from our analysis is that, with regard to criteria 2 and 5, the ECB has not met the requirements in full. This is an interesting point to observe. One explanation could be that the ECB intentionally did this in order to avoid the impression that its independence is endangered; that is, that it heeds the calls of some political body. The first conclusion is based on the fact that the ECB has published its economic projections (criterion 2) and econometric models (criterion 4) and stated that the best contribution monetary policy can make to a balanced and appropriate policy mix, with a view to promoting sustainable growth and employment, is to achieve and maintain price stability in the Euro area (criterion 5). After examination of criteria 2 and 5 in more detail we derive the second conclusion.[13]

Publication of staff economic projections has come under severe criticism from the panel of experts and ECON (see, for example, Svensson, 2001). Although it met the wish of the European Parliament by publishing projections for all requested variables, from the very beginning the ECB made it clear that these projections should not be confused with forecasts. It devalued its projections at the same time as these were published for the first time by stating that they 'do not cover all the information pertaining to the second pillar and do not take into account the information relating to the analysis under the first pillar of the ECB's monetary policy strategy. From this perspective, the staff projections play a useful but limited role in the strategy' (ECB, 2000).

With regard to the fifth criterion, ECON would have wanted to hear from the ECB how it sees its secondary objective, as described in Article 105 of the Treaty, involving some definition, as in the case of the primary objective. The ECB has responded to this on numerous occasions, however, by stating that the best way monetary policy can contribute to the goals described in Article 105 is to achieve and maintain price stability. It should be noted that strict interpretation of this statement means that, by achieving the primary objective, the ECB simultaneously also achieves its secondary objective. This in turn means that its secondary objective is in fact not a separate objective but rather only a derivative of the primary one.

The ECB itself cannot be praised for having been very consistent with its remarks on this subject, adding to uncertainty that already existed. During monetary dialogue on 18 January 1999, president Duisenberg stated that, once price stability is achieved, one should not 'change track and focus on other things, in the interest of economic policy in general. Our aim is not only to have price stability but also to maintain it'. Just a couple of months later, in April 1999, the ECB lowered its key interest rate by 50 base points, after the analysis showed that the major risk at that time was that the expectations regarding real economic developments were for a downturn. According to Duisenberg, this made it possible for the ECB to 'pay due attention to the secondary objective of monetary policy of the ECB'.

We would like once again to point to the fact that the ECB's interest rates have behaved as if the Taylor rule was being practised. This means that either the ECB is right and its actions geared towards achieving price stability do indeed help achieve its secondary objective or the ECB is informally looking at the size of the output gap and setting its interest rates accordingly. If the first explanation is the right one, there are no consequences and the ECB should maintain its practice. However, if the second is true, the credibility of the ECB will be seriously damaged and a strong case could be made for more transparency, including publication of minutes of meetings, despite the already stated disadvantages.

We have mentioned and discussed all the criteria above with the exception of criteria 3 (publication of a regular overall report of economic developments in each of the participating Euro area countries) and 6 (abolishing the first pillar and adoption of inflation targeting). On both we can be brief. With regard to criterion 3, Duisenberg, during monetary dialogue in November 2000, stated very clearly that 'the ECB is not a forecasting agency but a central bank . . . we take a look at the Euro area, not at individual countries', meaning that projections for individual countries will not be published by the ECB. Concerning the first pillar of the ECB's monetary policy strategy, after analysis of monetary dialogues there is absolutely nothing one could see as an indication that the first pillar will be abolished. Therefore we conclude that the ECB is holding strongly to this and that change in this matter is not to be expected in the near future. This does not mean that change regarding the first pillar, one might say the holy of holies of the ECB, should be ruled out. It simply means that, on the basis of the analysis of the monetary dialogues, there are no clues indicating change in this aspect. What the impact of the likely entrance of the Sveriges Riksbank and Bank of England, both inflation targeters, will be remains of course unknown. But this structural change, and we can easily perceive this to be one, could very well have an impact even on the first pillar.

In Table 6.3 we have given a total overview of the monetary dialogue 'transmission mechanism'. In the third column the ECB's reply is given as one of the following: 'yes', 'no' and 'unknown'. The criterion as to what to enter each time was the reply given by the ECB in the question-and-answer sessions of the monetary dialogue after the first time the ECON mentioned each subject (immediate response). This method allows us to monitor and detect change(s) at the ECB, as we can compare the final answer (change implemented or to be implemented) with the initial position. The third option 'unknown' was introduced to cope with the fact that often the reply cannot be classified as 'yes' or a 'no'. For each of the subjects the entries are based on the following elements.

Table 6.3   Reaction of the ECB to subjects discussed

Subjects, panel of experts[a]	Subjects, ECON[b]	ECB reply	Change	Success
Monetary policy strategy[c]	Monetary policy strategy	no	−	n.a. (not applicable)
			−	
The secondary objective	The secondary objective	no	+	+
Definition of price stability	Definition of price stability	no	−	n.a.
Minutes of meetings	Minutes of meetings	no	−	n.a.
Forecasts	Forecasts	no	+	+
	Econometric models	unknown	+	+
	Report of economic development for each Euro area country	no	−	n.a.

Notes:
[a] These subjects have been taken from Table 6.1, the only change being that the last two subjects that were mentioned apart in Table 6.1 are aggregated here under one heading (forecasts).
[b] Subjects appearing in this column are the criteria mentioned earlier.
[c] This subject concerns mainly (but not exclusively) the critique on the first pillar of the ECB's monetary policy strategy.

As the ECB views inflation as a monetary phenomenon, it has no intention to abolish its first pillar and has stated this on several occasions. Therefore for this subject a 'no' has been entered. As for the secondary objective, the given entry is based on the comment by the president of the ECB, made during the 18 January 1999 monetary dialogue, that the ECB should not change tack and stimulate the economy once it has achieved price stability. Regarding the following two subjects, based on comments made by the president during various monetary dialogues, for each subject a 'no' has been entered. With regard to the forecasts, the entry is based on EMI (1997), on page 16 of which inflation forecasts are rejected because of the difficulties in producing them, their adverse effects on financial markets and wage and price setting and of their possible harming effects for the ECB's credibility. In the case of the sixth subject (publication of econometric models), the entry 'unknown' has been used because this subject was not mentioned during any of the monetary dialogues up to October 1999, when resolution A5-0035/1999 was adopted. As an alternative, one could view this subject as a precondition for forecasts (fifth subject) as these must be based on some econometric model. Thus, if we see the fifth and the sixth subject as complementary, we would be inclined to replace 'unknown' with 'no' in this case. Applying this procedure, however, does not affect the final outcome of the analysis, as in this particular case 'unknown' is de facto treated as a 'no' for the purposes of the success rate (see below). Finally, a 'no' in the case of country reports is the interpretation of the comment made by the president during the November 2000 monetary dialogue (see previous section).

In the fourth column, a '+' was entered if the ECB had changed its arrangement and procedures with regard to each subject up to July 2002 (delayed response). A minus sign represents the no-change situation. These signs were given according to the results of the analysis from the first part of this chapter.

Finally, the fifth column defines whether ECON has been successful in its attempts to induce change(s) within the ECB regarding each subject. The procedure we used here is as follows: + has been entered in those cases where the ECB had taken a decision to implement change(s) with regard to each particular subject *within two years of the particular subject being mentioned for the first time by ECON in the question-and-answer sessions.* Otherwise a − or N.A. has been entered. To determine whether a decision was taken, the same procedure as in the first section of this chapter was applied. By definition, in this column plus signs are given only to those subjects which have a plus sign in the fourth column.

After applying this procedure a measurement, 'success rate' was calculated to be 42.9 per cent. This measurement provides a way to assess the performance of ECON. The success rate is calculated by dividing the number of pluses from the fifth column by the number of subjects raised by ECON as reported in column two. We can also calculate the success rate for the panel of experts by comparing the first and the fifth columns. This procedure yields a success rate of 40 per cent.

Two final points remain to be made in relation to Table 6.3. First, as will be shown later on, there are some changes that we can expect to occur in the near future in the field of communication policy (publication of minutes) and the primary objective (definition of price stability). This aspect was not accounted for in the above overview table based on the simple fact that, although there are some indications that changes are to occur, in practice and formally nothing has been changed to this day. However, it should be noted that, if and when the minutes become published and the definition of price stability changes, the success rate of ECON (and of the panel of experts, which would reach an amazing 80 per cent) will be higher provided that the definition we used here for 'success' is properly adapted to new circumstances. Second, given the fact that every subject that has been mentioned by the panel is also mentioned by ECON, this strongly indicates that the transmission from the panel of experts to ECON is equal to 100 per cent. In addition, and supporting this strong correlation, during monetary dialogues members of ECON have regularly referred directly to the briefing papers of the members of the panel of experts. From this we conclude that the panel's contribution to monetary dialogue is very important. It might even be stated that without it ECON would most certainly be much less effective.

Taking into account the above conclusions, is there anything that might be expected in the near future? There are several significant events that will happen in the not-so-distant future, such as the personnel changes within both the executive board and the governing council and the possible entrance of the United Kingdom and Sweden into the Euro area. It is possible that these events will have some impact on the internal procedures and arrangements of the ECB. Although this question might be interesting, it goes beyond the scope of this chapter to investigate possible effects of these changes, so attention will be focused on investigating whether any changes might be expected in light of the analysis of the monetary dialogues.

After careful analysis of the transcripts of question-and-answer sessions of the monetary dialogues, strong clues have been found indicating possible changes with regard to the criteria 1 (publication of minutes) and 7 (the definition of price stability).

Publication of Minutes

While in November 2000 Duisenberg strongly rejected any change with regard to publication of minutes by saying that 'We [the ECB] do not intend to meet that wish of the European Parliament', during the May 2002 monetary dialogue – when on one occasion the working of the governing council after future enlargement of the Euro area was discussed and publication of minutes was again mentioned – he did not exclude the possibility that, as the governing council would become even larger, voting would occur and become normal procedure and that, 'as a consequence, also . . . the so-called anonymous balance of votes might be published'. The possibility that minutes would be published increased recently when Lucas Papademos, the vice president of the ECB, on this subject remarked that the change of view in the governing council 'could be reflected in the publication of anonymous votes. This could provide an additional signal to the markets about prospects of changes in the monetary policy' and 'personally I would not feel that I would lose my independence if votes were to be announced in a group sense' (European Parliament, 2002), which in essence goes fully against one of the ECB's main arguments against publishing minutes and/or balance of votes. More importantly, this comment shows that 18 members of the governing council do not seem to have the same opinion on this subject.

Price Stability Definition

There is also a gradual change to be discovered, similar to that related to the publication of minutes. In the monetary dialogue of June 2000, Duisenberg stated that changing the definition of price stability would be 'a disaster' because it could give a signal that the ECB did not care about inflation any longer and that this issue is 'something that I categorically am inclined to withstand and to deny and I will not co-operate in this aspect'. Just a couple of months later, during the September 2000 monetary dialogue, he seems to have started paving the way for possible change as he indicated that change is possible, saying that, 'if the definition were to be changed it will be discussed fully in public and in no way would that infringe on the independence of the central bank, because ultimately it would still be the General Council of the ECB which takes the decision . . . However, it would be too early to change it now'. The door for change was opened even further[14] during the March 2001 monetary dialogue, where Duisenberg relaxed his strong original statement that he would 'not co-operate', saying 'I do not think there is a *need* to redefine price stability.'

The 'need to redefine price stability' might not be there yet in his view, given that the ECB might in time to come succeed in bringing inflation safely under the 2 per cent ceiling, that the views of members of the governing council might differ also with regard to this subject and that this definition is somewhat odd compared to that of other major central banks; with some of them being probable future members of the Eurosystem, any change in the future most likely would not damage the credibility of the

ECB. This means that one of the main arguments against changing of the definition would be taken away, paving the way for a new definition.

This gradual change can be noted also with regard to the forecasts which were eventually published. In 1998, Duisenberg commented that forecasts would 'obscure rather than clarify what the Governing Council is actually doing' (in relation to this, recall also arguments against their publication given in EMI, 1997). In April 1999, during that quarter's monetary dialogue, he made a comment that 'There will also come a moment – it is too early now but I personally have no doubt that there will come a moment – when we also, like many other institutions, will publish our forecasts . . . but in such a way that they will never become self-fulfilling prophecies.'

This was a first indication that some changes regarding this issue could be expected in the future. Again, some six months later, in October 1999, in his presentation of the ECB's Annual Report before the European Parliament, Duisenberg remarked that the forecasts would be made public in the course of the following year. In November 2000, before ECON, he finally announced that the ECB has decided to publish what it calls *economic projections for the Euro area*. ECON called the publication of economic projections 'a first step towards greater transparency' (European Parliament, 2000) and warned the ECB that they will first look at the publication and determine how satisfactory the projections are and that they 'will have to be refined and improved over the coming year so that they become economic forecasts in the true sense of the word'.

RECOMMENDATIONS

Both ECON and the ECB could make an effort to meet some of the criticism without compromising the ECB's current arrangements. We would recommend to ECON to demand that the ECB stick to its statute and to take a formal vote each time it meets, even if during its meetings it becomes clear that consensus can be reached. In this case, the argument that voting behavior cannot be revealed as voting had not taken place would not be applicable any more, making it possible to press for minutes. Second, when restructuring the ECB's general council, the initiative for this should not be left exclusively in the hands of the ECB. ECON should insist on setting up some sort of monetary policy committee. The reason is that the individual members of the governing council in that case would not share collective responsibility. This would also make it possible to build a stronger case for publication of minutes (this interesting point is mentioned in Hämäläinen, 2001).

It is a fact that one of the main reasons for ECON wanting minutes of the meetings is to be able to say something about the direction of monetary policy actions and that this wish is shared by the general public (as illus-trated in press conferences). In order to do this, without having to publish its minutes of meetings, we advise the ECB to start indicating, after every meeting at which it assesses the stance of monetary policy, whether it has a neutral, tightening or relaxing bias, similar to what the Fed has been prac-tising for some time. In this way, it would eliminate the most important reason ECON has to call for publication of minutes, while at the same time avoiding the negative consequences of publishing minutes and increasing the transparency and credibility of the monetary authority.

MONETARY DIALOGUE COMPARED TO THE HUMPHREY–HAWKINS TESTIMONIES

Monetary dialogue seems to serve the same purpose as the Humphrey–Hawkins testimonies in the United States. However, we feel obliged to point out some differences between the two. Apart from the obvious difference in frequency, with testimonies of the chairman of the Fed taking place bian-nually, while the monetary dialogue in the EU is a quarterly exercise, there are others. There is the fact that the preparation for monetary dialogue is far more intensive and in-depth than the preparation for the hearings in the USA. ECON has a panel of experts who advise it on what subjects to discuss with the ECB. In addition, ECON holds separate sessions with members of the panel of experts in order to discuss various issues in depth. Furthermore, the Humphrey–Hawkins testimonies have been forced upon the Fed by the Full Employment and Balanced Growth Act of 1978 (also known as the Humphrey–Hawkins Act).

The ECB and ECON on the other side have agreed that the president of the ECB would appear before ECON every quarter to discuss monetary policy of the ECB. One possible consequence could be that the Fed takes a somewhat more reserved stance during these hearings than the ECB during monetary dialogue. This is seen also in the form of questions presented to each central bank. The chairman of the Fed is faced with general questions on, for example, what the Fed can do about unemployment in a random constituency, to which he cannot present a simple but true answer, 'nothing'. Instead, he has to elaborate in order to give the members of the Congress the feeling of importance. The ECB, on the other hand, is faced with much more specific questions, fully supported by valid, academic arguments. Another important difference concerns the broader issue of the relationship between the US Congress and the Fed and ECON and the ECB. As Akhtar and Howe (1991) point out, the Congress has continuously challenged and debated the Fed's independence, trying to strengthen political control over the Fed. ECON, on the other hand, never took (or indicated that it might take) any steps that would jeopardize the ECB's independence. Finally, when we look at these testimonies of both central banks from the standpoint of accountability and transparency, we find that transcripts of monetary dialogue sessions are readily available on the home page of the European Parliament. In contrast, transcripts of the Humphrey–Hawkins testimonies are published with some delay.

CONCLUSION

There exists a relationship between politics and monetary policy. As human beings represent both, there is always some mutual influence between the two. This is only natural as it is inherent in our nature that we try to influence the behavior of others or, while taking decisions, take into account the possible effects on our surroundings. This certainly applies to central banks, which, by altering their interest rates, influence the lives of millions of people simultaneously. At the same time, it has become conventional wisdom that, regarding monetary policy, we cannot trust politicians and that it is therefore optimal to delegate powers in this field to an independent central bank. In order to comply with our democratic principles, the central bank must be held accountable through elected representatives. In this chapter we have looked at one of the, in many ways, specific relationships, namely that between the ECB and the European Parliament. This study was performed in order to answer the question whether it might be said that the European Parliament, through its relationship with it, in fact influences the ECB and, if so, what can be said about that finding.

With regard to the subjects raised by the panel of experts in briefing papers and in monetary dialogues by ECON, we conclude that both the panel and ECON have raised similar issues with the ECB. After establishing that ECON and the panel have similar points of criticism regarding the ECB, we have investigated whether the ECB had implemented any changes in its procedures and arrangements so far. Analysis of its press releases and press conferences led to the conclusion that, indeed, some changes were implemented. In order to investigate whether there is a relationship with monetary dialogue, these changes were compared to the list of changes ECON has suggested that the ECB implement.

In view of changes already implemented, we can conclude that the ECB has met three out of seven specifically defined wishes expressed by ECON. In terms of the success ratio calculated earlier the performance of ECON has been successful in 42.9 per cent of the cases. In addition, two other facts have been noted. First, with regard to those wishes that were met, the ECB did not always fully comply with the structure or form asked for by ECON. It can be said that the required form or structure simply was impossible to realize because of the lack of (credible) data and that great uncertainty also played a major role. On the other hand, the impression also exists that the ECB could have acted as it did deliberately in order to avoid giving the impression that it was influenced by others. The only way to exclude one of these possibilities would be to take a look at the minutes of the meetings of the governing council, as explicit statements or clues might be found in them. Not having access to these (yet) prevents the exclusion of either possibility at present.

Second, from detailed analysis of the transcripts of the question-and-answer sessions of each monetary dialogue, and of the ECB's press conferences over the years, we noted that the ECB seems to provide indications of changes that are to come. This is demonstrated by the publication of forecasts. In this case the ECB hinted on several occasions that these eventually would be published. Extrapolating from this finding and, assuming that the ECB's behavior in this aspect will remain unchanged (and there is no evidence that this assumption is false – on the contrary, given the fact that the ECB's goal is to increase its transparency, this assumption might even be considered conservative), we might witness more changes in the future. This especially applies to the publication of minutes and the change in the definition of price stability, which essentially also includes the secondary objective of the ECB, as its room for maneuver would increase with the adoption of some broader definition. With regard to the former, both ECON and the ECB could make it possible to achieve greater transparency and enhance understanding and credibility of the ECB, while preventing negative side-effects, regarding the independence of the central bank and/or its existing credibility.

Finally, we can also say that there will most probably be some effect as the Euro area expands, certainly if and when the United Kingdom and Sweden adopt the Euro, but we cannot point out exactly what this effect will be and in what degree it will facilitate further changes within the ECB.

On the basis of this research we conclude that the ECB has showed a high degree of responsiveness to criticism, or in other words, that there is some degree of influence running from Brussels to Frankfurt. It is important to note that, although the word 'influence' has been used here, it should not be interpreted as meaning that the ECB is, or has been, put under formal pressure. The next question is whether it can be concluded that it is only ECON that influences the ECB. If we define ECON (and therefore the European Parliament) in a broad sense as being the body representing citizens of the Euro area and assume that its preferences reflect those of European voters, a valid assumption as the European Parliament is elected by public ballot, then the answer is definitely positive. If we look at ECON itself (thus in a narrow sense), this implies that other variables, such as other pressure groups, have been omitted. This, however, does not impair the validity of the analysis and results, as there is some evidence that, regarding the amount of pressure from other interest groups, the ECB is in a comfortable position (Maier, 2001).

So far, evidence shows that the member states generally have refrained from putting a great deal of pressure on the ECB. This could be because the ECB firmly defied calls for lower interest rates that were raised on occasion and took a tough stance on this. On the other hand, it could also be because the politicians in the Euro area acknowledge that the ECB is still young and creating credibility is of the utmost importance for the success of the monetary union. As the creation of this union was a political deed, this could also explain the relatively moderate pressure on the ECB. Thus, as these other variables can safely be ignored, the same answer as before applies; that is, we may conclude that it is in fact ECON that influences the ECB. Even though we cannot fully exclude other factors, the European Parliament seems to remain the most important one. One could criticize this finding by arguing that the European Parliament, although democratically elected, does not have much political influence, compared, for example, to the ECOFIN Council. We think that political influence of the European Parliament has increased over recent years, certainly since the European Commission led by Santer was forced to resign. Granted, the European Parliament does not have the influence or the role of the US Congress, but, regarding the issue of holding the ECB accountable, it has shown itself to be more mature than its counterpart in the USA. We might say that, owing to the fact that it has chosen a typical European approach to holding its central bank accountable and the fact that it goes to considerable lengths to prepare the monetary dialogues as thoroughly as possible, the role and influence of the European Parliament certainly has increased during past years.

Still, one final and crucial question remains to be answered: does the conclusion that the European Parliament influences the ECB in some degree mean that the ECB is not as independent as its legal status implies? On the basis of our research, and having analysed numerous related documents (such as speeches by ECB officials), we are convinced that it does not as, first, the ECB's independence is firmly anchored in the Maastricht Treaty, which can be changed only after all signatory parties agree to this. Therefore, there is, legally speaking, nothing to prevent the ECB disregarding calls for any change whatsoever. The empirical results on independence of various central banks, where the ECB emerges as the most independent central bank in the world, support this view. Second, the ECB has on numerous occasions stated that it wants to increase transparency and to become easier to read, indicating that it does not rule out any changes even if others propose them. Third, the ECB has repeatedly stated that it views its relationship with the European Parliament as very useful and productive, and never as possibly dangerous to its independent status. Finally, in taking decisions, the ECB generally takes ample time, indicating that it is weighing all the pros and cons with due consideration. Ultimately, each decision is taken by and under full responsibility of the ECB and it is not forced upon it. So, taking all these factors into consideration, one thing should be pointed out: the ECB has shown a healthy attitude so far, indicating that it can deal with criticism and that it acknowledges the fact that it can learn from it. This not only does not endanger its independence, it increases the trust and credibility the ECB needs.

We have deliberately focused on issues regarding accountability, communication policy, procedures and arrangements, that is, monetary policy in a broad sense, and have not investigated whether monetary policy actions themselves were influenced by the criticism from ECON or by other factors, such as financial markets. Although we are under the strong impression that in this aspect the ECB has operated in a fully independent manner, further scientific research on this subject is needed in order to complete the picture of complex relationships regarding monetary economics in the Euro area.

Finally, regarding transparency or, more specifically, comments made by members of the decision-making bodies of the ECB, we would strongly advise the ECB's officials to stop giving mixed messages. Analysts around the globe are watching and analysing every aspect of the ECB and the success or failure of its (monetary policy) actions, in some part at least, depends on how well it is understood and read by the markets and the public. In addition to the fact that this central bank is young, which somewhat complicates its sincere efforts to be transparent and readily understood, the ECB itself, intentionally or not, is at the same time frustrating this process by sending out a range of mixed messages on various subjects and changing its remarks relatively frequently. President Duisenberg has on several occasions made remarks that are completely the opposite of his earlier comments. For a central bank that puts a high value on transparency, and attempts to increase it, this behavior is certainly eccentric. Should it persist, there is the dangerous possibility that it could impede the efforts to increase the transparency of the ECB. Granted, in its communications the ECB faces unique, great and challenging difficulties, but this does not make improvements impossible. The ECB has shown that it can cope with far greater challenges. The very reason for its existence, the third stage of the EMU, is a good example. ECON can play a major role here by alerting the ECB to this problem and calling for changes.

The importance of the European Parliament will increase even further in the near future as by then we will have reached the 'medium term', no matter how it is defined. This means that the European Parliament will be able to assess the performance of the ECB for the first time.

To conclude, we can, when referring to the monetary dialogue and on the strength of the results given above, call it a real dialogue and argue, albeit with hindsight, that the impression that 'Duisenberg is just repeating official positions' (Gros, 1999) is inaccurate, as these 'official positions' have a tendency to change, thanks to the European Parliament. The intensity of the monetary dialogue and the importance it has both for ECON and for the ECB fit perfectly in a world in which there is a still-growing need for accountability and transparency. Recent developments in the USA involving ENRON and Worldcom, for example, have led to the introduction of new laws concerning corporate governance. As central banks have enormous powers but are led by technocrats and enjoy a high degree of independence, society is calling for more accountability and transparency from them as well. The price to pay for being independent is apparently, and quite rightly we might add, the obligation to explain and give a full account of actions taken and their outcomes. The new laws introduced in the field of corporate governance therefore cannot be seen as standing on their own. They are a part of a wider need for accountability and transparency, not only from private corporations but also from the government, including the monetary authorities. In conclusion, this process of greater accountability and transparency should not stop at corporate governance but should enompasss governance in general.

We would hope that it will not take a scandal of ENRON proportions within the monetary policy world to find the weak spots, but rather that, regarding the European Union, the ECB and ECON will continue with their productive discussion, identifying possible improvements in order to maximize this need for transparency and accountability, without compromising the ECB's independent status.

NOTES

1. For a more detailed description of methodology used, see Mujagic (2002).
2. These other tasks are to conduct foreign exchange operations consistent with the provisions of Article 111 (ex Article 109) of the Maastricht Treaty; to hold and manage the official foreign reserves of the member states; and to promote the smooth operation of payment systems (ECB, 2001).
3. These criteria were constructed using Eijffinger and Geraats (2002).
4. Actually, 15 sessions have taken place during previous years. The monetary dialogue of 17 April 2000 was left out because the transcripts of this session are not available.
5. However, some empirical research shows that there is in fact a structural stability in European money demand function for M1 and M3 (Clausen and Kim, 2000). For a short

overview of research focusing on possible explanations for the supposed vanishing of the relationship between money and inflation, see Mujagic (2000).

6. The real money gap is the difference between the current real money stock (nominal money stock deflated by a commonly used inflation measure such as the consumer price index – CPI) and the real money stock that would result in a hypothetical long-run equilibrium, where y equals y^* and V equals V^* (velocity's long-run level).

7. Then again there is President Duisenberg's refusal to answer a question on the money gap because, in his words, 'I do not know precisely what a money gap is' (ECB press conference, 3 March 2002).

8. It is, however, interesting to note that there have been voices, mainly from Germany, that have called on the ECB to put monetary growth at the centre of its strategy, because the two-pillar strategy cannot be credible with markets, especially when the weights of the two pillars are not clear and change over time (Sachverständigenrat zur Begutachtung der gesamtwirtschaftlichen Entwicklung, 1999).

9. Meaning trying to achieve a prespecified target for expected inflation rate.

10. Taylor rule is a monetary policy rule that states that the nominal interest rate should be set using the equilibrium real interest rate: the rate of inflation over the previous year. The inflation objective and the output gap is given by:

$$i_t = r^{eq} + \pi_t + 0.5 \left[y_t + (\pi_t + \pi^*) \right]$$

where i_t is the nominal interest rate, r^{eq} is the equilibrium real interest rate, π_t is the inflation over the previous year, y_t is the output gap and π^* is the inflation objective. For more on the Taylor rule see Taylor, 1993.

11. This seems to be justified as even some members of ECON behave in this way. In September 2001, Abitbol raised concerns as 'one cannot understand that for two and a half years all the bank's forecasts have been wrong and you can still tell us . . . that these projections are going to be fine'. This is a perfect example of judging the ECB on something it does not have as an objective, in this case its forecasts.

12. The overview given here is highly simplified. For full version see Mujagic (2002).

13. The fourth criterion is left out as no criticism (or appraisal for that matter) was found specifically concerning econometric models. This might be the consequence of their detailed and rather technical nature.

14. However, to confuse things even further, during the press conference on 7 June 2002, Duisenberg stated that the ECB 'is not thinking of changing our definition of price stability'.

REFERENCES

Akhtar, M.A. and H. Howe (1991), 'The Political and Institutional Independence of the U.S. Monetary policy', *Banca Nazionale del Lavoro Quarterly Review*, 178: 343–89.

Bean, C. (1999), 'An Analysis of the ECB's Monetary Strategy and its Potential Contribution to Growth and Employment', Briefing paper for the Committee on Economic and Monetary Affairs of the European Parliament.

Begg, D., F. Canova, P. De Grauwe, A. Fatas and P.R. Lane (2002), 'Surviving the Slowdown', *Monitoring the European Central Bank*, Washington, DC: CEPR.

Bofinger, P. (1999), 'The Conduct of Monetary Policy by the European Central Bank according to article 105 of the Treaty versus the Real Economy', Briefing paper for the Monetary Subcommittee of the European Parliament.

Clausen, V. and J.-R. Kim (2000), 'The Long-Run Stability of European Money Demand', *Journal of Economic Integration*, 15(3): 486–505.

Dehesa, G. de la (2001), 'Is M3 a Useful Tool to Assess Price Stability?', Briefing paper for the Committee on Economic and Monetary Affairs of the European Parliament.

Duisenberg, W.F. (1998), 'The ESCB's Stability-oriented Monetary Policy Strategy', speech, 10 November.

ECB (2000), *Monthly Bulletin*, December: 6.

—— (2001), *The Monetary Policy of the ECB*, Frankfurt am Main: European Central Bank.

Eijffinger, S.C.W. (2001a), 'Should the ECB Governing Council Decide to Publish its Minutes of Meetings?', Briefing paper for the Committee on Economic and Monetary Affairs of the European Parliament.

—— (2001b), 'Should the European Central Bank Use M3 to Assess Price Stability?', Briefing paper for the Committee on Economic and Monetary Affairs of the European Parliament.

—— and P.M. Geraats (2002), 'How Transparent are Central Banks?', CEPR Discussion Paper No. 3188, Washington, DC.

European Monetary Institute (1997), *The Single Monetary Policy in Stage Three: Specification of the operational framework*, Frankfurt am Main: EMI.

Fitoussi, J.P. (2001), 'Economic and Monetary Conditions in the Euro Area: The ECB, the Fed and the Euro', Briefing paper for the Committee on Economic and Monetary Affairs of the European Parliament.

Gros, D. (1999), 'Improvement of the Democratic Accountability Process', Briefing Paper for the Committee on Economic and Monetary Affairs of the European Parliament.

—— (2001), 'The ECB's Unsettling Opaqueness', Briefing paper for the Committee on Economic and Monetary Affairs of the European Parliament.

—— and L.B. Smaghi (1999), 'Open Issues in European Central Banking', Centre for European Policy Studies, Brussels.

Hämäläinen, S. (2001), 'The ECB's Monetary Policy – Accountability, Transparency and Communication', speech, 14 September.

Horn, G.A. (2001), 'An Analysis of the ECB's Monetary Strategy and its Contribution to Growth and Employment', Briefing paper for the Committee on Economic and Monetary Affairs of the European Parliament, August.

Issing, O. (1999a), 'The Monetary Policy of the ECB in a World of Uncertainty', speech, 3–4 December.

—— (1999b), 'The Eurosystem: Transparent and Accountable, or "Willem in Euroland"', *Journal of Common Market Studies*, 37(3): 503–19.

—— (2002), 'ECB Watchers Conference: monetary policy and the role of the price stability definition', speech, 10 June.

Kydland, F.W. and E.C. Prescott (1977), 'Rules rather than Discretion: The Inconsistency of the Optimal Plans', *Journal of Political Economy*, 85(3): 473–91.

Maier, P. (2001), 'The Impact of Politics on Monetary Policy: A Study of the Bundes bank and Other Central Banks', Groningen, The Netherlands: Labyrint Publication.

Mazier, J. (2000), 'The Conduct of Monetary Policy and an Evaluation of the Economic Situation in Europe – 2nd Quarter 2000', Briefing paper for the Committee on Economic and Monetary Affairs of the European Parliament.

—— (2001), 'M3, Inflation and the ECB', Briefing paper for the Committee on Economic and Monetary Affairs of the European Parliament.

Mujagic, E. (2000), 'Monetary Targeting is Still the Best Monetary Policy', *Faces*, 2(3): 47–55.
—— (2002), 'Monetary Dialogue Between the European Central Bank and the European Parliament: Does it Influence Frankfurt?', thesis, Tilburg University.
Sachverständigenrat zur Begutachtung der gesamtwirtschaftlichen Entwicklung (1999), 'Wirtschaftspolitik unter Reformdruck', Wiesbaden.
Svensson, L.E.O. (1999), 'Inflation targeting as a monetary policy rule', *Journal of Monetary Economics*, 93: 607–54.
Svensson, L.E.O. (2000), 'What Is Wrong with the Eurosystem's Money-growth Indicator and What Should the Eurosystem do about it?', Briefing paper for the Committee on Economic and Monetary Affairs of the European Parliament.
—— (2001), 'What Is Good and What Is Bad with the Eurosystem's Published Forecasts and How Can They be Improved?', Briefing paper for the Committee on Economic and Monetary Affairs of the European Parliament.
—— (2002), 'A Reform of the Eurosystem's Monetary Policy Strategy is Increasingly Urgent', Briefing paper for the Committee on Economic and Monetary Affairs of the European Parliament.
Taylor, J.B. (1993), 'Discretion versus policy rules in practice', *Carnegie-Rochester Conference Series on Public Policy*, 38: 195–214.
Wyplosz, C. (2000), 'Briefing notes to the Committee for Economic and Monetary Affairs of the European Parliament', the third quarter of 2000.
—— (2001a), 'The ECB Communication Strategy', Briefing paper for the Committee on Economic and Monetary Affairs of the European Parliament.
—— (2001b), 'Briefing notes to the Committee for Economic and Monetary Affairs of the European Parliament', the first quarter of 2001.

7. Euro weakness and the ECB economic governance: a strategic institutionalist perspective

Miriam L. Campanella

INTRODUCTION

In transaction cost economics (Williamson, 1975; Ouchi, 1980; Perrow, 1981), economic governance is intended to be a remedial tool for market failures. Either when carried out by state-led institutions or when assigned to independent central agencies, mechanisms of economic governance are meant to restore the terms of market competition and (or) regulate the structure of property rights (North, 1981). European economic integration has given rise to a unique example of evolutionary economic governance generated by supranational institutions designed to deliver and monitor regulatory legislation in sensitive sectors of common interest, ranging from safety standards to market competition, which have normally been the exclusive province of national states.

This chapter argues that the ECB, a major EU-level institution designed to take charge of the Euro area monetary policy, has managed its monetary policy beyond the limit maintenance of price stability,[1] a major objective of its statutory assignments, keeping the Euro area interest rate policy in tune with macroeconomic responsibility. Whether this attitude developed from the objective rigidities of the European economy and the strictures of its fiscal policy, as some authors have argued (Begg *et al.*, 2002), or from the idiosyncrasy of the monetary area, which made it hard to pursue an inflation rate of less than 2 per cent, it is a matter of fact that the inflation reference value which the bank set as a self-defined target was not achieved. Further, the constant weakness of the Euro on exchange foreign markets (1999–2001) and the lack of an interventionist move signaled clearly its drive toward a pattern more concerned with the macroeconomic conditions of the Euro economic area than with the statutory objectives of its institution building – a pattern similar to the resilient model in use by the US Federal Reserve.

The ECB neglect vis-à-vis the Euro exchange rate on the forex market, with a loss of 25 per cent of its early value, and a constant inflation rate above 2 per cent in the Euro area led to the concern of many economists (such as Bergsten, 1997) that the ECB may have preferred to build up its own credibility to the detriment of Euro area economic growth.

The chapter's main argument is that there is some unambiguous evidence that during the period (1999–2002) the ECB acted as a major policy maker of the Euro area economic governance in spite of the fact that ECB institution building does not help it to satisfy such a role very fully. Because of its statutory constraints, the bank does not have the ability to react, or the promptness to switch its policy pattern enjoyed by US Federal Reserve or the Bank of England (Bini-Smaghi and Gros, 2000, p. 11).[2] Further, its monetary policy, which is based on a monetary growth benchmark (4.5 per cent yearly growth) and a loose reference value of the inflation rate (below 2 per cent on a yearly basis), is an obstacle to the bank pursuing a more activist policy (Gros, 2001). In spite of this, the ECB has followed a sensible and flexible policy while retaining the institutional and policy constraints of its statute, and has contributed greatly to benefiting Euro area GDP growth by about 3 per cent a year. The result has been achieved in spite of the political pressure of those who argued in favor of a 'target zone policy', fearing that the central bank was too eager to build up its own credibility and to match the success story of the German Bundesbank. The resistance of the ECB to a 'target zone policy' and its neglect vis-à-vis the exchange rate have succeeded in achieving the desired outcomes at negligible expense.[3]

The chapter's first section reviews some economic explanations of the Euro's weakness against the US dollar and finds that they cannot provide a completely satisfactory and appropriate explanation of the ECB's monetary policy making. After introducing the model of strategic institutionalism framed within the International Political Economy (IPE) theories, the chapter's second section works out a model of strategic institutionalism. The model applies especially to the ECB monetary policies which have hovered between too rigid commitments and a softer monetary stance. In the third section, there is an assessment of the benefits generated by a sliding Euro. The fourth section offers some conclusions.

THE EURO'S SLIDE: A PUZZLING QUESTION

The case of a weak Euro has challenged economists' predictions that a stronger Euro would be the logical consequence of European central bankers' zeal to match the reputation of the Bundesbank (Bergsten, 1997). Explanations range from systemic factors and the intrinsic volatility of the present freely fluctuating exchange rate regime (Fischer, 2001) to the theories of rational expectations in which the calculation of returns plays a major role (De Grauwe, 2000). There are other explanations based on the behavior of fuzzy Euro holders (Sinn and Westermann, 2001) where groups of currency holders are called in to explain why the Euro weakened on foreign markets, and still others which point out the institutional factors which impinge on ECB decision making (Gros, 2000; 2001; Bini-Smaghi and Gros, 2000). Euro weakness turns out to be a real puzzle.

On its record, the Euro has indeed performed very poorly on exchange rate markets. Starting on January 1999 at an agreed rate of $1.17, the Euro has fallen steadily, with very few interruptions. At the introduction of the Euro on the markets (January 2002), it was still below 90 cents, having lost 25 per cent of its initial value. Depending on how the exchange rate is measured, the Euro has devalued within a range of 17 to 25 per cent against the major world currencies and especially against the US dollar.

The idea that a weak Euro is the result of the present system of exchange rates is implicit in Fischer (2001), who believes a weak Euro comes largely from the present informal system of the market as it differs from a formal target zone system in three important ways: '1. There are no pre-announced target zones, and so no commitment to intervene at any particular level of exchange rates. 2. The informal system, which is in place, operates more through coordinated exchange market interventions than coordinated monetary policy actions. 3. Such interventions are rare' (ibid., p. 8). Systemic explanations risk, however, being neutral on the question why the downward trend of the European currency persists, and they do not seem to offer any indications of the causes.

Prior to the introduction of the Euro on the exchange markets, most pundits predicted a stronger rather than a weaker Euro. For those who predicted a strong Euro, among others Bergsten and the European Commission, there was the argument that, other things being equal (especially concerning the internal equilibrium), the real exchange rate should appreciate in countries accumulating current account surpluses (Euroland) and depreciate in those accumulating deficits (US dollar area). Referring to a study based on the Mimosa model (Aglietta *et al.*, 1997), the DG IV of the European Commission estimates that, given a positive increase on the current account of the EMU countries (including Greece) of 1 to 2 per cent between 1998 and 2005, against a negative sign in the current account of the USA for the same period, from −2.1 to −2.7 per cent, 'the dollar should depreciate in real terms against the Euro'. Further evidence of the Euro being a strong currency is argued by those (Bergsten, 1997; Alogoskoufis *et al.*, 1997) who stress portfolio reallocations.

For that tiny minority who judged that the Euro would be weak, the point is that the Euro area lacks fiscal and economic flexibility. The view was anticipated by Calomiris, with the argument that a weak Euro was to be expected, given the major financial factors related to the off-balance expenditures in the area. Calomiris draws attention to the two most important categories of the off-balance sheet looming in the Euro area: the pay-as-you-go pension systems and banking systems: 'The potential for massive fiscal expenditure to bail out insolvent and unfunded pension systems in Continental Europe poses a severe threat to public budget.[4] The banking system is the second big threat to public expenditure as the persisting bail-out policy in France and Italy is evidence' (1999, p. 147).[5] In such a scenario, not only is the Euro doomed to suffer from a weaker exchange rate against the US dollar, but it can put a lot of strain on global financial market efficiency. A weak Euro is likely to strengthen the attraction of the dollar as a numeraire and a store of value, and countries outside Europe will continue to peg their exchange rates to the dollar (ibid., pp. 147–53).

If Euro weakness were to be explained according to the rational expectations theory, it would be regarded as a consequence of growth and demand differentials, inflation rate differentials, the relative rate of return of US versus Euroland assets (both short- and long-term) and the current account of the USA and Euroland.[6] This explanation is not fully convincing. As Bofinger explains, the best way to forecast tomorrow's exchange rate (or next month's or next year's) is simply to take today's. This so-called 'random walk' model, though far from perfect, 'is at least as good as any sophisticated model based on "fundamentals or other factors"' (Bofinger, 1999b, p. 8). The structural explanation has its flaws, especially evident when its prediction failed to see the slowdown of the US economy and the underperformance of its stock exchange was not matched by a corresponding appreciation of the Euro. The Euro continued to fall throughout the first and second quarters of 2001 and did not even recover after the tragedy of 11 September. A 'puzzling phenomenon' indeed, as De Grauwe (2000) put it. A weak Euro challenges the theory of rational beliefs which predicts that exchange rate should match economic fundamentals. A viable explanation of Euro weakness should instead point out that the exchange rate should be taken as a 'signal to search for those variables that can explain the particular exchange rate movement' (ibid., p. 16). It is a matter of fact that, at the beginning of 1999, at the very time of the introduction of the Euro, a self-reinforcing mechanism was established. With the early and continuous appreciation of the US dollar against the Euro (see Figure 7.1), the signal was that market participants assessed the US economy as being in much better shape than the Euro economies.

All the good news was in favor of the USA, and the bad concerned Euroland. Market participants are usually successful in this search for signals about the real economy, De Grauwe argued, 'because there is often

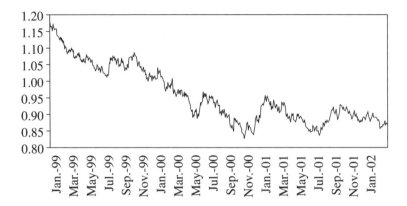

Figure 7.1   US$/Euro nominal exchange rate, January 1999 to January 2002

conflicting evidence of underlying strength and weakness'. And as investors need a practical way to simplify a complex world, the self-reinforcing
mechanism functions as a practical tool to reduce complexity. The process
should not be considered 'irrational'. On the contrary, it 'is a rational
response in a world of extreme uncertainty about how the economy works
and how future developments will affect it. These beliefs, however, work as
filters that allow the market to select the news that fits the prevailing beliefs'
(ibid., pp. 14–15). In a similar mood, Rzepkowski (2001) challenges the
structural fundamentals thesis and recalls that the expectations of Euro
strength were based on the huge US current account deficit and on the
USA's external debt. If traditional fundamental variables appear unsuit-
able to describe the evolution of the Euro/dollar exchange rate, explanations resting on short-term portfolio reallocations are likely to depict the
dynamics of the single currency better. Euro weakness should be related to
that herd behavior which is the source of 'mimetic contagion': traders
follow the behavior of unconfident agents as their confidence in information and assessment of fundamentals is weak (ibid., p. 22).

One line of approach in the literature (Clostermann and Schnatz, 2000 ;
De Grauwe, 2000; Rzepkowsi, 2001; Sinn and Westermann, 2001) appears
quite determined to challenge the 'prosperous explanation'. Assuming that
exchange rate movements of the Euro can be adequately approximated
using a synthetic exchange rate, which is computed as the weighted average
of the currencies which make up the Euro, Clostermannn and Schnatz
found three major determinants of the Euro/US dollar exchange movements: real oil prices, the relative price relationship between traded and
non-traded goods, and the public sector spending ratio of the Euro area in

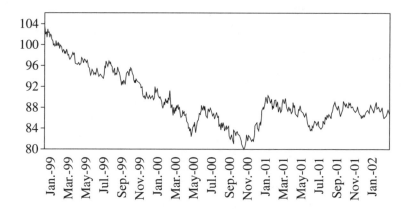

Source: European Central Bank, Monthly Bulletin, January 2002.

Figure 7.2   US$/Euro real exchange rate, January 1999 to January 2002

relation to that of the USA. Euro parity with the dollar has not been significantly outside its normal trading range over the 12 years from 1987 (see
Figure 7.3). As Patterson *et al.* acknowledge, the fall was what was 'needed
to "kick-start" economic activity in the Euro area. The lower exchange rate
has clearly stimulated Euro-area exports, playing a significant part, in particular in German economic recovery' (2000, p. 11).

Sinn and Westermann (2001) point out that the short-term frame of the
exchange rate seems to be quite disregarded in the 'prosperous explanation'
perspective. They argue that the persisting Euro weakness should be associated with the behavior of some special groups of Euro holders who shift
into US dollars, afraid to retain Euro currencies at the time of uncertainty
about the introduction of the real currency. Outside the Euro area, two
groups are especially sensitive to the Euro changeover: Eastern Europeans
and Turks and holders of black market currency in Western Europe. Both
groups are afraid of holding European coins and notes to show their wealth
at the bank counter (Sinn and Westermann, 2001). In their view, the weakness of the Euro is a very transitory phenomenon attributable to the virtual
nature of the Euro. For this reason the shift into the dollar is deemed to be
both temporary and reversible. The authors designate an explanatory
mechanism based on a two-country portfolio model made up of money,
bonds and shares. They argue that 'there is little reason to expect a
country's profit expectations to translate into the exchange rate, because
these are already reflected in share prices'. They stress that 'the demand for
money in the narrow sense of the word counts most', by recalling a class-
room definition that 'the exchange rate is the price of one type of money in

Source: ECB, Eurostat and US Department of Commerce, Bureau for Economic Analysis
(Patterson *et al.*, 2000, p.11).

Figure 7.3   Exchange rate and fluctuation band, US$ per Euro, 1987–2000

terms of another and not the price of interest-bearing assets, as portfolio
managers and economists who developed the portfolio balances approach
have claimed' (ibid., p. 40).

A fourth strand of explanations attributes the source of Euro weakness
to market participants' uncertainty about the evolution of the political and
institutional setting in the area. Incompleteness of the Eurozone polity has
indeed played greatly on the ECB's credibility. This point is underlined by
Naudin, who considers that the ECB, despite all the care and expertise its
founding fathers and present executives have devoted to it, is still a very new
institution (2000, p. 169), different from other major federal central banks
such as the US Fed or the German Bundesbank, not underpinned by political union (ibid., pp. 136–40; Buiter, 1999, pp. 198–99). The efforts made by
Wim Duisemberg to fill the political void by getting the ECB to open up
and be willing to face a more public assessment by publishing its inflation
outlook, have in fact not impressed the market's participants.

Even more relevant elements of uncertainty came out regarding monetary policy, especially over the bank's monitoring of M3 growth. The fact
that the ECB gave a numerical reference value as the first pillar and fixed it
at 4.5 per cent annual growth induced many market observers to believe
that the first pillar was to be considered more important than the second
(Harmonized Index of Consumer Price) and that the ECB monetary
framework was pretty similar to monetary targeting (an established target
of monetary growth) (BIS, 1999, p. 73). Despite the ECB's assertion that its
monetary policy was conducted on a two-pillar basis, during 1999–2001 the
two pillars gave contradictory signals and, in this circumstance, the ECB

was fated to attribute more weight alternately to the first and to the second. The two-pillar strategy, based on both monetary growth (M3) and the assessment of the medium-term outlook for prices and price stability based on a very broad range of indicators, is widely perceived as not being credible because, as Gros (2001, p. 4) argues, 'the ECB usually pretends that both pillars point in the same direction'.[7] Not only has M3 not played the role of mathematical transparency, but also the inflation assessment has not been fully transparent. As Gros has observed, the ECB should reconsider its self-imposed 'two pillar strategy', and should abandon the first pillar (M3), and should also reconsider and make 'a crystal clear choice between core inflation and headline inflation' (ibid.). The general perception has been that the ECB did focus on core inflation while claiming to take into account headline inflation rates.

From this erratic performance, the markets gained the impression that the European monetary framework was not as solid as the ECB claimed. Evidence came out during 1999, when the ECB first lowered (April 1999) and later raised (November 1999) Eurozone main interest facility with little or no relation to M3 growth rate, which continued to record levels above 5 per cent. While this attitude raised the question whether the ECB's self-definition of the two-pillar monetary policy made it prone to failure and/or collusion (Patterson *et al.*, 2000, p. 48), the ECB's uncertainty was inevitably transferred to the Euro's external value.

Some of the explanations (see Box 7.1), however, seem more complementary than others. The prosperous explanation is more comparable with those that stress perception and herd behavior (De Grauwe, 2000; Rzepkowski, 2001) than with inner determinants (Sinn and Westermann, 2001), while the latter seem to add to the systemic explanation, even if it seems too vague to answer this chapter's central question.

By zooming in on the institutional determinants explanation, some authors deal with the institutional factor in a very different way. Buiter (1999) and Gros (2000) focus on the ruling and self-ruling features of ECB monetary policy and suggest that they are at the root of the Euro weakness. Others hint at the bank's scant communication skills and its institutional setting (Gros, 2001; Eichengreen, 2000) to explain the forex market's slide in Euro currency. When the focus shifts to the market participants' behavior, two distinct points are stressed: first, by shifting portfolio into US dollar-denominated assets, market participants assessed Euro economies as being inadequately endowed with factors of production; second, by so doing, market participants seemed to have subjected ECB monetary policy to severe scrutiny.

As Gros argued, the focus on institutional factors is generally limited to the canonical question: 'Do institutions matter?', a question which should

---

BOX 7.1 MODELS OF EXPLANATIONS

Systemic: informal exchange rate arrangements and high volatility (Fischer, 2001).

Structural: prosperous economy explanation: strong US$, strong US economy; weak Euro, weak Euroland.

Rational beliefs: De Grauwe (2000) and herd behavior; Rzepkowski (2001).

Inner determinants of exchange rate versus structural explanation: Black money, Eastern European D-Mark holders: Sinn and Westermann (2001).

Institutional determinants: weak Euro as a consequence of the flaws of the entire ECB edifice: Buiter (1999); ECB monetary policy opaqueness: Gros (2000, 2001).

---

be widened so as to contemplate 'How do institutions matter on Euro external performance?' Here attention turns to the so-called 'unsettling opaqueness'[8] of the ECB monetary policy. As Gros put it, ECB policy making raises questions about many aspects of its monetary policy and the perception that market participants derive from it:

- Did the ECB authorities care about the negative perceptions stemming from the bank's opaque monetary policy?
- Did monetary and political authorities act promptly so as to persuade market participants to reconsider their negative perceptions?
- Can their non-activism be defined as a colluding drift on the way to a benign neglect?

If the answer to the first two questions is simply 'no', the third question calls for a deeper understanding of what expectations were related to the introduction of the Euro. As a narrative of the facts tells us, the ECB and the Council of Ministers, at the onset of the Euro, had different views about the question whether or not to activate an exchange rate policy (Campanella, 2000a). At a certain point in time, however, the Council of Ministers, and more explicitly the Euro-Group, converged with the ECB in underwriting a policy of indifference towards the exchange rate policy; that happened during Summer 1999, when it was clear that the Euro was on the track of a steady weakness. From then on, the problem of the Euro exchange rate was no longer an issue at stake between the ECB and Euro-Group, which, instead, showed it was quite at ease with a sliding currency.

A clear result of the battle for dominance between the ECB and the Euro-Group was that Euro monetary authorities endorsed a clear non-interventionist stance vis-à-vis the Euro's external value, a policy which shares many elements with the US 'benign neglect'. Since then, as Munchau has argued, the ECB 'lack[ed] the resolve to use what little control they have over the common currency's exchange rate' (*Financial Times*, 24 April 2000). What really matters is not whether intervention on the exchange rate was to be chosen, but whether the Euro authorities actually used their own room for maneuver in order to accommodate Euroland's sluggish economy.

STRATEGIC INSTITUTIONALISM AND ECB ECONOMIC GOVERNANCE

The weak Euro and the ECB monetary policy in the first three years of EMU encourage us to consider the ECB in a post-EMU scenario. If in the pre-EMU scenario it was used to portray the ECB institution building, based on the model of delegation, as a means to get lower inflation (Bini Smaghi and Del Giovane, 1996; Campanella 1996), in the post-EMU scenario (1999 onward) the focus should shift inescapably onto the ECB acting as a policy maker straining to bear economic benefits to the Euro economic area. With an emphasis on stability, the ECB's blueprints constrain the bank to deliver stable prices and interest rates, that is, a stable government in which growth takes care of itself. Given the initial constraints of the EMU blueprints, the new scenario is better described according to a strategic institutionalist perspective in which institutions are expected to derive collective net benefits for the incumbents (joint Pareto gains) rather than simply complying with the principles of delegation policy (Campanella, 1997). Theories of International Relations would predict that cooperative regimes governed by common institutions, geared up to reap benefits arising from cooperation, can trigger conflicts over distributional gains. The problem with a plain neoinstitutionalist approach is the vulnerability of that sort of institution (Moravcsik, 1996) as they are prone to be over-ruled every time the principals do not agree with the outcomes of their operation. In order to handle the principals' pressure, supranational institutions choose to accommodate their principals, though not giving up their own institution-building prerogatives. A survival exercise follows, in which supranational institutions struggle to deliver joint Pareto gains for all the participating parties, though at different rates. Without renouncing their role of preventing cheating and resolving distributional conflict, the actors of the common institutions are ready to undertake accommodative policies delivering the outcome(s) the principals have sought.[9]

Not only does the ECB, as a supranational institution, match the case of neoinstitutionalism, as discussed in the theories of International Relations, it also offers a model of how, once the common institution goes into full operation, it is prepared to survive the principals' pressure by means of accommodative policies. A review of the ECB executive board decision making in the three years following the introduction of the Euro is evidence. The ECB policy pattern diverges strongly from the one economists and ECB-watchers predicted. Reviewing the ECB monetary policy in the post-EMU scenario, the ECB board seemed more geared to achieve responsiveness and resilience toward economic factors than to stick to its statutory objectives. Whatever the impact of the environmental factors on its decision making, including the considerable dimension and diversity of monetary conditions, the shift to the post-EMU monetary policy has been facilitated and triggered by two major institutional factors: first, a certain dash of opaqueness, which the European Monetary Institute (EMI), the forerunner of the ECB, added to its self-regulated two-pillar monetary policy (Gros, 2001); and, second, the determination to escape the likely application of Article 109 of the Maastricht Treaty relative to exchange rate provision. The latter relates to a complex (Bofinger, 1999, pp. 33–4) and 'intricate and convoluted language' (Smits, 1997, p. 375) provision which gives heads of state (the Council of Ministers) the 'final say over Euroland's participation in any new global monetary system' (Eichengreen, 2000, p. 5). In other words, it can be perceived as a threat to ECB board independence if the Council fears the bank will fail to 'direct monetary policy to political ends'. The threat can materialize in exchange rates arrangements which will be faced by the ECB decision makers.

Both factors have triggered the ECB's shift from blueprints to actual monetary policy. The focus on the 'external value' of the Euro raises questions which have awakened little interest in studies of European integration. Has the Euro been introduced so as to gain a competitive advantage? How are the related institutions prepared to provide 'collective' gains? In what circumstances are the affected parties likely to retaliate?

In a rare analysis of the likely consequences of the achievement of EMU policies, Bergsten (1997) anticipated the analysis of the consequences of the Euro for the other parties. The major benefit expected is that of enjoying the benign neglect policy. The reasoning goes as follows. If the EMU countries fully adhere to the tenets of the Stability Pact (Amsterdam, 1997), serious consequences can follow for the Euro's value. 'If the EU truly abandoned all flexibility in the conduct of fiscal as well as monetary policy, the resulting absence of macroeconomic instruments could portend the use of other, far less desirable, tools to counter the region's severe unemployment and growth problems. One would be competitive depreciation' (Bergsten, 1997, p. 34).[10]

As a matter of fact, Bergsten's prediction seemed to materialize with the sudden devaluation of the Euro after its introduction and the persistent Euro weakness in the three years thereafter. Charges have been made that the Euro has followed a well-known pattern of competitive devaluation which is matched to reduction of interest rates. As Patterson *et al.* acknowledge, 'Far from being an unanticipated mishap (. . .) the fall of the Euro parity against the dollar was a deliberate policy, designed to boost the competitivity of, in particular, German industry. Given that inflationary pressures were negligible, the ECB was able to accommodate this strategy by reducing interest rates in early 1999; and during the first quarter of 2000, Euro-area and German exports were at a level over 20% higher than in 1999' (2000, p. 48).[11]

As Patterson *et al.* commented, this experience 'seems to suggest that a fall in exchange rate can boost economic growth; but that rising comparative economic growth does not necessarily boost the exchange rate' (2000, p. 49). Of course, this pattern can work on condition that no one or no one powerful international competitor is seriously affected or that this economic stimulus is confined to the economy in question. In times of general declining economic activity, 'widespread use of the exchange rate in this way may lead to a cycle of 'competitive devaluation', in which each economy attempts, at least temporarily, to export its unemployment' (ibid.).

How do theories of International Relations assess this outcome? Martin and Simmons (1998) argue that international institutions as objects of strategic choice are both dependent and independent variables (p. 757). While delivering benefits to the incumbents, they should be able to fix consequential distributional conflicts. The ECB case especially fits the above definition. The agreement of Germany to create the ECB was made in exchange for a continuing fiscal discipline, fixed in the Stability Pact (Amsterdam, 1997), with the twofold objective of policing member countries' fiscal stance and reducing distributional conflicts which would likely be lumped together in the new currency regime.

BOX 7.2   NEOINSTITUTIONALISM: RESTRICTED PARADIGM

- Benefits arising from cooperation.
- Conflicts over distributional gains.
- The problem of cooperation then turns out to be how to prevent cheating and how to resolve distributional conflict.
  Martin and Simmons (2000: p. 743).

When it comes to EMU strategic institution building, we cannot limit the assessment to intracooperative benefits and conflicts. Krasner (1983) acknowledged that cooperation and regime occur when state actors are likely to get two major payoffs: (a) Pareto joint gains for the benefit of the incumbents, (b) zero sum game for the non-participants. Strategic institutionalism should also account for the likely consequences that strategic institutions can generate for non-participants (Vaubel, 1985). By including the excluded parties, strategic institutionalism can be portrayed in the extended version below (see Box 7.3).

BOX 7.3   STRATEGIC INSTITUTIONALISM: EXTENDED PARADIGM

- Net benefits to incumbents are being gained at the likely expense of the excluded parties (Vaubel, 1985).
- Cooperative institutions aimed at solving time-inconsistency problems can mimic neoliberal arrangements with a view to gaining market participants' credibility, cheating market participants and circumventing market discipline.
- Cooperative institutions have built-in opaqueness relating to standard setting, policy pattern and enforcement.

In European Studies, Euro arrangements have frequently been described as a two-pronged device. On the one hand, they are aimed at gaining market credibility, while, on the other hand, they are designed so that the incumbents can regain their power over monetary policy, which they have lost in the wake of the globalization process (MacNamara, 1998, pp. 43–71). Examples of this two-pronged policy can be found in many EMU institutions, and include the following:

- the creation of the ECB, where the delegation of the Euro area monetary policy has solved the time-inconsistency dilemma faced by weak currency countries such as France or Italy (Campanella, 1996);
- fiscal discipline, as stated in the Stability Pact (Amsterdam, 1997), which is a delegation of fiscal discipline to a supranational institute but which is designed to be enforced by a peer group, the Council of Ministers, with a clear political bias (Campanella, 2000b).

The research agenda of students of European integration and more generally of regionalism should check systematically for strategic interests in order to consider the ad hoc nature of international institutions. That leads to the setting up of a research agenda in which 'collusion', either active or passive, represents a likely outcome of regional institution building. As Webb (1993) and Connolly (1995) argued, passive or active collusion can be at the root of 'macroeconomic policy'. The Euro exchange rate policy may turn out to be a further example of the EMU strategic interaction institution building. Free-floating exchange rate policy adopted by the ECB can lend itself to a market-driven policy, or it can conceal an aggressive 'beggar-thy-neighbor' policy by means of which to gain some competitive advantages.

The research protocol adopted centers on certain questions (see Box 7.4).

BOX 7.4   EXTENDED STRATEGIC
          INSTITUTIONALISM: A RESEARCH
          PROTOCOL

- Are colluding interests included in the analysis? What influence do they have in this or that policy or institution building?
- If there are 'Pareto joint gains', where is the zero-sum game? Who is (are) the loser(s)?
- What consequences are EMU and Euro competitive position- ing likely to produce in the international economy?

THE GAINS AND COSTS OF THE EURO BENIGN NEGLECT

Three major set data, the size of the Euro area, the effects of exchange rate weakness on cost and prices, and a short record of the ECB executive board policy,[12] feature the case of the Euro as a candidate for a 'benign neglect' stance vis-à-vis major international currencies. This policy can match the one run by the US Federal Reserve in the 1960s under the Bretton Woods arrangements. In that period, the North American monetary authorities were prone not to care about the dollar exchange rate movements because the dollar was linked through a system of fixed but adjustable parities to the European currencies and it was convertible in gold. Under this regime, US political authorities were allowed to freely pursue their aims, while the central banks of European countries continued to buy US dollars even if the dollar convertibility was clearly not credible. All three set data suggest, not only that Euro zone features all the circumstances leading to a benign neglect policy, but that the ECB actually adopted it, and delivered major dividends for the participating countries to the single currency.

Euro Big Size and 'Benign Neglect'

When we consider the Euro monetary area, its big size comes first (see Table 7.1). Although the ECB executive board has made it clear that the large size of the Euro area is, so far, of little or no interest to it, and it has made it clear that it is interested in building up the Euro's efficacy in terms of economic growth rather than extending its use worldwide (Noyer, 1999a), size is not something that we can ignore. Behind the US dollar and ahead of the Japanese yen, the Euro is the second most widely used currency in the world economy. As regards being considered a real 'international' currency, the Euro has still to gain credibility with the public at large. In technical terms, it has to show that it is able to cover all three basic functions a currency is expected to fulfill – as a store of value, as a medium of exchange and as a unit of account – and the Euro is functioning, to a lower degree, in all three (*ECB Monthly Bulletin*, January 2000, pp. 32–3). The major success story of the Euro as an international currency is to be found in Eastern Europe. In the case of using the Euro as a pegging currency, approximately 30 countries outside the Euro area currently have exchange rate regimes involving the Euro to a greater or lesser extent.[13] Although the Euro remains second to the US dollar in terms of its official use, the role of the Euro will certainly increase in the future, especially from the year 2002, when Euro banknotes and coins begin to circulate.

Table 7.1   Size: GDP and population

	Europe	USA	Japan
Population	292 mn With pre-ins[a] 376 mn	270 mn	127 mn
GDP	Euro 5.774 bn 76% of USA	Euro 7.592	Euro 3.327 bn

Note: [a] Pre-ins refer to the four member countries (UK, Sweden, Denmark and Greece) which are not included in the Euro area. The first three have opted out while Greece was not admitted in the first wave (1998) until 2001 when it was assessed to meet the Maastricht criteria.

For Noyer, the Vice-President of the ECB, taking the current situation as a starting point, the Eurosystem's position concerning the future international role of the Euro is crystal clear: the bank will not adopt a belligerent stance in order to force the use of the Euro upon the world economy, as the Euro as an international currency will come about anyway. It will happen spontaneously, slowly but inexorably, without any impulses other than those based on free will and the decisions of market participants, without any logic other than that of the market. In other words, the internationalization of the Euro is not a policy objective of the ECB. In Noyer's words: 'the Eurosystem neither promotes nor hinders the development of the Euro as an international currency as we consider that the international role of the Euro will and should develop through the interaction of market forces (Noyer, 1999a, p. 3).

The international positioning of the Euro is being established with the extension of its use in Eastern Europe pegging systems and because of the portfolio holdings. Padoa-Schioppa, a member of the executive board of the ECB, commented: 'The Euro, which fulfils the necessary conditions to be a leading international currency with the USD, aims to cooperate with the dollar and not against it. There is enough room for both currencies in the world economy' (1999).

If the necessary conditions for a currency to become an international currency are based on two broad factors, low risk and large size, the Euro authorities are prepared to fulfill their duties to improve the first, as the latter is a matter of fact. The low risk factor is related to the confidence inspired by the currency and its central bank, which in turn mainly depends on the internal and external stability of the currency. The low risk factor tends to lead to diversification among international currencies, since diversification is a means to bring down the overall risk; it acts, so to speak, as a centrifugal force. By contrast, the large size factor relates to the relative demographic economic and financial importance of the area, which supports the currency; in other words, the 'habitat' of the currency. The large size factor, which – in Padoa-Schioppa's words – includes the demographic, economic and financial dimension, generally tends to lead to centralization around one or a few key international currencies. It can be seen as a centripetal force, as a virtuous circle, which will tend to lead to an increasing use of the Euro as an international currency. The ECB executive board is unanimous in declaring the stability of the Euro, measured by safeguarding its 'purchasing power of savings', rather than its strength, as the major achievement. As a consequence, the Euro exchange rate does not constitute an element which should be considered in the second pillar of the ECB's monetary policy strategy. The exchange rate is only one among many factors which contribute to the bank's outlook on price developments.

If the size factor or the habitat of the Euro is far more important than the exchange rate when it comes to assessing the international role of a currency, the question which naturally comes up is whether the ECB executive is willing to stabilize the single currency at the expense of higher volatility.

The Weak Euro and its Dividend: Some Figures

'The exchange rate flexibility is as Churchill's democracy: *it is the worst system, with the exception of all the others*' (Bergsten *et al.*, 1999, p. 1). Since the dismissal of the Bretton Woods arrangements of the early 1970s, the free fluctuation of exchange rates has become textbook economics. It is regarded as a stabilizing force in the world economy, allowing each country to pursue 'the mixture of unemployment and price trend objectives it prefers, consistent with internal equilibrium, equilibrium being secured by appreciation of the currencies of "price stability" countries relative to currencies of "full-employment" countries' (Johnson, 1972, p. 410). From a critical perspective, however, a free fluctuation of the exchange rate is regarded as a genuine source of macroeconomic instability. The reason for rejecting floating an exchange rate is the evidence that asset markets, and the foreign exchange markets in particular, are driven by herd behavior rather than rational expectations. Large countries can get a clear advantage by adopting a free fluctuation of exchange rates. According to Bergsten *et al.* 'The advantage of large countries vis-à-vis smaller and developing ones can stagger now with the introduction of the Euro as the EMU authorities can be tempted to emulate the USA in their attitude to run a "benign neglect policy" – a calculated indifference to the movements in their country's exchange rate' (1999, p. 4).

Since 1997, the ECB's precursor, the European Monetary Institute, had supported a free-floating exchange rate and rejected exchange rate targeting (a policy aimed at maintaining a currency exchange rate within an established value) for the Euro area on the grounds that this strategy was not appropriate for an area as large and closed as the European one, and that an externally oriented strategy might have been inconsistent with domestic price stability . The argument goes that establishing an external objective, such as a well defined value for the Euro, could lead to conflicts between the internal and external price stability objectives, precisely because extra Euro trade has only a relatively small impact on the Euro economy and, thus, economic developments within the Euro area might easily have diverged from those of the countries to which the exchange rate target would be linked. This risk is nowadays accentuated by the integration of the financial markets, which has made the choice between internal and external orientations even more explicit.

For that reason, the ECB was poised immediately after its installation to oppose the interventionist policy aimed at introducing exchange rate target zones (Campanella, 2000a) and stated that stable exchange rates of the new single currency are best served by stability-oriented policies that are consistent with economic fundamentals (see Duisemberg, 1999, p. 2, quoted in

Bofinger, 2000, p. 5). Subsequently, however, market participants and specialist observers sensed a certain indifference to exchange rate movement and the fear that the ECB was taking a benign neglect attitude was confirmed in an ECB press conference, when Duisenberg declared: 'Not having an exchange rate policy – and we have no policy – does not mean that there is benign or malign neglect. For the time being there is neglect.' This position was shared by Pedro Solbes, the commissioner to monetary affairs of the European Commission, who declared there was 'no clear relationship between a well-defined monetary policy and the exchange rate' (Patterson *et al.*, 2000, p. 35).

What benefits are likely to accrue if a 'benign neglect policy' is fully agreed to? And whom has that policy mostly benefited? If public support for the single currency has fallen along with the downward trend of its exchange rate, as the Euro barometer records,[14] the international competitiveness of the Euro against the US dollar and Japanese yen has led to a loss in cost competitiveness of the US dollar of around 30 per cent. In historical perspective, 'the unit labour cost position of the Euro area producers is currently very favourable relative to US producers as the real exchange rate of the US stands 31% above its long-term average (Figure 7.4) higher economic growth and employment. Euro weakness has affected the Japanese yen by recording a deterioration of 15 per cent in cost competitiveness for Japanese competitors against EU-12 producers since the launch of the Euro'.[15]

The price and cost competitiveness has spread differently in Euroland (see Table 7.2). Diverging movements in costs and prices affect cost

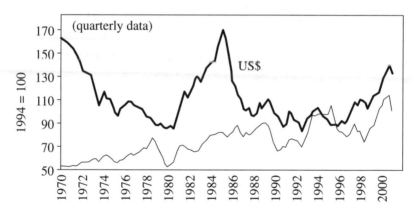

Note: Deflated by unit labour costs in total economy.

Source: European Commission (2001), *Quarterly Report,* first quarter.

Figure 7.4   Real exchange rates, US$ and Japanese yen versus EU12

Table 7.2 Cost and price indicators of individual countries relative to the Euro area (EU-12)

% change	Over the last year (Q1–01/Q1–00)			Over the last two years (Q1–01/Q1–99)			Relative to 1980–2000 average (Q1–01/Average 87–00)		
	ULCE	ULCM	PGDP	ULCE	ULCM	PGDP	ULCE	ULCM	PGDP
Euro area member states									
BLEU	-0.1	1.1	-0.3	-0.2	3.0	-0.4	3.1	-1.8	0.8
Germany	-1.5	1.8	-1.6	2.6	-3.0	-3.2	-3.1	5.1	-3.2
Greece	-1.1	-3.0	-1.4	-4.0	-4.4	-3.1	11.3	11.0	9.3
Spain	1.6	1.8	1.9	3.1	4.4	4.3	1.8	7.8	1.3
France	-0.5	0.0	-0.7	-1.1	-1.2	-1.1	1.4	-6.6	-1.8
Ireland	2.3	3.9	3.0	3.4	4.8	6.3	0.5	-21.1	12.1
Italy	0.4	-0.5	0.8	0.9	-0.3	1.5	-4.5	-1.0	0.5
Netherlands	2.2	1.8	1.9	4.2	3.7	3.2	6.2	2.1	2.6
Austria	0.7	1.9	-0.3	-1.4	2.8	-0.1	-0.7	-0.6	0.2
Portugal	2.6	2.7	0.4	6.2	5.2	1.6	13.0	8.9	13.7
Finland	0.2	-2.7	1.7	0.5	-6.3	3.0	-10.9	-20.5	-4.5
Non-Euro area member states									
Denmark	0.6	0.7	0.8	2.7	2.0	2.9	7.9	9.7	6.5
Sweden	-4.3	-3.0	-5.5	1.3	3.8	0.2	-3.8	-11.2	-7.5
UK	-2.2	-2.1	-2.0	11.4	13.6	10.9	25.6	34.3	21.0

Notes: ULCE and ULCM for Italy relative to any period before 1998 are distorted by the 1998 tax reform which shifted taxation from labor costs to value added but did not significantly change competitiveness.
ULCE = based on unit labor costs in the economy as a whole; ULCM = based on unit labor costs in manufacturing industry; PGDP = based on GDP deflator. A minus means an improvement in cost competitiveness.

Source: European Commission (2001), *Quarterly Report*, first quarter, p. 8.

competitiveness positions of Euro area member states. If in Belgium, Luxembourg and Italy the price and cost competitiveness has been broadly constant over the two years following the introduction of the Euro, Germany, France and Greece have improved considerably. While in France this reflected low cost pressures due to moderate wage pressure, in Germany low price pressure results from weaker cyclical conditions (weaker consumer demand[16]) than for the average of the Euro area (European Commission, *Quarterly Report*, 2001, pp. 7–8). For the other six member economies, there was a deterioration in the cost competitiveness positions. Especially relevant are the positions of Ireland, Spain and Portugal, three of the 'four poor'. In Ireland, following rising wage and price pressures due to continued strong growth and an increasingly tight labor market, cost competitiveness indicators have deteriorated after the introduction of the Euro of about plus 5 per cent for unit labor cost for the manufacturing sector (ULCM). In Spain and Portugal, the appreciation of the real exchange rate may be warranted as the economies catch up with other Euro countries. In Portugal, the large current account deficit (10 per cent of GDP) is an alarming signal of a serious deterioration in the country's competitiveness in a phase of persistent Euro weakness.

When competitiveness gains of EU-11 are compared to figures for Denmark, Sweden and the United Kingdom, it transpires that Denmark has seen a further deterioration in its unit labor cost (ULC) competitiveness of about 3 per cent, which increases to 10 per cent in manufacturing sector. The UK has seen its ULC deteriorating by about 26 per cent of its 1987–99 ULC average. Conversely, in Sweden, a 3 per cent improvement of ULCM comes from a 9 per cent depreciation of the Swedish krona.[17]

Adding figures for the Euro extra-area trade to the above labor cost competitiveness, there is clear evidence that a weak Euro has helped export performance considerably. Data released by the ECB indicate that the importance of the international trade sector is still growing for the Euro area (Figure 7.5). In 1999, the Euro area accounted for 19.5 per cent of world exports, compared with 15 per cent and 8.5 per cent for the USA and Japan respectively.

Even more significant is the fact that the Euro area's exports of goods and services represent around 17 per cent of the Euro area's GDP, compared with just over 11 per cent for the USA and 9 per cent for Japan, while its imports are equivalent to around 15 per cent of its GDP, compared with about 13 per cent and 8 per cent for the USA and Japan respectively. Hence, in terms of exports, at the moment the Euro area is approximately 50 per cent more open than the USA. From this perspective, there are grounds to believe that the influence of the Euro exchange rate on the Euroland economy is greater than that of the dollar on the US economy. As Patterson

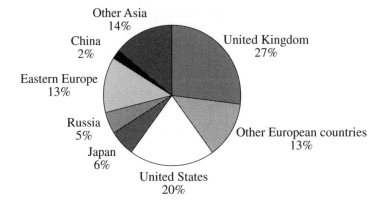

Figure 7.5   Share of Euro exports

et al. argued, it is reasonable to say that a depreciation of the Euro exchange rate could be a relevant factor in sustaining exports and, thus, all of economic growth. Evidence is particularly striking with respect to the Euro–dollar and the Euro–sterling exchange rates, as the USA is the second most important trading partner of the Euro area, after the UK. 'Therefore, a real depreciation of the euro with respect to these two currencies would imply an effective stimulus for European exports towards both the United States and the United Kingdom and, thus, an important contribution to economic growth' (Patterson *et al.*, 2000).

Figure 7.5 shows the relative importance of the UK and the USA as trading partners for the Euro area. In sum, a weaker Euro has clearly contributed to European economic growth, given the fact that European internal consumption is low and the Euro area remains a quite open economy. The outcome, however, did not get here as an effect of the Ecofin-11 activism in exchange rate policy, though in theory according to the provision of Article 109 of the Maastricht Treaty, the Finance Ministers might operate in this direction. If put into action, the exchange rate policy as granted to Ecofin-11 would probably have conflicted with the ECB's mandate regarding price stability and ended in a relevant negative impact on inflation and on interest rates (Campanella, 2000a). In fact, in the first year of its working, the ECB was 'justly praised for having entirely fulfilled its primary task of ensuring price stability' by ensuring that headline inflation in the Euro area remained below 1.5 per cent, despite a substantial rise in the price of oil. Doubts were raised about its 'two pillar strategy' as the monetary aggregate (M3) was seen to grow beyond its reference value of 4.5 (monetary growth) at a rate above 6 per cent per annum.

Euro Monetary Policy and ECB Decision Making: a Short Record

On raising the issue of 'no one being in charge' of the Eurozone exchange rate policy, some authors have linked the Euro's lasting weakness on forex markets to the ambiguities of its institutional environment. In fact, ex Article 109 of the Treaty on Economic and Monetary Union, it emerges that, although the Council and ECOFIN should have the 'ultimate responsibility' to conclude 'formal agreements', the ECB decides the substance of exchange rate arrangements. According to Henning, 'If the ECB objects to fixing a parity, first, one of two sources of initiative is effectively blocked. Second, it is highly unlikely that the Council would muster the necessary unanimity in the face of strenuous objections from the ECB. Third, public knowledge of the ECB dissent would rob the formal arrangement of most if not all of its credibility in the foreign exchange markets' (1997:41). This also means the reverse, that the ECB would not embark on an exchange rate policy which would lead the Council and ECOFIN to take action on entering formal agreements (target zone policy) or suggesting 'general orientations' to the ECB, a move which could only lessen the ECB's room for maneuver, and one which the bank is therefore unlikely to adopt (ibid., p. 42).

Henning's analysis made a case for the ECB to come out as the strong man in exchange rate policy. Such a conclusion seemed to materialize during the first eight months of stage three of EMU in the stances taken by the former finance ministers of France and Germany, who were set to confront the ECB on the 'exchange rate policy'. The outcome confirmed Henning's prediction, in that the ECB showed itself to be the strong man. The ECB–ECOFIN-11 confrontation ended with the resignation of the German finance minister and the abandoning, at least for the time being, of any idea of target zone policy (Campanella, 2000a).

If the ECB turns out to be the strong man in the game, there is clear reason to survey the bank's policy and decision making. Major insights do not necessarily come from ECB exchange rate policy, which is not among the policy instruments endowing the ECB, but, as Gros *et al.* (2000) and Gros (2001) say, from its interest rate policy, which represents its major instrument for achieving price stability. There is no reason to doubt that exchange rate stabilization is not an objective of ECB monetary policy. In support of this view, Eugenio Solans (1999), a member of the executive board of the ECB, argued that the success of the Euro cannot be measured by the evolution of its exchange rate in relation to other currencies. The fact that since 1 January 1999 the effective nominal exchange rate of the Euro has depreciated is of much less relevance than the sound inflation rates. In the long run, the strength of a currency and its stability move together. The

ECB should assume responsibility for the level of inflation. The exchange rate is 'only one among other variables' which the ECB should take into account when deciding monetary policy. As a consequence, the exchange rate of the Euro depends on the 'macroeconomic fundamentals of the Euro area, the evolution of other currencies and market expectations' which are beyond the reach of the bank's policy, or in Solans's words 'against which it is preferable not to act'. In conclusion, the evolution of the Euro (that is, its depreciation) reflects the strength of the dollar rather than the weakness of the Euro (ibid.).[18]

One can argue that, for the ECB's executive board, the Euro exchange rate does not matter, in that intra-exchange rate instability has been definitely removed by fixing exchange rate parities within the 11 (now 12) participating countries – a clear reference to the disruptive effects that volatility did inflict on the member economies under the fixed but manageable exchange rates. Some figures recall these effects: the Italian lira depreciated by 65 per cent against the D-Mark after the 1992 exchange rate crisis, which resulted in a staggering public debt of above 124 per cent of GDP.

Volatility is not seen to be a matter of great concern for the Euro vis-à-vis its external partners and competitors as it is unlikely to inflict any serious harm on the Euro economies, and would instead offer a welcome boost to Euro economies unable to regain competitiveness by introducing unappealing and badly needed structural adjustments. On 27 September 1999, Noyer, ECB deputy, did not make any secret of the fact that the recovery of the Euro economies from the slowdown observed around the turn of 1998–9, caused by the Asian financial crisis, should be attributed to the Euro dividend; that is, to its relative depreciation against the US dollar. In his forecast the process, which was expected to gain momentum with a sustained strengthening of real GDP growth in the second half of 1999 and was forecast to grow further in 2000, is led by exports and a weak Euro.

While the possibility of a pronounced slowdown of the US economy with negative repercussions on world trade is not excluded, Noyer (1999b) hints at a stronger recovery in Asia as a boosting factor of the Euro area economy. In conclusion, he clearly points to the external environment and a weak Euro as major factors of Euro area economic growth.

Before the summer break of 1999, the ECB president took a conscious 'neglect' attitude towards the Euro's fall against the dollar. One statement in his introduction to a press conference in June 1999 addressed the issue as follows: 'Turning to *exchange rate developments*, the Governing Council noted that from the start of Stage Three to 1 June the Euro depreciated by 7.7% when measured in nominal effective terms. Vis-à-vis the USD the exchange rate declined from around 1.18 to 1.04 over the same period. The current effective exchange rate level broadly corresponds to those observed in summer 1997 and spring 1998.' In the view of the governing council, the cause of the fall is 'cyclical divergences between the Euro area and the United States', which, in the view of the council, are expected to 'diminish over the course of this year and thereafter'. After mentioning an optimistic, and groundless, economic forecast, Duisenberg produced a bizarre mosaic of self-confident statements so as to inculcate the idea that the bank runs the monetary policy appropriately and cannot be blamed about the Euro's weak exchange rate: (1) it is a currency 'firmly based on internal price stability'; (2) 'therefore [it] has a clear potential for a stronger external value'; (3) 'since the start of Stage Three of the EMU the Euro has become the second most important international currency in the world'; (4) 'the policy of the Eurosystem will be to safeguard its internal purchasing power, thereby also supporting the international role of the Euro'; (5) 'as already mentioned, nominal long-term interest rates are low by any historical standard, reflecting the confidence of global investors in the Euro.'

In the same circumstance, when he was put under pressure by a question referring to O. Issing, chief economist of the ECB and member of the executive board, who had expressed no concern at the Euro's fall and, instead, had admitted that 'this level might have some advantages, because it would stimulate activity and exports outside the Euro zone', Duisenberg's answer was as sibylline as usual: The weakening of the Euro 'is not something we strive for. But that it has the effect you mentioned cannot be denied. As always, I see no reason whatsoever to disagree with what my esteemed colleague Issing has said' (Duisenberg, 1999a).

Later, on 9 September 1999, in the ECB questions-and-answers session, the ECB president was asked again about the Euro's level against the US dollar (see Duisenberg, 1999b). This time the question was raised to find out whether the president shared the contentment of Ernst Welteke, the Bundesbank president, with 1.05 Euros to the US dollar, and whether this value was as an appropriate level for the currency. The question caught Duisenberg off guard. The response was as circumspect as possible. He said that he would not be tempted to indicate any specific level which was desirable, and made a public declaration that the level at which the Euro was at that time being traded, and had been traded in the previous five to six weeks, was, to his mind, 'an understandable level' (Duisenberg, 1999b).

In mid-January 2000, the Euro exchange rate started to fall steadily below parity with the US dollar. Since January 2000, it has been traded below parity, and in mid-January, ECB executives started to prepare public opinion for a future move by the bank. On 31 January, Duisenberg declared that 'The exchange rate plays an important role in the strategy of the ECB and its further weakening could be a risk to the ECB's goal of maintaining price stability' (reported in Barber, 2002, p. 3). The exchange rate indicator is being reranked in the bank's monetary strategy; Issing affirms that it is 'an important variable for the Eurosystem as it is one of the determinants of the outlook for price stability'. Imported goods, not only oil commodities, which are still to be paid for in dollars pose a threat to price stability in the Euro area, and 'this threat will be taken into account together with the information on price developments revealed by all other indicators'. Though, he adds that 'exchange rate, on the other hand, in the context of the clear mandate and the appropriate strategy, cannot be a target of monetary policy' (Issing, 2000).

On 3 February 2000, at the end of a troublesome week, in which an ECOFIN-11 meeting in Brussels witnessed serious disagreement over the weakness of the Euro, and a reversal of tradition,[19] with the French set to favor a 'strong Euro' and the Germans encouraging a weaker and more profitable one, the ECB president announced at a press conference that the reference interest rate could be raised by 25 base points. Though the size of the rise is similar to the one the FOMC of the USA Fed announced on 2 February 2000, the ECB governing council did not act in coordination with or on the example of the Fed (Figure 7.6)

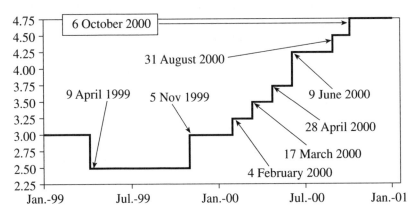

Figure 7.6   ECB's policy interest moves, 1999–2000

The rise of the interest rate by a tiny 25 base point happened at the end of February 2001, and after a steady below parity level of the Euro value against the US dollar. The ECB executives, as Duisenberg candidly revealed during the press conference held after the governing council meeting (3 February 2000), 'have prepared markets well enough in their, as it so happens, justified expectation that something would happen. And I do not think that today's decision will have come as a big surprise to any of you here' (Duisenberg, 2000b). But the rise was almost a non-event, as the market participants were impressed neither by the ECB rise nor by the rhetoric that ballooned in the ECOFIN-11 joint promise about structural reforms. What seems to be the reason for the rise which occurred on 3 February 2000?

- Was the ECB move aimed at stopping the Euro's depreciation or even to reverse the below-parity bias that had set in?
- Was it a necessary move, made so as to comply with the markets and to add credibility to the Euro monetary authorities, showing that the ECB was watching the evolution of prices and inflation in the area carefully?
- Was it a move aimed at signaling to wage setters that the ECB would not tolerate inflationary pressure?
- Or, in a more captious explanation, was the tiny rise dictated by a 'colluding drift' with ECOFIN-11 ministers, who did not conceal their sympathy for a weak Euro?

The market's response was to continue to trade the Euro at below parity against the US dollar. This persistence below parity may mean that the size of the rise has not been considered sufficient to reverse capital outflows from the Eurozone. The movement (Table 7.3) reveals increasing residents' outflows of DI which were not offset by similar inflows.

Table 7.3   Euro area capital flows in the first 10 months of 1999

Direct and portfolio investment abroad, total	Net outflows of DI	Residents' investments
1999 Euro 149.4bn	Euro 98.3 (+50%)	Euro 151.5bn
1998 Ecu 140.4bn	Ecu 64.1bn	Ecu 126.0bn
Capital inflows in the first 10 months of 1999 (FDI)		
1999 Euro 53.2bn		
1998 Ecu 62.0bn		

Source: ECB (2000), *Monthly Bulletin*, January: 33.

In a recent survey, IMF (2001) attributes the weakness of the Euro to its being driven by two basic objectives of investing: maximizing expected returns and minimizing risk. As a consequence, the IMF warns, this trend could be suddenly reversed if perceptions of relative rates of return were to worsen for the US dollar area.[20]

The second question raises the problem of the ECB as a credibility seeker, and its move, though tiny, can be interpreted as that of a 'price stability' guardian. The upswing that a fall in the exchange rate is likely to cause to the Harmonized Index of Consumer Prices (HICP) in the Euro area has been calculated at a 0.2 per cent. According to the Commission's forecast, the inflation rate in the Eurozone should be 1.5 per cent in 2000 and 2001, so the bank's rise does not have much influence on immediate inflation pressures relative to imported inflation. If anything, the rise to 25 base points should be regarded as a pre-emptive move directed towards somebody or some group which can *really* push up inflation pressures. For whom was this signal intended? There are many to whom the bank wanted to send its signal: to markets, so as to gain credibility, and to social partners so as to discourage wage increases. The intensity of the signal, however, seems to have been directed especially at the German company IG Metall, which had asked for a wage rise three times the actual level of German inflation, that is, a 5 per cent wage rise.

As Issing declared: 'We face a dangerous, fragile situation as wage negotiations are just starting in Europe' (21 January 2000). Welteke, president of the Bundesbank and member of the ECB governing council, stressed, 'Price risks are now on the upside. We are very vigilant' (28 January, reported in Barber, *Financial Times*, 2 February 2000, p. 2). The drama concerning mounting inflationary pressure reached its peak at the same time as the Euro exchange rate began a downward trend. A sense of urgent need for the bank to intervene spread among some monetary analysts. Callow of Crédit Suisse First Boston warned, 'A weaker Euro implies higher import prices and faster growth, which in turn can create domestic inflationary pressures. In fact, the Euro's woes add a sense of urgency' (quoted in Barber, *Financial Times*, 2 February 2000, p. 2). According to the OECD, a 10 per cent depreciation of the Euro adds 0.6 percentage points to inflation, with a one-year lag. A $10 a barrel increase in oil prices (which tripled in 1999) is expected to boost inflation even more, by 0.6 percentage points in one year, and by another 0.5 percentage points after two years. In January 2000, the Eurozone's inflation rate reached 2 per cent, which is the ECB's limit for price stability.

Nonetheless, the increase in the reference interest rate made on 3 February 2000 can hardly be interpreted as having been triggered by exchange rate erosion. Though the circumstance could have suggested the ECB was facing a panic, this was not the case. Social partners and the impending wage negotiations in Germany and in other member economies are by far the most important factor of inflationary concern. The increase in the reference interest rate was clearly aimed at unions and was meant to impose a moderate wage policy on them. In Duisenberg's own words: 'Our expectation is that we shall see higher inflation rates in the next few months. Inflation rates are now approaching higher levels than expected earlier, and larger and more protracted commodity and producer price increases are heightening the risk of second-round effects. Against this background it is crucial for wage negotiators to be able to rely on the maintenance of price stability in the medium term' (Duisenberg, 2000).

As far as exchange rate policy is concerned, the survey of the ECB's attitude vis-à-vis the Euro external value provides evidence for the case made by this chapter. The ECB's 'benign neglect' attitude is not only part of its own self-ruled monetary policy. This chapter suggests that the bank, amidst some understandable 'confusion' arising from the adoption of the two-pillar strategy (Gros, 2001, p. 4),[21] has enjoyed considerable leeway so as to bolster economic recovery in the Euro area by a 3.5 per cent per year increase in GDP, matched by a significant reduction in unemployment rates, a record performance for the Euro economies in a decade. This result seems to confirm the existence of a relationship, though a rather complex one, between interest rate and exchange rate which is included in theories such as Uncovered Interest Parity. However, considering this a one-way relationship could be misleading. As a matter of fact, it is also true that movements in interest rates are the instrument used by monetary authorities to react to exchange rate developments in order to offset, for instance, their impact on inflation' (Patterson *et al.*, 2000).

As Figure 7.6 shows, the bank's small step policy vis-à-vis a depreciating Euro points towards the professed desire of the ECB to 'give growth a chance'. In December 1999 and in January 2000, ECOFIN11 expressed concern that a tightening of monetary policy could jeopardize the nascent recovery of the Euro economies (P. Norman, *Financial Times*, 8 February 2000, p. 2). The German finance minister especially had clearly warned the ECB against taking any action to back the Euro. Although a conflict between internal and external objectives and, thus, between the ECOFIN-12 (includes the admission of Greece in January 2001) and the ECB could arise again, it is the ECB which is better equipped to provide an internal stability policy linked to economic performance.

CONCLUSION

Challenging ECB watchers who have assessed a depreciating Euro as a puzzling factor which eventually could have caused imported inflation, and have criticized the ECB policy makers for their inadequacy in setting the bank's monetary policy and their inability to run it appropriately, this chapter has worked out a perspective from which the two above critical points should, instead, ber praised. Firstly, the depreciating Euro exchange rate, as many independent observers and EU reports widely recognize, has been an 'ally factor' (Richter, 2002, p. 2) of the Euro area, as it has stimulated the GDP growth rate and international competitiveness (EUROFRAME, 2001, p. 44). It has also been an ally factor to Euro area political authorities otherwise compelled to undertake costly structural reforms. Secondly, a survey of the ECB monetary policy shows striking evidence of the bank's move to advance its monetary policy from a rule-bound course to a real-world approach, distancing itself from the academic expectations of pre-EMU scenarios. After repelling political pressures (Campanella, 2000a), the bank moved towards monetary moderation, challenging economists' predictions of its being prepared to match the 'hard-nosed' Bundesbank.

By working out a strategic institutionalist perspective, this chapter allows us to see instead the ECB as prepared to be responsive to the demands of economic governance, and to adopt a smooth monetary stance, when it has deemed it to be crucial to assist sluggish growth of the Eurozone. Its monetary conduct has made evident the ECB's sensitivity to economic performance and preparedness to act in a responsive way to the problems of economic governance, to a rather similar degree to that of its closest sister, the US Federal Reserve. This attitude may bring about a major problem as it may lead the bank to fall into the 'liquidity trap' of being more responsive to economic growth than monetary stance (Steindl, 2000, pp. 215–20). The consequence can be a monetary policy colluding with social and economic corporate interests and political elected governments. The latter can see this as a way to circumvent the implementation of painful structural reforms.

NOTES

1. Hall (1992) reviewed the Bundesbank executive as a central actor of Germany's economic governance.
2. Irrespective of inflation targeting, which should be the primary objective of the bank of England, Sir Edward George is being praised for 'cutting interest rates sharply – by more than the European Central Bank' (*Financial Times*, 22–3 December 2001, p. 7).
3. Initial attempts in late 1999 and the first half of 2000 to take action that would raise the value of the Euro failed. Subsequent concerted efforts made by major central banks, in late 2000, to resort to a series of direct interventions in the foreign exchange market had little effect.
4. As Jonathan Gruber and David Wise (1998) show, high retirement benefits encourage declining labour participation, which is adding to the fiscal problems the pension funds face. The unused labor capacity of workers between the ages of 55 and 65 is 67 per cent in Belgium, 60 per cent in France, 59 per in Italy, and 58 per cent in Netherlands, compared to 48 per cent in Germany and 37 per cent in the United States.
5. At the time of writing (February 2003) the German banking system is experiencing an even worse situation than the one mentioned in Calomiris (1999). See *The Economist*, 22 February 2003, p. 73.
6. Though generalization has no place in exchange rate dynamics, IMF (2001) admits: 'it does appear that there is some evidence that an important factor driving exchange rates

between the Euro area and the United States over the past years may have been net equity flows, apparently based on perceptions of future growth'.

7.   For a technical assessment of the confusion about M3 and the forward inflation index, see Gros (2001).
8.   The expression is used by Andrew Bevan of Goldman Sachs in *Daily Bond Strategy*, 11 May 2001.
9.   The argument applies to 'Agenda 2000' and the budget policy carried on by the European Commission (Laffan, 1997; Campanella, 1998) and at the time of writing it can be extended to the case of the issuance of an 'early warning' against Germany. On the collusive course of the Stability Pact, see Campanella (2000b).
10. Bergsten argues in favor of exchange rate management policies or exchange rate targets, as he fears that either a strong Euro, which could be encouraged by the ECB, eager to gain a reputation and credibility as the guardian of the new currency, or a competitive depreciation of the Euro, can cause disruptive volatility in the international monetary market (1997, pp. 39–47).
11. On Oskar Lafontaine and ECB conflict over exchange rate policy, see also Campanella (2000a).
12. As Patterson *et al.* (2000, p. 5) sum up, the external value of a currency can affect the internal economy in a number of ways: long-term misalignment will affect relative international competitivity; depreciation/appreciation may increase/decrease inflation and boost/dampen growth; exchange rate volatility can raise costs, destabilize markets and misallocate capital.
13. These exchange rate regimes are currency boards (Bosnia-Herzegovina, Bulgaria, Estonia); currencies pegged to the Euro (Cyprus, the Former Yugoslav Republic of Macedonia and 14 African countries in which the CFA franc is the legal tender); currencies pegged to a basket of currencies including the Euro, in some cases with a fluctuation band (Hungary, Iceland, Poland, Turkey and so on); systems of managed floating in which the Euro is used informally as the reference currency (Czech Republic, Slovak Republic and Slovenia); and, last but not least, European Union currencies pegged to the Euro through a cooperative arrangement, namely ERM II. As is well known, Denmark and Greece joined ERM II on 1 January 1999, with a ±2.25 per cent fluctuation band for the Danish krone and a ±15 per cent fluctuation band for the Greek drachma.
14. The Commission's Eurobarometer opinion poll, for example, found support in Germany down to only 50 per cent in April/May 2000.
15. European Commission, *Quarterly Report*, first quarter, 2001, p. 6.
16. Data relative to 2001 show domestic demand and investment were at the root of Germany's problems. Although household disposable income rose by 3.6 per cent in 2001, up from 2.8 per cent in 2000, Germans put much of their extra money into savings. The savings rate went up in 2001 for the first time in a decade to 10.1 per cent of disposable income, from 9.8 per cent in 2000. The weak Euro has continued, in spite of global trade recession, to be the very positive factor of the German economy at an annual rate of 5.1 per cent, well below 13.2 per cent, 'but enough to ensure that overall gross domestic product was positive' at its 0.6 for 2001 (Barber, 2002, p. 5).
17. European Commission, *Quarterly Report*, first quarter, 2001, p. 9.
18. In the Bofinger perspective, this conclusion does not seem to have much justification, as a data panel for the period from 1982 to 1999 relating to the USA and Germany reveals that there is no systematic relationship between the real GDP growth differentials and the D-Mark–dollar exchange rate (1999, pp. 6–7).
19. Jean-Claude Trichet, governor of the French central bank, speaking in a radio interview over the weekend 5–6 February 2000, said that European bankers (central bankers of course) 'are not satisfied with the current level of the Euro' since it imports more inflation than is necessary'. Instead, Germany's Social-Democrat-led government 'has made it clear that it can live with the Euro's low level. It believes inflationary risks are minimal in Germany and that a weak Euro has been good for economic growth' (Barber, *Financial Times*, 8 February 2000, p. 29).
20. Similarly, IMF (2001).

21. As Gros argued: 'The two pillar approach is widely perceived as not credible because the ECB usually pretends that both pillars point in the same direction. There is a growing consensus among academics that the ECB is de facto following an inflation strategy (focusing on core inflation) although this is officially denied' (2001, p. 4).

REFERENCES

Aglietta, Michel *et al.* (1997), *Mimosa Project*, Brussels: European Commission.
Alogoskoufis, George and Richard Portes (1997), 'The Euro, the Dollar, and the International Monetary System', in Paul R. Masson, Thomas H. Krueger and Bart G. Turtleboom (eds), *EMU and the International Monetary System*, Washington, DC: IMF, pp. 58–78.
Bank for International Settlements (1999), *69th Annual Report*, June.
Barber, Tony (2000), 'Improved growth needed to boost Euro', *Financial Times*, 2 February, p. 2.
Barber, Tony (2002), 'Economic downturn originates from home', *Financial Times*, 18 January, p. 5
Begg, D., F. Canova, P. DeGrauwe, A. Fatas and P.R. Lane (2002), *Monitoring the European Central Bank 4: Surviving the Slowdown*, London: Centre for Economic Policy Research.
Bergsten, Fred C. (1997), 'The Impact of the Euro on Exchange Rates and International Policy Cooperation', in Paul R. Masson, Thomas H. Krueger and Bart G. Turtleboom (eds), *EMU and the International Monetary System*, Washington, DC: IMF, pp. 17–48.
Bergsten, Fred C., Olivier Davanne and Pierre Jaquet (1999), 'The Case for Joint Management of Exchange Rate Flexibility', Institute for International Economics Working Paper 99–9, Washington, DC.
Bini Smaghi, Lorenzo and Paolo Del Giovane (1996), 'Convergence on Inflation: A necessary prerequisite for EMU?', *Open Economies Review*, 7: 117–26.
Bini Smaghi, Lorenzo and Daniel Gros (2000), *Open Issues in European Central Banking*, Houndmills: Macmillan and St Martin's Press.
Bofinger, Peter (1999a), 'The Monetary Policy of the ECB under Treaty Article 105', Directorate General for Research, Brussels, European Parliament, Economic Affairs Series ECON-112
(*www.europarl.eu.int/dg2/ECON/EMU/EN/default.htm*).
Bofinger, Peter (1999b), 'Options for the exchange rate management of the ECB', Directorate General for Research, European Parliament, Economic Affairs Series ECON-15, September.
Buiter, W.H. (1999), 'Alice in Euroland', *Journal of Common Market Studies*, 37(2), June: 181–209.
Calomiris, Charles W. (1998), 'The Collapse of the European Monetary Union', Cato Institute's 16th Annual Monetary Conference, 22 October, Washington, DC.
Campanella, Miriam L. (1996), 'Central Bank Independence and European Central Banking Institution-Building', *Economia delle Scelte Pubbliche*, 1: 57–76.
Campanella, Miriam L. (1998), 'Central Eastern European Enlargement and EU Budget Policy: A strategic agenda setter for joint (Pareto improving) gains', TKI working papers on European Integration and Regime Formation, South Jutland University Center.
Campanella, Miriam L. (2000a), 'The Battle between ECB and Ecofin-11', in Maria

Green Cowles and Michael Smith (eds), *The State of the European Union: Volume 5 Risks, Reforms, Resistance and Revival*, Oxford: Oxford University Press.

Campanella, Miriam L. (2000b), 'European Monetary Union: Economic versus political integration and the limits of supranationalism', in Svein S. Andersen and Kjell A. Eliassen (eds), *Making Policy in Europe*, 2nd edn, London: Sage, pp. 167–86.

Clostermann, Joerg and Berd Schnatz (2000), 'The determinants of the Euro–dollar exchange rate: Synthetic fundamentals and a non-existing currency', 'Discussion Paper 2/20 Economic Research Group', May (*www.dresearch.com*).

Connolly, Bernard (1995), *The Rotten Heart of Europe: The Dirty War for Europe's Money*, London and Boston: Faber and Faber.

De Grauwe, Paul (2000), 'The Euro–dollar exchange rate in search of fundamentals' (*www.202.pair.com/sterckx/publicatie.php3?pub=eurokoers/euroDollarRate 2000.htm*).

Duisenberg. Willem F. (1999a), Press Conference, 2 June (*www.ecb.int*).

Duisenberg. Willem F. (1999b), Press Conference, 9 September (*www.ecb.int*).

Duisenberg. Willem F. (2000), Press Conference, 3 February (*www.ecb.int*).

Economist, The (2003), 22 February: 73.

Eichengreen, Barry (2000), 'The Dollar Vs. The Euro: Do We Care?', American Foreign Service Association (*www.afsa.int*).

EUROFRAME (2001), European Commission: Brussels.

Fischer, Stanley (2001) 'Exchange rate regimes: is the bipolar view correct?', Distinguished Lecture on Economics in Government, New Orleans, 6 January (*www.imf.int*).

Gros, Daniel (2000), 'The Euro: strong economy, weak currency', *CEPS Commentary*, September (*www.ceps.be*).

Gros, Daniel (2001),'The ECB's Unsettling Opaqueness', CEPS, Brussels (*www.ceps.be*).

Gruber, Jonathan and David Wise (1998), 'Social Security and Retirement: An International Comparison', *American Economic Review*, 88(2): 158–63.

Hall, Peter A. (1992), 'The movement from Keynesianism to monetarism: institutional analysis and British economic policy in the 1970s', in Sven Steimo, Kathelen Thelen and Frank Longstreth (eds), *Structuring Politics. Historical Institutionalism in Comparative Analysis*, Cambridge: Cambridge University Press, pp. 90–113.

Henning, Randall C. (1997), *Cooperating with Europe's Monetary Union*, Washington, DC: Institute for International Economics.

International Monetary Fund (IMF) (2001), 'Prospects and Policy Challenges', *World Economic Outlook*, May, Washington, DC.

International Monetary Fund (IMF) (2001), 'What is Driving the Weakness of the Euro and the Strength of the Dollar?', *World Economic Outlook*, May, Washington, DC.

Issing, Otmar (2000), 'The Euro area – first experience and perspective', 26 January (*www.ecb.int*).

Johnson, Harry G. (1972), 'Political Economy Aspects of International Monetary Reform', *Journal of International Economics*, 2: 401–23.

Krasner, Stephen D. (ed.) (1983), *International Regimes*, Ithaca, NY: Cornell University Press.

Laffan, Brigid (1997), 'An Elusive Budgetary Peace: Santer', 5th Biannual ECSA Conference, Seattle.

MacNamara, Kathleen R. (1998), *The Currency of Ideas: Monetary Politics in the European Union*, Ithaca, NY: Cornell University Press.

Martin, Lisa L. and Beth A. Simmons (1998), 'Theories and Empirical Studies of International Relations', *International Organization*, 52(4), Autumn: 729–57.

Moravcsik, Andrew (1996), *Studying Europe After the Cold War: A Perspective from International Relations*, TKI working paper, South Jutland Univeristy Press.

Naudin François (2000), *The European Central Bank: a bank for the 21st Century*, London: Kogan Page.

North, Douglass (1981), *Structure and Changes in Economic History*, New York: Norton.

Noyer, Christian (1999a), 'The Euro Area in the Global Economy', 19 July (*www.ecb.int*).

Noyer, Christian (1999b), 'The European Central Bank: The Economic and Financial Driving Force behind Future Europe', 26 October (*www.ecb.int*).

Ouchi, William G. (1980), 'Markets, Bureaucracies and Clans', *Administrative Science Quarterly*, 25(1): 129–41.

Padoa-Schioppa, Tommaso (1999), 'Eurosystem: new challenges for old missions', 15 April (*http://www.ecb.int*).

Patterson, Ben, Dagmara Sienkiewicz and Xavier Avila (2000), 'Exchange Rates and Monetary Policy', Directorate General for Research, European Parliament, Economic Affairs Series ECON-120.

Perrow, Charles (1981), 'Markets, Hierarchy and Hegemony', in Andrew Van de Ven and William Joyce (eds), *Perspectives on Organization, Design, and Behavior*, New York: Wiley, pp. 371–86.

Richter, Stephan (2002), 'The unappreciated Euro', *The Globalist* (*http://www.TheGlobalist.com*).

Rzepkowski, Bronka (2001), 'Heterogeneous Expectations, Currency Options and the Euro/Dollar Exchange Rate', CEPII, Document de travail N.01–03.

Sinn, Hans-Werner and Frank Westermann (2001), 'Why has the Euro been falling?', CESifo working paper no. 493.

Smits, Robert (1997), *The European Central Bank: Institutional Aspects*, The Hague: Kluwer Law International.

Solans, Eugenio (1999a), 'The Euro as an International Currency', 18 September (*www.ecb.in*).

Solans, Eugenio (1999b), '100 Days of EMU' (*www.ecb.int*).

Steindl, Frank G. (2000), 'Does the Fed Abhor Inflation?', *Cato Journal*, 20(2), Fall.

Vaubel, Roland (1985), 'International Collusion or Competition for Macroeconomic Policy Coordination? A Restatement', *Recherches Economique de Louvain*, 51, 233–40.

Webb, Michael (1991), 'International Economic Structures, Government Interests and International Coordination of Macroeconomic Adjustment Policies', *IO*, 45(3): 309–42.

Williamson, Oliver E. (1975), *Markets and Hierarchies: Analysis and Antitrust Implications*, New York: The Free Press.

Index